Inclusive Design

The reality of the built environment for disabled people is one of social, physical and attitudinal barriers which prevent their ease of mobility, movement and access. In the United Kingdom, most homes cannot be accessed by wheelchair, while accessible transport is the exception rather than the rule. Pavements are littered with street furniture, while most public and commercial buildings provide few design features to permit disabled people ease of access.

Inclusive Design is a documentation of the attitudes, values and practices of property professionals, including developers, surveyors and architects, in responding to the building needs of disabled people. Legislative and regulatory controls, particularly in western countries, increasingly require development teams to design the built environment in ways which are sensitised to the needs of disabled people. Disabled people are also demanding adaptations and changes to buildings to permit them a greater use of the built environment and, consequentially, a fuller role in society. Such demands are leading to new pressures on the property and building industries with implications for project design, costs, management and related processes. This book documents the way in which pressure for accessible building design is influencing the policies and practices of property companies and professionals, with a primary focus on commercial developments in the UK. The book also provides comments on, and references to, other countries, particularly Sweden, New Zealand and the USA.

Rob Imrie is Professor of Human Geography at Royal Holloway, University of London. He is co-author of *Transforming Buyer–Supplier Relations* (1992), author of *Disability and the City* (1996), and co-editor of *British Urban Policy* (1999). **Peter Hall** is a researcher in the Public Policy Research Unit, Goldsmiths College, University of London.

Inclusive Design

Designing and Developing Accessible Environments

Rob Imrie and Peter Hall

London and New York

First published 2001
by Spon Press
11 New Fetter Lane, London EC4P 4EE

Simultaneously published in the USA and Canada
by Spon Press
29 West 35th Street, New York, NY 10001

Spon Press is an imprint of the Taylor & Francis Group

Typeset in Frutiger Light by Wearset, Boldon, Tyne and Wear
Printed and bound in Great Britain by St Edmundsbury Press,
Bury St Edmunds, Suffolk

British Library Cataloguing in Publication Data

A catalogue record for this book is available from the British Library

Library of Congress Cataloging-in-Publication Data
Imrie, Rob 1958–
    Inclusive design : designing and developing accessible
environments / Rob Imrie and Peter Hall
        p. cm.
    1. Architecture and the physically handicapped–Great Britain.
2. Universal design–Great Britain. I. Hall, Peter. II. Title.

NA2545.P5 H339 2001
720'.87–dc21

00–069812

ISBN 0–419–25620–2

To Mike and Claire

Contents

Notes on the authors   viii
Preface   ix
Acknowledgements   xii
Illustration credits   xiii

PART I
Debates   1

1 Inclusive design and development in the built environment   3
2 Barriers to disabled people's inclusion in the built environment   27
3 Access directives in the development and design process   48

PART II
Illustrations   67

4 Developers' responses to the building needs of disabled people   69
   Case study: Bluewater, Dartford, UK   86
5 Architects and disabling design practices   92
   Case study: Ikon Gallery, Birmingham, UK   113
6 Shaping access through institutional and project team dynamics   120
   Case study: Crescent Theatre, Birmingham, UK   136

PART III
Reflections   141

7 Alternative directions in property development, disability and design   143

Endnotes   154
Appendices   162
References   168
Index   181

The authors

Rob Imrie is Professor of Human Geography at Royal Holloway, University of London. His research interests include the geographies of mobility and movement of disabled people, urban design and disability, and urban politics and governmentality. He is co-author of one book (*Transforming Buyer–Supplier Relations*, 1992, Macmillan, Basingstoke), author of another (*Disability and the City*, 1996, Paul Chapman Publishing, London, and, St Martin's Press, New York), and co-editor of *British Urban Policy* (1999) published by Sage.

Peter Hall was, until recently, a full-time researcher in the Department of Geography at Royal Holloway employed on a Leverhulme Trust funded project on 'architects and disabling design in the built environment'. He is now a research assistant in the Public Policy Research Unit, Goldsmiths College, University of London. His previous research experience includes work in the Division of Policy Studies, University of Humberside; the Public Sector Management Group, London School of Economics; and the Local Economy Policy Unit at South Bank University. He has written articles for a range of journals, including *Environment and Planning B: Planning and Design*, *Urban Studies* and *Policy Studies*.

Preface

The reality of the built environment for disabled people is of social, physical and attitudinal barriers which prevent their ease of mobility, movement and access. In the United Kingdom (UK), the majority of homes are not wheelchair accessible, while accessible transport is the exception rather than the rule. Pavements tend to be littered with street furniture, while most public and commercial buildings provide few design features to permit disabled people ease of access. Induction loops are rare while colour contrasts and tactile paving are poorly designed or often non-existent. In the British general election in May 1997, for instance, 75 per cent of polling offices were inaccessible to people in wheelchairs, while few had the technical aids to permit visually impaired people to mark their votes on the polling papers. Such illustrations indicate that physical barriers to disabled people's inclusion in buildings, the wider built environment and society, are considerable.

Physical barriers are compounded by social and attitudinal barriers which tend to regard disabled people as inferior and of little value. As Ellis (2000: 21) notes, modern society is averse to 'risky bodies', and anxieties about the disabled and diseased body revolve around concerns to preserve independent bodies, of 'health, fitness, and youth'. Hawkesworth (2001), refers to the bounded and barriered geographies of people with facial disfigurements, or those individuals who fail to measure up to, or present, an acceptable aesthetic appearance. As Hawkesworth shows, such individuals are often regarded as 'dirty' and 'disordered' or 'abject things', objects of disdain and a danger to be distanced from society. Indeed, disabled people often feel 'out-of-place' because of social and attitudinal markers of difference, ranging from people's indifference to them, to acts of hostility and even physical violence. Not surprisingly, in combination with the physical configuration of the built environment, the socio-attitudinal nature of society is a powerful mechanism of social exclusion.

This book considers the attitudes, values and practices of property professionals, including developers, surveyors and architects, towards facilitating inclusive design, with the focus on providing for the needs of disabled people. Legislative and regulatory controls, in western countries, increasingly require development teams to provide for disabled people's building needs. Disabled people are also demanding adaptations and changes to buildings to permit them a greater use of the built environment and, consequentially, a fuller role in society. Such demands are leading to new pressures on the property and building industries with implications for project design, control, costs, management and related processes. This book is a documentation of how pressures for accessible building design are influencing the policies and practices of property companies and professionals, with a primary focus on commercial developments in the UK. The book also provides comments on, and references to, other countries, particularly Sweden, New Zealand and the United States of America.

In doing so, we provide first-hand testimonies from property professionals about their understanding of, and responses to, disabled people and their building needs. Developers' responses to disabled people are not necessarily invariant, predictable, or reducible to a cost calculus. Rather, the evidence is illustrative of a heterogeneity of developers' attitudes, values and responses to the needs of disabled people. Given this heterogeneity, we are not attempting to produce a design guidance manual to inclusive design, nor do we seek to offer prescriptive advice or measures on how to achieve accessible environments. Indeed, we firmly believe that there is no such thing as a singular prescriptive approach to access because each and every situation will demand different types of responses by professionals and others involved in the process. As we argue, the attainment of inclusive design, in part, is dependent on property professionals' sensitivity to the development contexts and knowledge of the building needs of people with physical and mental impairments.

This book is primarily based on information generated from an Economic and Social Research Council (ESRC)-funded project (grant number R000236997) entitled 'Commercial property development and providing for disabled people's building needs in Sweden and the United Kingdom'. The research involved postal surveys of architects and chartered surveyors in Sweden and the UK, and in-depth interviews with property developers, architects, project managers, surveyors and other property professionals in both countries. This was supplemented by case work of development practices and projects in the UK and Sweden, seeking to show the diversity of attitudes and approaches of developers and other professionals to the building needs of disabled people (and users more generally). The book primarily reports on UK experiences in relation to commercial property, such as office, retailing, hotel and leisure developments, although we make a range of comments in relation to housing and the residential built environment. In addition, interview material generated by a Leverhulme Trust-funded project (grant number ID19980496), entitled 'Architects and disabling design in the built environment', is also drawn upon in the book.

In producing this book, we are indebted to many people. We would especially like to thank the participants in the research for giving up their valuable time to share their experiences with us. We are indebted to a number of individuals who supported the research by commenting on various drafts of questionnaires and advising on different stages of the research process. These include, amongst others, Mike Batty, Keith Bright, John Chatwin, Paul Clark, Richard Cullingworth, Sarah Fielder, Julie Fleck, Jacqueline Green, Brendan Gleeson, Marian Hawkesworth, Marian Kumar,

Sarah Langton-Lockton, Carla Nailer, Greg Penoyre, and the architects who attended a project workshop in July 1999. Thanks also to anonymous referees of the original research application and final report to ESRC, and to an anonymous reader of a draft of the book. We are particularly grateful to Peter Cleland for his support over the years and his willingness to share his knowledge and wisdom with us. He has been a significant source of encouragement and has always had time to comment constructively on the various research papers we have produced associated with this, and related, research projects.

Thanks are also due to Göran Cars in the Department of Spatial Planning, Regional Institute of Technology (KTH) in Stockholm, for providing us with a base to work from in Sweden and for his participation in some of the research. We were also supported by other staff at KTH, and we would like to thank Joakim Bergström, Jonas Hagetoft, Inger Normann and José de Silva for conducting interviews, translating documents and for being warm and friendly hosts. Sián Putnam was a vital part of the research in transcribing interviews and we thank her for this. The Department of Geography at Royal Holloway has proved to be a supportive environment and we are especially grateful to Sue May, Xingmin Meng and Nigel Page for helping us in the production of this book. In particular, Sue was a critical part of the process in producing the book's figures, while a term's sabbatical, granted by Royal Holloway to Rob Imrie, was important in helping to bring the research to a conclusion. Rob Imrie is especially indebted to the ESRC, who have generously supported his research over the years and made it all possible.

Finally, we owe a special thanks to Mike Dolton and Claire Edwards for their friendship and support over the last few years and for providing us with a rich and stimulating environment in which to develop our ideas. We dedicate this book to them.

Rob Imrie and Peter Hall, November 2000

Acknowledgements

Sections of Chapter 1, and a substantial part of Chapter 5, are based on the article 'Architects and disabling design in the built environment', first published in 1999 in the journal *Environment and Planning B: Planning and Design*. We are grateful to Pion Ltd for granting permission to reproduce parts of this article. In addition, Chapter 4 is largely drawn from an article entitled 'An exploration of disability and the development process ', first published in 2001 in *Urban Studies*. Again, we are grateful to the publisher, Carfax Publishing, for granting us permission to reproduce parts of this article.

Development company interviewees included Charlie Spencer, Grainhurst, London; Richard Robinson, John Laing Property Holdings, London; Nick Roberts, Chelsfield plc, London; Peter Lackey, Berkeley Group, Cobham; Daniel Carter, Arrowcroft Group, London; James Scott and Hugh Thomas, Asda Property Holdings; Derek West, St Modwen Developments, Birmingham; Ian McKee, Slough Estates, Slough; Bob Wright, MEPC, London; Harvey Smith, Capital Shopping Centres, London; Ian Beaumont, Rose Project Services, Birmingham; Jon Miller, Tarmac Design, Birmingham; Graham Field, Land Securities, London; Andy Thomas, Great Portland Estates, London; John Hayman, British Land Co., London; Julian Vickery, Greycoats, London; Andrew Fursdon, Kajima Properties, London; Steve Burton, Castle Estates, London; Ian Bond, Howard Holdings, London; Tony Giddings, Argent Group, London; Ian Reid, Tarmac Building, Birmingham; Gary Warburton, Tarmac Building, Birmingham; Ian Betts, Silk & Frazier, Birmingham; Peter Jacobs, Bovis Interiors, London.

The authors and publisher are grateful to all who gave their permission for the use of copyright material. They apologise if they have inadvertently failed to acknowledge any copyright holder and will be glad to correct any omissions that are drawn to their attention in future reprints or editions.

Illustration credits

The authors and the publishers would like to thank the following individuals and institutions for giving permission to reproduce illustrations. We have made every effort to contact copyright holders, but if any errors have been made we would be happy to correct them at a later printing.

Adler, D., Butterworth Heinemann Publishers, 1.3
Alvar Aalto Archives, Helsinki, 1.4
The British Museum, 2.1
Judy Monahan, Sadler's Wells, Example 1.1
Neufert, E. and Neufert, P., Blackwell Science Ltd., 1.2
Office of Population Censuses and Surveys, 2.2

In addition, the following organisations and individuals provided us with photographs to illustrate case studies: Argent Estates Ltd.; Bluewater Management; Ikon Gallery; the Lighthouse, Glasgow; Penoyre & Prasad Architects; SECC, Glasgow; Adrian Burrows; Alastair Carew-Cox; Martin Jones.

Part I
Debates

1 Inclusive design and development in the built environment

Introduction

The provision of access to buildings for disabled people is becoming a more important dimension of property development in developed countries. In recent years, government directives on access have proliferated, with the recognition that the built environment, and associated development, design and building processes, are inattentive to the needs of disabled people. For instance, many commercial and public buildings are inaccessible to wheelchair users, while few buildings provide appropriate design features and navigational aids to enable people with a range of sensory impairments to move around with confidence and ease. Accessible transport is a rarity, while most housing lacks basic adaptations or design features to facilitate independent living for disabled people. Inaccessible and poorly designed built environments are an infringement of disabled people's civil liberties or, as Barnes (1991: 179) observes, 'the physical environment . . . has been constructed without reference to the needs of disabled people'.

The sources of disabled people's exclusion from many facets of the built environment are multiple and complex yet are linked, in part, to the policies, practices and values of professionals involved in property development, design and construction processes. In particular, some argue that developers, architects and designers tend to operate in ways which are inattentive to end users (Darke, 1984a, b; Matrix, 1984; Willis, 1990). For instance, Darke (1984a: 391), in researching the role of architects in public housing schemes in London, concluded that 'architects' images of their users are generalised, imprecise, and stereotyped'. For Darke, architects of public housing only envisage a limited range of household types which primarily conform to the nuclear family and the elderly. Others also note the singular and reductionist conceptions of users which underpin development practices, ones which tend to be insensitive to racial and gender differences, while ignoring the multiple physiologies of the body (Colomina, 1994; Hayden, 1985; Imrie, 1999a; Matrix, 1984; Thomas, 2000; Weisman, 1992).

Such observations are part of a wider recognition of the inappropriateness of much building, and other, design in relation to the needs of users.

For instance, as the European Commission (1996: 7) have argued, 'to ensure equal chances of participation in social and economic activities, everyone of any age, with or without any disability, must be able to enter and use any part of the built environment as independently as possible'. Other studies highlight the interrelationships between physical design and the (in)ability of people to perform daily tasks and live independent lives. Thus, the Royal National Institute for the Blind's (RNIB, 1995: 6) 'Needs Survey' shows that many people with vision impairments are isolated and trapped in their homes, 'with many dependent on sighted assistance for such tasks as shopping'. Likewise, as a range of publications have high-lighted, many wheelchair users are part of a 'captured community', often dependent on assistance to move from one place to another (Drake, 1999; Gleeson, 1999a; Imrie, 1996; Oliver, 1990).

In exploring the interrelationships between property development, design and disability, we divide the chapter into a number of themes. We begin by outlining the broader patterns and processes which, we argue, orientate the values and actions of the development industry towards project strategies and outcomes not necessarily sensitised to the multiple building needs of potential users. In part, this is because property profes-sionals' conceptions of building users are either non-existent or revolve around an 'identikit' which reduces users to technical categories often bereft of human or social ascriptions. However, developers are conditioned and constrained by a broader range of socio-political and economic processes which, as we shall argue, influence the forms of building provi-sion (see also Ball, 1998; Guy, 1998; Healey and Barrett, 1990). These processes include pressures to standardise building design, or to reduce design to a common set of parameters not necessarily sensitised to bodily variations or capacities.

This proposition is amplified in the chapter, where we consider the role of design theories, ideas and practices in influencing the form and content of the built environment. We develop the argument that designers and architects tend to perpetuate aesthetic ideas and practices which are based on one-dimensional conceptions of the human form, and are preoccupied with ornamental and decorative aspects of a building rather than its use. We explore Ward's (1996: 31) allegation that 'when we revisit the history of the [architectural] profession, we find that serious attempts to place the social at the center of design theory have been silenced and an attempt has been made to produce and maintain a seamless image of professional theory and practice associated with a depoliticised fine art'. Indeed, for Lewis Mumford (1928), and others, modern design is characterised by its estrangement from the affective desires, emotions and needs of people; while, for Frank Lloyd Wright (1992), the rise of what he termed the 'plan factories', or corporate architectural businesses, is core to architects' loss of contact with individual needs and feelings.

These views are part of a broader critique of the development process, and the chapter also describes and evaluates alternative ways of conceiv-ing of the design and development of the built environment, or perspec-tives which challenge the mainstream social relations of building design, construction and provision. In particular, the term 'social architecture' has been coined to describe a disparate range of ideas which, at their core, are committed to development and design processes which, in Mumford's (1928: 298) terms, 'create a culture capable of extending and nurturing life in all its forms'. We explore the core ideas associated with social architecture and, in particular, the popularisation of the universal design movement. In the penultimate part of the chapter, we evaluate the possibilities for a development and design philosophy around the notion of inclusive design. We conclude by outlining the book's main themes and structure.

Social exclusion and the development process: preliminary observations

Most of us expect to be able to move around the built environment with ease of access and entry into buildings. For Blomley (1994: 413), 'rights and entitlement attached to mobility have long had a hallowed place within the liberal pantheon and, as such, mobility is part of the democratic revolution'. For instance, in the USA and Canada mobility rights are formally enshrined in legislation and, for Hobbes (1996), mobility is fundamental to the liberty of the human body. As Hobbes (1996: 57) has argued, 'liberty or freedom, signifieth, properly, the absence of opposition; by opposition, I mean external impediments of motion'. However, immobility, and restrictions on movement and access, are defining features of the lives of many people, particularly for those with physical and mental impairments. As Figure 1.1 illustrates, the built environment is characterised by obstacles and physical impediments which render ineffective the efforts of many disabled people seeking independence of movement and mobility.

Some researchers see disabled people's estrangement from the built environment as the result of wider, pejorative, societal attitudes towards disability, particularly amongst policy professionals, while others note the weaknesses of disabled people's organisations, such as the charities, as crucial in failing to politicise the demands of their constituents (Barnes,

1.1 Inaccessible and barriered built environments.

The photographs in this montage illustrate different aspects of design which inhibit disabled people's movement and mobility. 1.1a exhibits contradictory design elements, whereby smooth paving is intersected by cobbled stones which tend to prevent ease of movement of wheelchairs. 1.1b is a shopping centre directory board, characterised by information which is presented in lettering too small for most vision-impaired people to see. 1.1c shows a step into the rear of a shopping centre which prevents wheelchair users from gaining access.

1.1b

1.1a

1.1c

1991; Drake, 1999; Imrie and Kumar, 1998). Other researchers have highlighted the absence of strong regulatory controls, over the actions and operations of developers, as the key to understanding the design and development of disabling environments (Gleeson, 1999a; Imrie, 1997). Indeed, most research has focused on the attitudes, values and operations of planning regulators, yet, in doing so, has generally ignored the socio-institutional dynamics of property development in contributing to, and ameliorating, the physical barriers that disabled people have to confront. To date, there has been little or no research of the interrelationships between property development processes and the production of disabling and disablist built environments.

However, the socio-institutional structures and relations of the development process are, we would argue, implicated in the production and perpetuation of disabling barriers in the built environment. Inattentiveness to, and exclusion of, the needs of disabled, and other, people is evident at all stages of the design and development of the built environment. For instance, few disabled people are architects or hold positions of power within the development industry, while formal educational training for property professionals, on the building needs of disabled people, is more or less non-existent. Statutes reinforce the rights of developers to determine, broadly, the form, content and location of building projects, while minimising third-party representations. Land markets also tend to respond to profit signals and opportunities, and are less attentive to the supply of property, and related infrastructure, sensitised to non-profit uses or activities. For most developers, the provision of access facilities and features in buildings falls into this latter category.

This is evident from statements by developers, investors and other agents involved in the development process, who tend to dismiss disabled people's access and mobility requirements because of the perceived cost and profit implications (Guy, 1998; Imrie, 1996). For instance, the House Builders' Federation (HBF, 1995: 1–2), in objecting to the possibilities of legislation requiring housebuilders to construct dwellings to specified accessibility standards, have argued that the effect 'will be to add to the cost of dwellings in key sectors of the market . . . this will make them non-viable' (also, see the arguments in Chapter 2). Likewise, Imrie's (1996, 1997, 2000a) research indicates that developers in the UK need to be persuaded by planning regulators to build accessible buildings, with many property companies unwilling to do so because of cost concerns and the belief that accessible buildings are not needed (see also Gleeson, 1997, 1999a; Kitchen and Law, 2001).

Such notions tend to confirm mainstream economic conceptions of property development and dynamics in suggesting that the provision of buildings and ancillary infrastructure is driven by the demand for property. It is also assumed that the requisite demand for, for example, accessible buildings will be unproblematically provided (or not) through the collective interactions between the various agents involved in the development process. However, as Guy (1998: 265) suggests, the supply of a building, and ancillary design features, is not reducible to a simple demand equation given the complexities of the socio-institutional, technical, legal and investment contexts within which property development takes place (see also Ball, 1998; Healey, 1992; Healey and Barrett, 1990). For Guy (1998), the development process is underpinned by a complexity of social actors and interactions, framed by judgements and decisions not reducible to specific forms 'of agent rationality' (Healey and Barrett, 1990: 92; quoted in Guy, 1998: 265).

In recognising such complexity, and moving beyond reductive models of the development process, we concur with D'Arcy and Keogh's (1997: 690) observation, that it is necessary to consider property in 'physical and legal terms, and the nature of the property market process through which the functional requirements of property for use, investment, and development are addressed' (see also Healey and Barrett, 1990). As D'Arcy and Keogh (1997) note, changes in the urban fabric are constrained by factors such as the existing built environment, and mediated through land and property markets which are often highly specific to particular bundles of land. For instance, in relation to the provision of accessible properties, developers are more likely to provide access in new buildings than old due to technical and cost differences in provision (Imrie, 2000a). Variations in building regulations, between different countries, also conditions contrasting levels of provision, while the attitudes and practices of key actors, such as architects, project managers and locally active disabled people and their organisations, can be important in influencing developers and their clients to incorporate access (see Imrie, 1999b).

The matrix of factors which, potentially, influence development projects requires researchers, as van der Krabben and Lambooy suggest, to acknowledge the social relations of building provision which, in turn, 'recognises the variety of agencies, agency relations, activities, and events involved in development projects' (1993: 1385). Such ideas have been, in our opinion, best expressed and developed by Ball (1981, 1985, 1998) through the formulation of 'structures of building provision' (see also Ball *et al.*, 1988; Ball and Harloe, 1992). For Ball (1998: 1513), the structures of building provision (hereafter referred to as SBP) refers to 'the network of relationships associated with the provision of particular types of buildings at specific points in time'. Each network is organisation- and market-specific and, as Ball (1998: 1514) suggests, 'associated with historically specific institutional and other social relations'. Thus, the contingent nature of property dynamics is core to the SBP approach or, as Ball (1998: 1514) notes, attention should be focused on the intricate webs of the development nexus, defined as 'the whole gamut of development, construction, ownership, and use'.

SBP are also dynamic in that the provision of accessible buildings for disabled people is subject to continual change resulting from, as Ball (1998: 1514) argues, 'factors like market pressures, changes in technologies . . . and because of the strategies of the organisations involved'. Changes in social attitudes and legal and regulatory frameworks are important too, as are the actions of particular interest groups, such as disabled people's organisations. For Ball, then, the potential range of institutions, and institutional relations, involved in a SBP is wide, variable and usually case-specific, and this is especially important where international comparisons are concerned. While acknowledging Ball's (1998: 1514) observation that SBP is not a 'complete theory in itself', and lacks explanatory utility, it offers a non-deterministic, non-reductive, and anti-essentialist view of socio-institutional processes. In doing so, SBP is part of an important, broader, genre of methodological approaches which seeks to situate theory in context and, as Ball (1998: 1514) notes, 'so guides the research focus rather than directly provides answers'.

Determinants of developers' responses to disabled people's building needs

In utilising and developing aspects of the SBP approach, in relation to developers' responses to the building needs of disabled people, it is possible to identify, at a general level, three aspects of the development process which are implicated in disabled people's estrangement from building and development projects and which are important in framing developers' attitudes and responses to the building needs of disabled people (see also Chapters 4 and 6). These are the economics of real estate; the legal frameworks underpinning developers' actions; and the technical discourses and knowledge systems of real estate. While these categories are not mutually exclusive nor exhaustive, they provide a broad base by which to contribute not only to an understanding of property professionals' attitudes and responses to the building needs of disabled people, but also to the limited stock of substantive research seeking to understand some of the specificities of property development processes (see also Healey and Nabarro, 1990).

First and foremost, the development process has been characterised by some as 'a struggle by property developers and investors to extract as much surplus exchange value as possible from building construction with little regard to the eventual use value of the building' (Guy, 1998: 267; see also Luithlen, 1994). The underlying economics of real estate are underpinned by cost pressures towards the maximum utilisation of space, while minimising the use of features which are perceived to add little value to property. In particular, fixtures and fittings, to facilitate disabled people's access to buildings, are often perceived by developers as a threat to the marketability of property. This was one of the HBF's main observations about the proposed extension of Part M of the Building Regulations to residential dwellings in England. As the HBF (1995: 4) said, 'the provision of ramped access will in itself be ugly, increasing the amount of concrete or tarmac in front of houses'. Adaptations to facilitate access, like ramps and handrails, were also presented by the HBF (1995: 5) as giving 'an institutional feel to developments, which is contrary to the image house builders need to create to sell to homeowners'.

Disabled people's inability to develop or exercise their capacities, or to influence such debates, is also linked, in part, to the power of corporate property development and its drive towards standardisation. The rise of large-scale corporate investments in buildings, since the early 1980s, sought to provide high levels of design specification. As Guy (1998) suggests, much of this, particularly in offices, was an over-specification of items such as air-conditioning. However, such specifications were never extended to access features and little or no thought was, or is, given to issues about users' mobility, manoeuvrability, or access into and around buildings. Off-the-shelf, standardised fittings and fixtures, were (and still are) common place, revolving around industry standards which are inattentive to bodily diversity or differences. This is not an invariant process, however, with competitive and commercial pressures, in different segments of the property market, producing contrasting developer responses. Some retail developers, for instance, are increasingly sensitised to volatile markets by seeking to cater for the building needs of all possible consumers, including the provision of access facilities and features for disabled people.[1]

The legal underpinnings of property development is also a basis for the estrangement or exclusion of disabled people from land and property processes (see Chapter 3). Access codes and statutes have been established in most countries yet, as a number of observers have noted, they are generally vague and provide regulatory control for substantial new constructions while doing little to regulate access provision in the refurbishment of existing buildings (Gleeson, 1999a; Imrie, 1996). As a result, much of the built environment remains unaffected by access directives, while some research indicates that developers seek to 'dumb down' standards by rarely providing more than is required by the regulations (Imrie, 1996, 1997, 2000a; Imrie and Hall, 1999). Developers are not legally obliged to consult directly with disabled people over development proposals, and disabled people and their organisations rarely meet developers or their agents (see Chapter 4). Many legal frameworks do little or nothing to influence developers to be pro-active towards meeting the building needs of disabled people, or to educate the property industry about the diversity of people's bodily capacities (Barnes, 1991; Imrie, 1996).

In particular, the dominant narratives and knowledge bases of the property industry serve to underplay the importance of responding to the needs of disabled people. For developers, profit and cost margins, adherence to technical standards, time scheduling and related matters, are project priorities. Real estate education and training is also implicated in producing property agents and professionals with partial views of users. These tend to project disabled people as wheelchair users and a vocal minority who rarely need to use buildings or, as a local authority officer, in interview, said, 'developers' perception is still that disabled people do not live normal lives – not going out spending money . . . they're not seen as a commercial asset so why build for them?' (quoted in Imrie, 1997: 443). Such views are not isolated to specific segments within the development industry but are evident across a broad range of contexts. For instance, in response to a questionnaire administered by the authors, on disabled people's access needs, a partner in a firm of chartered surveyors argued that:[2]

> I think that it is a waste of the country's resources to spend millions of pounds making every building accessible to wheelchairs, for example, when it is much easier to provide two able-bodied men to lift a wheelchair up the steps on the rare occasions when some buildings need access by the occasional visitor in a wheelchair. We are getting so hypersensitive on the subject that we feel we must fall over backwards to cope with people who will only occasionally need the facilities which are being so expensively provided.

Such pejorative conceptions of disability and disabled people are common-place in the development industry. For instance, in relation to the steepness of ramps, the HBF argue in favour of gradients of up to 1 in 10 despite evidence to suggest that such inclines do not facilitate independent movement by wheelchair users (Imrie, 1996). However, for the HBF (1995: 4) the issue is resolvable because 'a ramp of 1 in 10 is no steeper than commonly found in access to many public buildings where it is anticipated the wheelchair user will be assisted'. For most mobility-impaired people, such views are seen as demeaning because they deny them, potentially, the right to independence of mobility and movement. While the HBF's view is not reducible to all aspects or operations of the development industry, it highlights an underlying tension within the social relations of the development process to, on the one hand, maintain profit margins, while, on the other hand, having to respond to emergent societal demands for alternate design and development solutions.

Design culture, buildings and users

Designing for the needs of disabled people has never been a significant feature of the development process, nor of urban design theories and practices. As Figures 1.2 and 1.3 show, design texts, such as Neufert and Neufert's *Architects' Data* (2000), or the *Metric Handbook* (Adler, 1999), reinforce architects' commonly-held conception that the bodies they seek to design for revolve around a range of physiological norms. These norms tend to reduce the body to a universal type or a standard, characterised by fixed body parts (Imrie, 1999a). They are a potential source of denial of bodily diversity and difference (see also Chapter 5). Where design professionals, such as architects or interior designers, incorporate disabled people's needs into projects, there is the tendency to reduce disability to a singular form of mobility impairment, that of the wheelchair user.

Such observations have led some researchers to suggest that design and development processes are disabling and disablist by failing to recognise, and respond to, the needs of disabled people (Gathorne-Hardy, 1999a; Walker, 1995). Disablism in urban design is identifiable in a number of interrelated ways. Foremost is the broad and, arguably, enduring (and durable) value bases of modernism as a key philosophical and practical informant of design theories and practices in the twentieth century (see Bloomer and Moore, 1977; Knox, 1987). While modernism was predicated on breaking down social divisions and differences, for Weisman (1992) it was closely aligned with an abstract engineering aesthetic which sought to propagate what was presented as 'the intellectual purity of rational, geometric, forms, and a mass produced industrial technology' (Imrie, 1996: 135). This aesthetic, in turn, was premised on a conception of the body, and related human behaviour, as knowable, predictable and invariant, or a potential denial of differences in bodily experiences and forms.

Sandercock (1998), for instance, notes how the power of modernist ideology promoted, post-Second World War, specific conceptions of design and space which, while claiming to be neutral and inclusive, failed to acknowledge social multiplicity or difference. The claimed neutrality of modernist design, with its emphasis on de-contextuality, standardisation

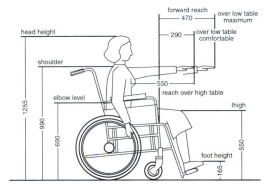

1.2 Man's dimensional relationships.

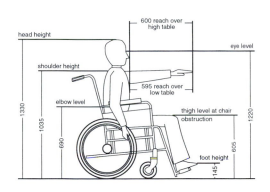

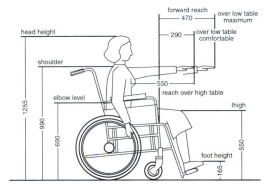

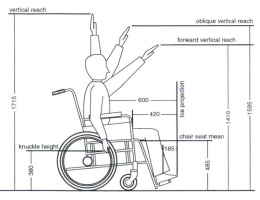

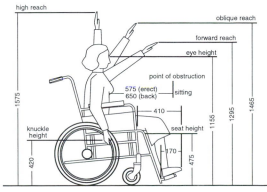

1.3 Dimensions of adult male and female wheelchair users.

and a homogeneous public, was often little more than a re-affirmation of existing socio-spatial dispositions and practices or responding to what Young (1990: 4) calls the mainstream, that is, 'white European male norms of reason and respectability'. This was a world without disabled people or where gender was little more than the perpetuation of patriarchal relations. It was also a world where bodies were reduced to an asexual status and where architecture and design was conceived of, as Bloomer and Moore (1977: ix) argue, to a 'highly specialised system with a set of pre-scribed technical goals rather than a sensual social art responsive to real human desires and feelings'.

The estrangement of building users from architectural and design processes was particularly heightened by the inability of modernism to break with past traditions, especially the idea of architecture and design as artistic endeavours and expressions, or the notion that the designer is con-veying beauty and truth through the context of their work (see, for example, Curtis, 1994; Knesl, 1984; Knox, 1987). Indeed, a concern with the decorative and the ornamental remains a powerful part of the design professions and, as Bloomer and Moore (1977: x) argue, 'architecture, to the extent that it is considered an art, is characterised in its design stages as an abstract visual art and not as a body-centred art'. Such ideas, in per-meating architectural and design theories and practices since classical times, are, as Davies and Lifchez (1987) note, problematical in ignoring the multiplicity of human needs in the built environment, given that the focus is more about the aesthetic, or the building form, not the user or the func-tioning of the building.

The broader processes and practices of the design and building profes-sions have, however, not gone uncontested by alternative ways of conceiv-ing the social and technical relations of building and design. For instance, Venturi (1966), in reflecting on the legacies of modernist architecture and the machine aesthetic, has argued for architects to recognise the complexi-ties of modern life and to address multi-functional programmes and needs. Others have propagated similar views in seeking to influence professionals to acknowledge the importance of 'social architecture', or perspectives which recognise the multiplicity of needs of building users and the need to accommodate them in building projects. For instance, the Finnish architect Alvar Aalto noted that responsible designers ought not to inflict any harm on building users nor provide environments unsuitable for their use. As Aalto (1940; quoted in Ventre, 1997: 12) argued, 'to provide natural or an artificial light which destroys the human eye or is unsuitable for its use means reactionary architecture even if the building should otherwise be of high constructive value' (see Figure 1.4). As Ventre (1997: 13) notes, in relation to the ideas of Aalto:

> personal, individual advantage – even in the sublimated forms of aes-thetic gratification of technical mastery – is not to be gained at the expense of the welfare of the larger social unit. Aalto went further: for him, no single user should suffer.

This lineage can be traced through a range of architectural or design ideas which, in their various ways, have sought to (re)centre the human subject

and to assert the ethical foundations of design ideas and practices (see Sommer, 1983; Turner, 1987). For instance, seeking to inscribe the social in architecture was, in part, a reaction against the primacy of abstract, often one-dimensional aesthetic knowledges and practices and their documented failings in relation to unmet building requirements and needs. Thus, as Aalto (1940, quoted in Ventre, 1997: 11) noted, 'the only way to humanise architecture is to use methods which always are a combination of technical, physical, and psychological phenomena, never any one of them above the others'. Likewise, Louis Mumford wanted to (re)centre architectural ideas in a broader, holistic understanding of people and nature or, as he suggested, 'we must look for a finer relationship between imaginative design and a whole range of biological, psychological, and sociological knowledge' (Mumford, 1928: 298; quoted in Luccarelli, 1995: 60).

For Mumford, the aesthetic and social were mutually entwined, or as Luccarelli (1995: 59) observes, it was Mumford's belief 'that the aesthetic shapes the practical and technological and has moral and social implications'. In Mumford's terms, then, social architecture is concerned with relational and processual matters, or how and why particular places come to acquire the form that they do. A variant of such ideas is 'architecture of the everyday', or what Harris and Berke (1997: backcover) define as 'building that is emphatically unmonumental and anti-heroic, an architecture rooted in the commonplace and the routines of life'. For disabled people, an architecture of the everyday has attractions in its resistance to the commodification of architectural objects, or an architecture that, in Hatch's (1984: 10) terms, 'avoids idealistic utopias but ... insists that the

1.4 Architects Aarne Ervi, Alvar Aalto, and Aino Aalto in the entrance hall of Viipuri Municipal Library, Finland.

For Curtis (1994: 230) the Viipuri Library 'was such as to suggest already the rejection of mechanistic qualities in earlier modern architecture; moreover, the functional discipline of the work was bound up with a poetic reaction to human needs rather than with arid calculation'.

process of conceiving and producing the man made [sic] world involves moral choices'. This, then, suggests that design ought to be less concerned with the production of marketable products, and more with the conception of living environments which embrace the spectrum of human values, both spiritual and material.

The popularisation of universal design

The potentially radicalising nature of social architecture or design has barely resonated with, or influenced, developers, designers or architects in relation to their thinking about the needs of disabled people. This is a pity because the core values and philosophies of social design are a concern with environmental and social justice and human rights. Its messages are fundamentally political and processual and demand changes not only to technical or physical infrastructure but also to social, attitudinal, political and policy structures. However, much of its radicalising edge has been either ignored or blunted by alternative ideas and practices which have ascended to a position of pre-eminence in debates about developing and designing for the building needs of disabled people. This is particularly so with what we regard as the problematical idea of universal design, or a 'catch-all' phrase which has become an increasingly popular concept by which to describe and gauge how far designers and their practices are sensitised to disabled people's building needs.

Ideas about universal design are prominent in the USA and have spawned a myriad of major research programmes and practical applications (see, for example, Greer, 1987; Ostroff, 2000; Salmen and Ostroff, 1997; Steinfeld, 1994; Steinfeld and Danford, 1999; Walker, 1995; Weisman, 1992, 1999).[3] In its broadest terms, universal design is a social movement primarily concerned with making products, environments and communication systems usable to the greatest extent possible by the broadest spectrum of users. As Greer (1987: 58) suggests:

> improved design standards, better information, and new products and lower costs make it possible for design professionals to begin designing all buildings interiors and products to be usable by all people all of the time instead of responding only to the minimal demands of law that requires a few special features for disabled people.

The proponents of universal design are highly critical of compensatory approaches to architecture, or where accessibility is added 'to otherwise inaccessible objects and standard designs' to compensate disabled people for their functional limitations (Connell and Sandford, 1999: 35; see also Salmen and Ostroff, 1997; Weisman, 1999). Additive design is seen as demeaning and drawing attention to a person's impairment with the potential for stigma and social exclusion, or as Steinfeld (1994: 3) argues, it provides little more than a 'token response to the needs of people with disabilities'. Steinfeld (1994: 4) further notes that, 'accessible design acknowledges that people with disabilities have a right to access and use of products and environments, but it doesn't go far enough because it doesn't express social integration'.

In contrast, universal design, so it is claimed, seeks to integrate the accommodation of disability with the basic concept of the design, by sensitising the environment to the broadest possible range of bodily shapes, dimensions and movements (see Table 1.1). The objective is, as intimated above, to draw attention away from people's impairment as a source or site of difference to minimise the possibilities of social ostracism. There is also a recognition that people's needs are never static, and that the design of buildings and other products ought to enhance, rather than inhibit, 'the changing abilities of humans throughout their life-span' (Salmen and Ostroff, 1997: 3). Moreover, universal design is seen as a complex process which requires an integrative, team approach to transcend the limitations of any one perspective or professional viewpoint (Ostroff, 2000). As Salmen and Ostroff (1997: 6) suggest, 'designers cannot get . . . information from books, databases or design criteria alone. Designers must involve the future users, the customers of the design', and develop a process which is 'broadly representative, user responsive and participatory'.

Such views underpin universal design's support for equitable use or the development of design which does not disadvantage any group of users. As Salmen and Ostroff (1997) suggest, universal design ought to be democratising in facilitating the use of product facilities and buildings for all. The reduction of energy expenditure is also a core principle or, as Steinfeld (1994) notes, people need an environment that eliminates unnecessary expenditure of effort. As Steinfeld (1994: 2) amplifies: 'this can be achieved by organising space and designing devices to simplify the task of using them . . . useless movements should be eliminated'. Likewise, the illegibility of the built environment, and related products, is a constraint on

Table 1.1 The key principles of universal design

Principle	Description
Simple and intuitive use	The use of the design is easy to understand regardless of the user's experience, knowledge, language skills or concentration levels.
Equitable use	The design does not disadvantage or stigmatise any groups of users.
Perceptible information	The design communicates necessary information effectively to the user, regardless of ambient conditions or the user's sensory abilities.
Tolerance for error	The design minimises hazards and the adverse consequences of accidental or unintended fatigue.
Flexibility in use	The design accommodates a wide range of individual preferences and abilities.
Low physical effort	The design can be used efficiently and comfortably and with a minimum of fatigue.
Size and space for approach and use	Appropriate size and space is provided for approach, reach, manipulation and use, regardless of the user's body size, posture or mobility.

Source: Center for Universal Design, 1995.

their use and universal design seeks, as Figure 1.5 indicates, to simplify environments by the use of colour and texture contrasts. While Steinfeld (1994: 3) acknowledges that not all environments will 'be usable by all people from the beginning', a remit of universal design is promoting the flexibility, adaptability and interchangeability of fittings and fixtures to ensure 'an adaptable environment, one that can be easily adjusted to meet the needs of any person' (Steinfeld, 1994: 3).

The principles of universal design are important, and potentially progressive, in seeking to restore disabled people's self-esteem, dignity and independence, while encouraging the development and implementation of user-friendly design. However, it is difficult to see how far transformations in disabled people's lives can occur without the development of a social or political programme for change and, in this respect, the core philosophies of universal design are unhelpful. Indeed, its principles are apolitical in that there is little or no recognition of the interrelationships between the social, technical, political and economic processes underpinning building and design. Universal design largely proceeds on the basis that environmental change is a matter of developing and implementing a technical or design solution (Gordon, 1983; Sokolowska *et al.*, 1981; see also Chapter 2). Facilitating access, for universal designers, is a matter of adaptation from one type of design to another, reconfiguring the fixtures and features of a building and developing new procedural mechanisms for deploying resources and their management.

1.5 Simplifying and codifying the built environment
Source: Jeremy Bailey, Jeremy Bailey Architects, London, 1999.

The following text is an extract from an interview with an architect who has experience in seeking to simplify the built environment. Here, he is referring to the re-design of a doctor's surgery used predominantly by ethnic minorities with a limited understanding of the English language:

We organised the various consulting rooms in different parts of the building in very simple colour coding. We had a red section, a blue section and a yellow section – primary colours – and on each of the consulting room doors there was a large number from one to four. So for patients, the minimum grasp of English they need is a colour and a number between one and four. This proved to be extremely helpful in what is quite a difficult building because it's an existing building that's been extended and it's become quite spread out. From the start we were concerned about how easy it would be to understand one's way around the building from the patient's point of view. Our clients – the doctors and their staff – obviously knew the building and it wouldn't be very difficult for them, but we could see that the existing premises, which were much smaller, were already difficult for their patients and they explained that they had a language problem with a number of patients and so we were keen to find a device to simplify and to make it possible to know where you were in the building at any one time. This led quite naturally onto zoning in terms of colours and large numerals. We had quite an interesting discussion with the staff once we'd proposed this idea, where they didn't like the idea of bright red, yellow or blue and they wanted more pastel colours. So we tried to explain that it would be rather difficult to explain the difference between a sort of terracotta and a beige to someone who didn't understand what either word was and that we had to keep it simple. We had to reduce it to a very powerful and simple form.

A technical and procedural response is, however, necessarily partial because it leaves intact the social and attitudinal relations which influence the form and content of design. Given that these attitudes are, at present, broadly discriminatory, there is no reason to suppose that technical adaptations, in and of themselves, will significantly change the lives of disabled people. Gleeson (1999b) goes further in arguing that some regard assistive technologies as corrective mechanisms or a means to transform disabled people into 'normal' human beings (see Chapter 2 for an amplification of these debates). The objective is 'social integration' or 'to integrate people with disabilities into the mainstream' (Center for Universal Design, 2000: 1). However, for Linton (1998: 58), such mainstreaming revolves around standards set by the dominant majority, or those allied to a definition of disability as 'not-normal' or abnormal. In this sense, impairment, as far as universal design ideas are concerned, is regarded as something to be overcome or to be eradicated, rather than to be accepted as an intrinsic feature or part of a person and their identity.

Universal design also appears to be totalising in its message of wanting to cater for all within the context of its design solutions. Its proponents claim, however, to be able to accommodate difference and variation by using adjustable and interchangeable design elements and designing spaces that can be easily customised. However, some have raised doubts about such solutions and, as Hind (1996) has noted:

> there are so many different types of sight loss and you can't create 'access for all'; universal design is not possible – there are too many contrasts and types with visual impairment and also depth of vision varies so much – you can get two-dimensional vision and distance just goes and you have to re-educate yourself about your environment.

In this sense, universal design may be promising much more than is technically achievable or feasible. It is also unclear as to how conflicts, between different types of users, with contrasting design needs, can be accommodated within the overall ethos propagated by universal design (see Goldsmith, 1997; RNIB, 1995). For instance, can a singular design respond to all types of vision impairment?

Universal design is characterised by a particular conception of the user as a consumer or customer of design products. As Ostroff (2000: 1) states, 'in universal design, where the needs and limitations of users may be unfamiliar, the designer can learn a great deal from the experiences of the potential consumer'. The customer analogy is, however, problematical because it does little to challenge or change the design professionals and their position as knowledgeable experts. As Salmen and Ostroff (1997: 6) suggest, 'designers must listen to and hear from perceptive spokespeople who can articulate the needs and responses of people of all stages of life' (see also Turner, 1987). Users are seen as consumers of a service, and only active in its production through market-based testing or exercises similar to those carried out by large private corporations prior to the development of its latest product. Thus, for Salmen and Ostroff (1997: 6), a legitimate exercise is that 'designers must involve the future users, *the customers of the design*, through universal design reviews' (emphasis added).

Inclusive design and the development of the built environment

Some of the limitations of universal design have been recognised by influential institutions. For instance, in an important document, the Royal National Institute for the Blind (RNIB, 1995: 13) in the UK, a registered charity that campaigns for the rights of vision-impaired people, have suggested that the objective of developers and designers 'should be to design any building or environment in such a way that all people . . . can move around as independently and freely as they would like. These fundamental issues need to be understood and incorporated from the very beginning of the design process.' While this statement seems to reaffirm the potency of universal design, the RNIB qualify their viewpoint by arguing that designers ought to adopt 'a certain type of design approach that sets out to include as many people as possible', without denying the need for design solutions to meet the needs of specific types of impairments (RNIB, 1995: 13). As the RNIB (1995: 13) have noted:

> It does not look for the lowest common denominator, nor does it attempt to reconcile the often conflicting needs of every possible minority group in society. Rather, by considering many varieties of special needs inclusive design tries to break down unnecessary barriers and exclusiveness.

Inclusive design, as defined by the RNIB, is, then, a development of the principles of universal design and, as we argue, more likely to lead to some of the necessary changes in the social relations of development and design processes. Inclusive design, as Table 1.2 suggests, is much more than a technical response to the needs of disabled people or just an 'add-on' to the existing stock of knowledge of building professionals. It is part of a lineage of ideas which seek to prioritise building users' views and values and to challenge the social and institutional, as well as technical, relations of design and building processes. Inclusion in the design and development of the built environment is not a disability issue per se; it is an equity and quality (of life) issue for everyone.

Inclusive design has much in common with Sommer's (1983) conception of social design or a process which seeks to place building users at the fulcrum of design processes rather than at their margins. As he notes, the crux of social design is working with people, rather than for them. Indeed, user control and involvement in the design and development of the built environment is a core clarion call and, as Hatch (1984: 4) suggests, inclusive design can, in part, be defined by 'users having the ability to take control of their environments'. Likewise, Towers (1995: 172) notes that 'participation can be justified on the grounds that people have a right to greater control over their environment', while, for others, the absence of participatory democracy in development and design processes is a form of environmental injustice (see, for example, Gleeson, 1999a; Hester Jr, 1987). A construction director of one of the UK's largest development companies, in interview with the authors, said:

Inclusive design	Non-inclusive design
Concern with meaning and context	Concern with style and ornament
Participative	Non-participative
Human oriented	Corporate or institution oriented
Client re-defined to include users	Owner as exclusive client
Low cost	High cost
Grassroots design approaches	Top-down design approach
Democratic	Authoritarian
Seeking to change design attitudes	Acceptance of prevailing design attitudes
Use of appropriate technology	Use of high technology
Use of alternate models of the development process	Development process controlled by corporate interests
Heterogeneity	Homogeneity

Table 1.2 Inclusive and non-inclusive design: a comparison

Source: Adapted from Sommer, 1983: 7.
Note that the contrasts drawn in the figure are purely for heuristic reasons. The contrasts cannot hope to capture the diversity or complexity of design relations and processes which lie between the two positions.

I think that when one says disabilities it is highly political as to how you say it. I always see it as making buildings available for everyone. I think that disabilities is one way of saying it. Sometimes there's no difference in my view to someone in a wheelchair as there is to someone pushing a pushchair. You've got to make things available to children as well and similarly when you look out for concerns for people who are hard of sight. Similarly you've got to look out for children who are wonderful at falling over balustrades and getting their heads stuck in things and you've got to think about them. Now that's nothing to do with disabilities and I just call it common sense access to buildings and public rights of way.

Such conceptions challenge the singular understanding of users propagated by design and building professions, with users often defined as inherently masculine, able-bodied and, as Weisman (1999: 4) notes, 'made up of middle class white people living in nuclear families'. Yet, people, and their uses of the built environment, are multiple, differentiated and complex. So much so, that Gathorne-Hardy (1999a, b: 5) notes that designers ought 'to recognise themselves as users and the fact that they share with all people a corporeality and physical vulnerability that renders the "normal" body grossly misleading'.

Inclusive design also seeks to challenge the expertism underpinning the production of the built environment by encouraging designers to re-think their relationships with those who they design for (Bentley, 1999; Sommer, 1983; Ventriss, 1987). The design and building professions, like all professional trades, are hierarchical, and users' knowledge is rarely deployed in the design and development of buildings. However, Example 1.1 (see pages 22–23) shows that users' knowledge is potentially a key resource and the point is not to challenge the architectural or design skills of professionals per se, but to interlink them more effectively with the experiential knowledge of lay people. Such ideas were formative in the writings of John Turner (1987: 273) who developed the notion that the property professional ought to be an enabling practitioner or 'one who is not only a reflexive listener but also an active collaborator with the client'.[4] As Bentley (1999: 239) suggests, 'the problem, therefore, lies not so much in the fact that designers feel they are experts, as in the kinds of experts they believe themselves to be'.

Inclusive design should not, however, preclude the possibilities of the utilisation of special or exclusive design features to facilitate the movement of those with specific physical or mental impairments. Indeed, inclusion can be thought of as the provision of special facilities and design features. As Figure 1.6 indicates, this is a recognition of the specificity of bodily impairment or the limitations on movement, or other physical and mental capacities, which are related, in part, to people's physiological and cognitive capacities (see Marks, 1999). Moreover, an important part of the process is user feedback and evaluations of building use and performance after its completion. However, as the RNIB (1995: 16) have noted, 'it is not normal practice to invite designers back to review their work'. In interview, an architect concurred with these views. As he suggested, 'feedback is the thing that most people learn from and it very rarely happens . . . constructive criticism is useful for the next time, rather than keep repeating the same mistakes'. Likewise, a member of an access group, in commenting on architects, noted that, 'if they had pride in their work they would go back to check . . . they could learn something from it'.

These and related ideas are, however, anathema to the development industry and are usually resisted. As Towers (1995) notes, developers often refer to user involvement as inefficient, in that it delays the development process. Likewise, Ventriss (1987: 282) notes that property professionals resist participation with users because of the belief that 'modern society is suffering not from a paucity of participation but too much'. Others, though, argue the reverse (Towers, 1995; Turner, 1987). Thus, Turner's (1987) research, on low-cost housing schemes, indicates that genuine participation in design is essential for an increase in material construction and creative work at lower cost. Disability groups deploy similar arguments to highlight that if only their advice on design had been incorporated into building projects, then expensive re-adaptations might have been avoided (see Chapter 4). As a member of an access group, in interview, suggested, 'we told the architects the shopping centre needed another lift but they ignored us . . . now they're having to put it in and it's costing them £50,000 more than if they'd put it in to begin with'.

However, inclusive design is not without its problems. For instance, the term 'user' is characterised by a high level of application but a low level of meaning and, as Hill (1999: 197) suggests, the problem with the idea of building users is that it is 'difficult to predict who they will be'. Indeed, the user is, in many respects, a mythical figure, or as Venturi (1966: 25) said, 'you don't know precisely how a place will be used'. Moreover, debates

1.6 The tree-top walk.

The photographs show an elevated tree-top walk amongst eucalyptus trees in Walpole-Nornalup National Park, locally known as the 'Valley of the Giants', in south Western Australia. With an underpinning philosophy of minimising disturbance to the bush, the idea of the tree-top walk was conceived of in 1990 by the Department of Conservation and Land Management (CALM). Inspired by similar structures in Malaysia, Queensland and New South Wales, CALM planned the entire area to be accessible to wheelchairs. The winning design came from Donald and Warn (Architects), leading a team that included engineers Ove Arup and Partners, environmental artist David Jones, and quantity surveyors Ralph Beattie and Bosworth. The design for the tree-top walk features six lightweight bridge spans, each 60 metres long and 4 metres deep, supported by guyed pylons. The resultant structure permits mobility-impaired and elderly people ease of access 40 metres up into the tree–tops by virtue of the low incline of the bridge span (which is never steeper than 1:14). The surfaces also permit ease of traction for wheelchairs. The tree-top walk shows that technical means are available to enable mobility-impaired people to get to places that many might argue are impossible to access.

Example 1.1 A study of inclusive design – Sadler's Wells, UK

Demolition of the old Sadler's Wells started in July 1996. The original building comprised two theatres; the main theatre seated 1600 and was inaccessible to a large number of people. The other, the Lillian Baylis studio theatre, was built with the needs of disabled people in mind but had become outdated. A disabled person's consultative group called 'Free for All' was set up to determine the detailed designs for access provision for the new building after National Lottery funding was granted. 'Free For All' included the project director, the architects and design team, Sadler's Wells staff, and a number of people with different physical and mental impairments.

The Group's design philosophy noted that disability access means ensuring that a building can be entered by everybody and that all its facilities are available to all, whatever their disability, without relying on the goodwill of strangers. Full disabled access not only guarantees that disabled people can travel around the building, but that they can open doors, turn on lights, buy a drink, get onto the stage, communicate with other people or make themselves a cup of tea. Also essential to disability access is Disability Equality Training for management and staff.

'Free For All' was set up prior to the submission of the outline planning application. Their remit was to produce a 'wish list' for the architects to research, work on and report back to the Group. The process was based on the premise that 'disabled people know best what they need', and Sadler's Wells wrote a commitment to disability access in the contract of every design and building consultant employed on the project. Part M was seen as a starting point and the commitment was to setting 'our own standards.'* Funding to pay for access was never an extra and the structural access costs and most of the technical access requirements were included from the start, within the overall budget.

As Emma McMullan, one of the committee members, stated:

I felt that it was vital that Sadler's Wells should look at disability access for all disabled people and not just those with mobility problems and sensory impairments. This is because most people see access as a physical issue forgetting that access is as much about attitudes, language and control of the environment.

Bold signage

Automatic opening doors with sight lines to improve ease of access for mobility and vision-impaired people

In responding to this, 'Free for All' were involved in a seven-phase process, from contributing to the design of structures to 'honing the process' to fit in with other regulations, such as building and health and safety rules. As one of the architects on 'Free for All' said, 'in the 30 to 40 private sector projects I had worked on, there had never been consultation with disabled people. We relied on Part M . . . I wanted to get things right.'

Gently sloping ramp with two-tone tactile and colour contrasts

Members learnt a lot from the process, or as Rachael Collinge said: 'there was enormous scope for improvement in disability access. A great deal can be done through the minutiae, not just the structure. The positioning of the light switch, the type of loo handle – this costs very little but can make a great difference.' One example of the process was providing access through the stage door entrance. The immediate problem was the cramped nature of the area and space only for a 1:12 ramp. There were no clear sightlines from the outside door through to the reception. Thus, the Group lobbied the local council to give the adjoining building to Sadler's Wells. This acquisition freed up the space and provides clear sightlines and a more spacious reception area. A longer, less steep ramp can also be accommodated.

The cost of the overall access consultation for Sadler's Wells was £16,805 including the cost of participation by the core members of 'Free For All' in the detailed design process and production of a final report. Access provision is varied and includes, amongst others, high contrast signage and attention to size and simplicity of typefaces; low-level duplicate touch signage in primary positions; infra-red systems for audio descriptions of performances; textured floor surfaces, automatic opening entrance doors; visual indicators for curtains up; vibrator alarm for audience/staff members; induction loops in auditoria and so on.

Text derived from Monahan, McMullan and Jentle, 1998.

* Part M of the Building Regulations stipulates the minimum conditions of access to be adhered to in new developments and substantial refurbishments of buildings. Chapter 3 provides a detailed discussion of Part M and related access directives in the UK.

Sadler's Wells

about inclusive design are part of a broader genre of critiques of the social relations of the development process which have rarely moved beyond general platitudes and well-intentioned statements. Thus, from the development of perspective on community planning in the 1960s, to the recent debates about universal and inclusive design, the dominant images projected are, in Dempsey and Foreman's (1997: 287) terms, ones 'of righteousness, growth, fulfillment, and triumph' (see, for example, Sommer, 1983; Towers, 1995; Turner, 1987; Wates, 1976; Wates and Knevitt, 1987).

There are, however, few examples of inclusive design in action or discussion of how far, and in what ways, it is possible, or feasible, to re-orientate the social relationships between property professionals and those that use the built environment. Indeed, debates about social inclusion and democracy have little to say about how to increase the transparency and accountability of private sector corporate property firms, or of how users might be able to politicise the development process in order to gain greater control over it. The development professions are characterised by, as Towers (1995: 195) notes, 'narrow and fragmentary pre-occupations' which are resistant to the principles of inclusive design. As subsequent chapters will suggest, the attainment of inclusive design will not be easy bearing in mind, as Adair *et al.* (1999) note, the risk averse nature of the property industry.

Themes and structure

Inclusive design is as much about processes as products, or about the social, attitudinal and institutional relations which underpin and shape the practices of professionals. In most countries, property and building professions are characterised by hierarchical social and technical networks and relations which are often inattentive to the diverse physiological and emotional needs of building users. Most property professions have little exposure to, or knowledge of, the needs of disabled people and only react to them when forced to do so by legislation (see Chapter 3). The dynamics of the development process, as we have argued, revolve around profit/cost criteria, and often the utilisation of standardised design features which are not necessarily sensitised to bodily differences. The provision of access features (for disabled people) is generally perceived, by property professionals, as something to be 'added on' to a building, a special feature, rather than an integral component of good design. Not surprisingly, most disabled people are estranged from the built environment, and the broader sociopolitical and technical processes which give shape to it (see Gleeson, 1999a; Imrie, 1996, 2000b, c).

The rest of this book develops these broader points by describing and discussing the attitudes, values and practices of property professionals in relation to responding to the building needs of disabled people. We divide the book into six further chapters. Chapter 2 develops the argument that the general attitudes and practices of the development industry towards disabled people are part of wider societal value systems which often regard disabled people as inferior and of little worth. We characterise the dominant value system as 'disablist', or one which is underpinned by biomedical discourses. These conceive of disabled people as abnormal or characterised by physical and/or mental bodily limitations which can only be overcome by corrective medical treatment, cure and rehabilitation. Thus, restrictions on mobility and movement are due to the malfunctioning of an individual's impaired body, rather than broader social and environmental barriers. Such values are entrenched and etched across generations of socio-attitudinal practices by state and society, and comprise an antipathy towards, and often hostility to, the needs of disabled people (see Barnes *et al.*, 1999; Oliver, 1996).

Chapter 3 evaluates the role and importance of legal frameworks in determining the types of provision of accessible design and environments. As the chapter indicates, while many countries have access statutes and related Codes of Practice, most legislation is weak, requiring little more than minimal responses by property professionals to the building needs of disabled people (see Doyle, 1995; Goldsmith, 1997; Gooding, 1994, 1996; Scott, 1994). Only a minority of countries interconnect disabled people's access needs with anti-discrimination legislation, with even fewer having statutes relating disabled people's access needs to human rights issues. Most countries are underpinned by voluntaristic legal frameworks or ones which are dependent on the goodwill of clients, and their professional teams, to provide access beyond what many regard as inadequately specified minimum legal standards (see, for example, Fleck, 1996; Gleeson, 1997; Imrie, 1996, 1997, 2000a). Enforcement of legislation is also lacking, with few countries monitoring the effectiveness of access statutes.

Part II of the book, 'Illustrations', develops the broader concepts and ideas outlined in Part I by investigating, empirically, the attitudes, values and practices of property professionals towards the building needs of disabled people, with the focus primarily on the UK. Chapters in Part II are based on primary research of property professionals, including postal questionnaires administered to architects and chartered surveyors, semi-structured interviews with the range of property professionals, and case studies of ten building projects (see Appendix I for a fuller discussion of the research methods and process, and also discussions in Part II). The research also involved interviews and meetings with local authority officers in planning and building control departments, interviews with local authority politicians, meetings with access groups and discussions with disabled people and representatives from their organisations. Documentary research was also integral to the project, and the case studies were compiled, in part, from the collection of minutes from meetings, gaining access to letters and other correspondences between key actors, the inspection of development control case files, the compilation of newspaper records, etc.

In summary, the evidence suggests that there is no singular or essential set of attitudes or responses by property professionals to disabled people's design and building requirements, but rather a complexity of possibilities conditioned by specific socio-institutional, market and political settings. Chapter 4 develops this proposition by exploring property developers' knowledge of, and attitudes and responses towards, disabled people. It shows that developers have limited knowledge of disabled people, and often regard them as a minor consideration in building projects. However, developers are not necessarily averse to responding to access issues, nor are they unaware of the industry's legal and, sometimes, moral obligations. In Chapter 5, the role of architects, in influencing the attitudes and responses of development teams to the building needs of disabled people, is considered. The chapter describes the contrasting ways in which architects define and design for disability, the types of competencies that they have acquired to do so, and the range of assumptions and attitudes that they bring to bear upon architectural production and designing for disabled people's needs.

In Chapter 6, we explore the proposition that how disabled people's access is defined and drawn into building projects is dependent on the social interactions between the variety of agents and agencies involved in project design and development processes (see also Ball, 1998; Guy, 1998). In so doing, we seek to develop the point made by Haviland (1996: 55), that 'design often begins deep within a project – it is nurtured and given shape in complex negotiations among powerful stakeholders and is hardened in the crucible of financial and regulatory review'. As the evidence suggests, there is no typical response to the needs of disabled people; rather, there is a range of possible responses dependent upon the socio-institutional context of development projects. Thus, responses to disabled people's needs can vary according to the time and cost pressures of any particular projects, or depending on the knowledgeability, motivation and understanding of the key professionals in the process.

The final part of the book, 'Reflections', draws out the broader relevance of the research findings. In Chapter 7, we develop the argument that inclusive design needs to evolve into a framework underpinned by 'a recognition of difference and responsiveness to individuated needs, as well as the protection of the rights of difference' (Gould, 1996: 86). In particular, we suggest that inclusive design ought to be aligned to a politics of movement, mobility and access to enable professionals to think about, and respond to 'the diversity of mobility, networks and access required by diverse groups in their daily lives' (Huxley, 1997: 2). We also explore the possibilities for learning and transferability of access practices between building contexts, and draw out some of the policy and practical relevance stemming from the case studies and testimonies reported in Part II of the book.

Further reading

There are a number of good books about design, development and discrimination. One of the best is by Weisman, L. (1992) *Discrimination by Design*, University of Illinois Press. Readers should also look at the marvellous book by Bloomer, K. and Moore, C. (1977) *Body, Memory, and Architecture*, Yale University Press, New Haven, and the text by Madanipour, A. (1996) *Design of Urban Space*, John Wiley, London. In relation to inclusive design, Sommer's (1983) text on *Social Architecture* is a good read. Likewise, Towers (1995) book, *Building Democracy*, is to be recommended for providing a very good and readable account about community development and architecture.

2 Barriers to disabled people's inclusion in the built environment

Introduction

This chapter describes and evaluates the role and importance of social values and attitudes towards disability and disabled people in influencing the practices of property professionals. The development process does not operate in a vacuum from broader societal norms and values, and it is our contention that any understanding of the former is dependent upon an understanding of the latter. For instance, in countries like Germany and Norway, social attitudes towards disabled people are conditioned by the widely-held and accepted, although not necessarily practised, idea that the socio-economic problems confronting disabled people are the result of systemic forms of societal discrimination, not disabled people's individual physiologies, pathologies or bodily impairments. This, then, implies that what ought to be overturned are less the individual bodily impairments and more the broader dynamics of institutional discrimination and social exclusion. In contrast, it is commonplace in the UK for the reverse conceptualisation to be centre-stage, or one which sees the eradication or adaptation of the impairment as the means for disabled people to fit into the prevalent forms of building provision. The latter is taken as given, the former as the source of the problem or the problem to be redressed.

In developing and discussing these ideas, we divide the chapter into three parts. First, we explore contrasting conceptions and definitions of disability and the physically and mentally impaired body, and their implications for professional policies and practices, with the focus on the UK. Second, we describe a number of common, and problematical, fallacies propagated by property professionals about disabled people and their building needs. These, we will argue, are critical in conditioning a combination of negative attitudes and actions by property professionals towards disabled people, with the consequences of contributing to disabled people's marginalisation from the built environment. In particular, we seek to contest the argument that providing for disabled people's building needs adds, abnormally, to development costs, while evaluating the contention that disabled people do not constitute an effective demand in terms of building utilisation. We conclude by noting that the provision of

accessible environments is increasingly not an option for property professionals and ought to become part of everyday practices and procedures.

Social and attitudinal barriers to inclusive design and development practices

Attitudes towards disabled people, world-wide, are generally negative and
demeaning, and society is characterised by a lack of interaction with, and
ignorance of, disabled people. Lévi-Strauss (1955) refers to modern societies as anthropoemic or, as Young (1999: 56) defines it, societies that
'vomit out deviants, keeping them outside of society or enclosing them in
special institutions'. Disabled people have, historically, been categorised as
outsiders, as 'not normal', or people to be controlled through the context
of special measures. Such measures have varied from the adoption of
asylums as places of refuge for disabled people, to special educational
systems and housing, and modes of transportation based on segregation
of provision. The segregation of disabled people has more or less rendered
them invisible, or as a population requiring particular forms of regulation
and control by state programmes and policies.

Segregated responses were, and still are, inscribed across the social, economic and political landscapes of disability. In the eighteenth century, the
asylum became associated with the aversion of 'normal' society to the
public presence of 'defective and degenerate' people. The term 'asylum'
became popularly understood as a place to lock away those that society
was unable to deal with, seeking, in part, to capture and cure mad minds
(see Figure 2.1). Thus, for Schull (1979: 8), the asylum was part of the
moral machinery 'through which the mind was to be strengthened and
reason restored'. Asylums, however, were only part of a broader institutional framework which sought to manage disabled people by excluding
them from the mainstream of society. For instance, the Education Act for
England and Wales (1921) was a mechanism for segregation in instructing
parents 'to cause [their disabled children] to receive effective elementary
instruction . . . in a certified class or school suitable for the child' (quoted in
Drake, 1999: 48).

These attitudes, and related policy measures, were, and still are, commonplace and did little to dispel popular ideas about disability as a 'personal tragedy' or an infliction which ought to be pitied and be the subject
of charity. Under the pathologising gaze of the medics, disability became a
conception of the 'abnormal' or the thing to be overcome or eradicated
through appropriate medical treatment and cure. Such attitudes, in and of
themselves, de-valued disabled people and gauged their worth only in as
far as they measured up to the bodily 'norms' of 'able-bodied' people
(whoever they were). There was a denial of disabled people's individuality
and vitality and, as Morris' (1991: 85) personal testimony notes:

> the general culture invalidates me both by ignoring me and by its particular
> representations of disability. Disabled people are missing from mainstream
> culture. When we do appear, it is in specialised forms – from charity
> telethons to plays about an individual struck down by tragedy – which
> impose the non-disabled world's definitions on us and our experience.

2.1 Plate 8 of A Rake's Progress by William Hogarth depicting his famous image of Bedlam.

Such definitions and experiences extend to most spheres of disabled people's lives, including policies and programmes to regulate and control the incidence of impairment (Barnes, 1991; Drake, 1999; Imrie, 1996; Oliver, 1990). One instance is where disabled people have been, and continue to be, the objects of those concerned with creating perfect bodies and the routine monitoring and manipulating of defective genes (Hubbard, 1997). As Drake (1999: 96) notes, in June 1995 the Chinese government outlawed marriages between people 'where there was a risk of a congenital deformity in their offspring' (see also Barnes *et al.*, 1999; Rufford, 1995). Likewise, Marks (1999) documents the forcible sterilisation of those deemed to be 'feeble-minded' and hereditarily unfit in the USA. As she comments, by 1920, 25 states had laws to enable authorities to sterilise those thought to be genetically inferior and 'by 1958 over 60,000 American citizens had been forcibly sterilised' (Marks, 1999: 35; see also Hubbard, 1997.)[1]

These programmes were more common than not and reflect the dominance of the medical model of disability or a conception of the disabled person which reduces their impairment to the category of a disease.[2] Here, the focus is on 'bodily abnormality, disorder or deficiency and the way in which this causes some degree of disability or functional limitation' (Barnes *et al.*, 1999: 21). It conveys the idea that disability is not normal or a bodily state which ought to be subjected to medical cure and, if appropriate, a period of rehabilitation. Disabled people are seen as victims of disease and/or misfortune and in need of 'care and attention'. Such thinking, until recently, was enshrined in the World Health Organisation's (WHO, 1980) influential International Classification of Impairment, Disabilities, and Handicap (ICIDH). As Table 2.1 shows, the WHO conceived of impairment as causing disability which, in turn, produces handicap, a relationship which they posited as linear and straightforward.

The framework is, however, problematical for reducing disability to the physical and mental impairment and assuming that the appropriate response is for the individuals to adapt themselves to their environments. This is, potentially, a 'blame-the-victim' approach. It conceives of disability as a social burden which is a private, not public, responsibility (Barnes, 1991; Barnes *et al.* 1999; Oliver, 1990; Shakespeare, 1998). The (medical) condition is the focus of concern; biological intervention and critical care by professionals, and the welfare state, are seen as key responses. Moreover, medical discourses are underpinned by 'medicine's drive to make normal that which it considers to be pathological and dysfunctional' (Marks, 1999: 51). Thus, as the WHO (1980: 4) note, disability is 'not being able to perform an activity considered normal for a human being'. However, there is little consensus as to what normality is, nor the recognition that normality is socially and culturally constructed and not a naturalised bodily state or something which is pre-given.

The medical definition of disability is important because it has consequences for policy and action in relation to the building needs of disabled people. Thus, the problems of an inaccessible environment can, potentially, be seen as personal and specific to the impairment, that it is the impairment per se that needs to be eradicated rather than the environmental barriers confronting disabled people. For property professionals, amongst others, this theoretically absolves them of responsibilities for addressing or overturning inaccessible design in the built environment (see Gleeson, 1999a, b; Imrie, 1996, 1997). However, in stressing the need to rehabilitate disabled people, the medical model also emphasises the possibilities of using techniques, or technical aids and supports, to enable

Table 2.1 The World Health Organisation's International Classification of Impairment, Disabilities, and Handicap (1980)

Category	Definition
Impairments	'Disturbances in body structures or processes which are present at birth or result from later injury or disease.'
Disabilities	'Limitations in expected functional activity or as restrictions in activity due to an underlying impairment.'
Handicap	'Difficulties in performing activities of daily living, like walking . . .'

Source: World Health Organisation, 1980.
(In its 1980 classification, the WHO utilised a threefold categorisation by which to define disability and its definitions have become the standard bearer which most countries in the world have adopted.)

disabled people to circumvent environmental barriers. Thus, prosthetic devices, such as artificial limbs, or special features, like ramps or lifts, are conceived of as a legitimate means to redress inaccessible places.

In relation to the built environment, statutory frameworks on access are broadly conceived within a medical conception of disability (see Chapter 3 for an amplification of this point). For instance, the definition of disability in the building regulations for access in England and Wales is impairment-specific in noting that disabled people are those 'who have an impairment which limits their ability to walk or which requires them to use a wheelchair for mobility or have impaired hearing or sight' (DETR, 1999a: 5). Likewise, in countries as diverse as Australia, Indonesia and India, definitions of disability in their respective building regulations are impairment-based and biased (United Nations, 1995). In all instances, the source of the problems for disabled people is located within their impairments, not broader social, attitudinal or other external phenomena. The UK building regulations also assume, or at least do nothing to dispel the view, that it is sufficient to devise technical or building responses to cater for the needs of disabled people independent of broader social, attitudinal and political responses (Imrie, 1996).

In response to the limitations of the medical perspective, revisions of the World Health Organisation's ICIDH are, at the time of writing, being made, and draft versions show a departure, in part, from the medical conception of disability. ICIDH-2, as it is known, proclaims that 'the issue is therefore an attitudinal or ideological one requiring social change, which at a political level becomes a question of human rights. Disability becomes, in short, a political issue' (World Health Organisation, 1999: 25). This view emphasises the importance of broader social and environmental factors in conditioning disabled people's lives (see also Butler and Bowlby, 1998; Gleeson, 1999a, b; Imrie, 1996, 1997). This was the underpinning of the social definition of disability in the UK, originating from the Union of the Physically Impaired Against Segregation (UPIAS) in 1976. As UPIAS (1976: 1) defined it:

> disability [is] the disadvantage or restriction of activity caused by a contemporary social organisation which takes no or little account of people who have physical impairments and thus excludes them from participation in the mainstream of social activities. Physical disability is therefore a particular form of social oppression.

Causality is ascribed to the social context or networks of socio-economic, attitudinal and political relations of disability. For Oliver (1990), disability, far from being a bodily state of impairment, is the socially inferior status that people with physical and mental impairments are forced to occupy by virtue of the social attitudes, prejudices and practices of an 'able-bodied' society. In policy terms, what has to be transformed is less the technical, design, configurations of the built environment but more the social attitudes and practices of society.

This, then, conceives of disability as socially and culturally produced, and invested with meanings which are continuously being challenged and re-shaped. As Barnes *et al.* (1999: 31) suggest, the social model's understanding of disability is not reducible to 'the level of individual psychology, or even interpersonal relations'. Rather, it seeks to understand how values,

Table 2.2 Contrasting ways of conceiving of disability: medical and social conceptions compared

Office of Population, Censuses and Surveys	Mike Oliver
Can you tell me what is wrong with you?	Can you tell me what is wrong with society?
What complaint causes your difficulty in holding, gripping or turning things?	What defects in the design of everyday equipment like jars, bottles and tins causes you difficulty in holding, gripping or turning them?
Are your difficulties in understanding people mainly due to a hearing problem?	Are your difficulties in understanding people mainly due to their inability to communicate with you?
Do you have a scar, blemish or deformity which limits your daily activity?	Do other people's reactions to any scar, blemish or deformity you may have limit your activities?
Does your health problem or disability prevent you from going out as often or as far as you would like?	What is it about the local environment that makes it difficult for you to get about in your neighbourhood?
Does your health problem or disability make it difficult for you to travel by bus?	Are there any transport or financial problems which prevent you from going out as often or as far as you would like?
Does your present accommodation have any adaptations because of your health problem or disability?	Did the poor design of your house mean that you had to have it adapted to suit your needs?

Source: Oliver, 1990: 7–8.

The table compares and contrasts the medical and social perspectives of disability in terms of their identification of the determinants of disabled people's everyday living experiences. It compares the UK's Office of Population Censuses and Survey's (OPCS, 1987) medically-derived questions, about barriers to disabled people's participation in society, with alternate questions, composed by Oliver (1990), re-framed through the context of the social model of disability.

attitudes and related practices condition disabled people's experiences. For instance, in the context of the development process, the medical model notes that a disabled person's inability to gain access to a building is a function of their impairment. Eradicate the impairment and the problem is solved. In contrast, as Table 2.2 implies, the social model argues that inaccessible buildings are a function of thoughtless and inappropriate design, underpinned by a development process which lacks knowledge of, and is insensitive to, the needs of disabled people (Imrie, 1996). The eradication of a particular impairment will do little to change this. For Barnes *et al.* (1999: 30), the social model, therefore, highlights the 'obstacles imposed on disabled people which limit their opportunities to participate in society'.

These obstacles are, for Abberley (1993), neither naturalistic nor inevitable, but are historically specific and culturally relative. In particular, Abberley regards disability as social oppression because disabled people are denied full participation in society. For instance, in Sweden in 1997, 31 per cent of disabled people, compared with 22.7 per cent of the total population, received comprehensive school education of 9 years or less, while less than a fifth (or 18.4 per cent) of disabled people have had higher education compared with a quarter (27.6 per cent) of the total population (Handikapp Ombudsmannen, 1997). Likewise, in the UK, disabled people are on the margins of society. Thus, while disabled people account for 20 per cent of the working-age population, they only make up 12 per cent of all people in employment (DfEE, 1999). Moreover, disabled people are more than twice as likely as non-disabled people to have no qualifications, while unemployment rates for long-term disabled people are nearly twice as high as those for non-disabled people (DfEE, 1999).

As Abberley (1987) suggests, such patterns are generated less by impairment-specific limitations and more by particular work-related institutional practices and attitudes (see also Doyle, 1995; Kavka, 1986). Thus, as Barnes *et al.* (1999: 112) note:

> the industrial infrastructure of western societies has developed without reference to the needs of people with impairments . . . inaccessible buildings, work processes, and public transport systems, and poorly designed housing, prevent many from working where or when they want.

Others point to employers' attitudes and discriminatory practices which, as research shows, are implicated in disabled people's uneven participation in the labour market (Barnes, 1991; Hall, E., 1999; Prescott Clarke, 1990). For instance, Fry's (1986) study shows that employers are more likely to discriminate against disabled people than non-disabled individuals at the initial stages of job application. Thus, as Graham *et al.* (1990: cited in Barnes *et al.* 1999: 113) suggest, disabled job applicants 'are six times more likely to get a negative response to a job application than non-disabled applicants'.

For proponents of the social model, such disablist, and disabling, socio-attitudinal value systems are apparent in most spheres of disabled people's lives and, arguably, may be thought of as perpetuating practices which are unjust. In relation to access to the built environment, Gleeson (1999a: 148) develops the useful idea of 'enabling justice' to describe new social spaces based on responding to the diversity of people's material and emotional needs (see Chapter 7 for an amplification of these debates). For Gleeson (1999a: 149), enabling justice provides all with material satisfaction (i.e. minimum access to food and shelter) and socio-cultural participation (i.e. cultural respect and political inclusion) with the broader objective of enabling disabled people 'to meet their own needs within a network of mutual obligations rather than within a hierarchy of dependency relationships (e.g. care giver/care receiver)'. Likewise, Marks (1999: 94) notes 'that discussion of disability needs to be part of a wider debate about citizenship and social inclusion, or who has what rights to material and environmental resources' (see also Finkelstein and Stuart, 1996).

The social model is, however, not without its detractors and, as Table 2.3 suggests, the social model of disability, like the medical model, is partial in emphasising selective or particular aspects of disability (Bury, 1997, Morris, 1991, Thomas, 1998). For instance, it has been criticised for ignoring how impairment, in and of itself, has the potential to debilitate the body whatever the nature of the underlying values, or attitudinal basis,

Table 2.3 Models of disability: a comparison

Medical	Social	Bio-social
Personal tragedy theory	Social oppression theory	Bio-social theory
Personal problem	Social problem	Personal/social problems
Individual treatment	Social action	Individual/social action
Medicalisation	Self-help	Medical/self-help
Professional dominance	Individual/collective responsibility	Collective responsibilities
Expertise	Experience	Expert/lay experiences
Individual identity	Collective identity	Individual/collective identities
Prejudice	Discrimination	Prejudice/discrimination
Care	Rights	Care combined with rights
Control	Choice	Control combined with choice
Policy	Politics	Political and policy change
Individual adjustment	Social change	Individual adjustment and social change

Source: adapted after Oliver, 1996; Barnes *et al.*, 1999: 30.

of society (see, in particular, Bury, 1996, 1997; Crow, 1995; Thomas, 1998). As Morris (1991: 10) notes:

> there is a tendency within the social model of disability to deny the experience of our own bodies, insisting that our physical differences and restrictions are entirely socially created. While environmental barriers and social attitudes are a crucial part of our experience of disability – and do indeed disable us – to suggest that this is all there is, is to deny the personal experience of physical and intellectual restrictions, of illness, of the fear of dying.

Others concur, with French (1993) noting that the restrictions caused by impairment would remain whatever the social conditions. As French (1993: 17; quoted in Thomas, 1998: 5) argues,

> While I agree with the basic tenets of the [social] model and consider it to be the most important way forward for disabled people, I believe that some of the most profound problems experienced by people with impairments are difficult, if not impossible, to be solved by social manipulation.

These and related criticisms have led to a re-appraisal of disability theory and the development of an alternative conception which seeks to develop an understanding of the interrelationships between biology and social values and attitudes (see especially, Bickenbach, 1993; Bury, 1996, 1997; Butler and Parr, 1999; Marks, 1999; Thomas, 1998). Bio-sociological approaches to disability, as they are termed, are in their infancy but are an attempt to move beyond the duality of the social and medical models of disability by seeking to interconnect them in ways which recognise the complex interactions between physiology, culture and wider socio-economic and political relationships (see, for example, Barnes *et al.*, 1999; Bickenbach, 1993; Butler and Bowlby, 1997; Marks, 1999; Shakespeare, 1998). Marks (1999), for instance, notes that impairment is not irrelevant to an understanding of disability but integral to it (see also Bickenbach, 1993; Bury, 1997). For Marks, impairment, in combination with broader social and cultural values and practices, combine to produce, potentially, debilitating and disabling situations for disabled people (see also Table 2.3).

The emergence of bio-social perspectives underpins recent changes to the WHO's (1999) classification of impairments, disabilities and handicaps. As the WHO (1999: 25) note:

> ICIDH-2 is based on an integration of these two extreme models. In order to capture the integration of the various dimensions of functioning, a bio-psychosocial approach is used . . . to achieve a synthesis thereby providing a coherent view of different dimensions of health at biological, individual and social levels.

In advocating a bio-psychological approach to the understanding of disability, the WHO, like others, is acknowledging the importance of what Bickenbach (1993: 178) refers to as the 'relationships between a medical and functional problem and the social responses to it' (see also Butler and Parr, 1999; Hall, E., 1999; Imrie, 1996, 1997). The bio-social perspectives argue that the physiology or make-up of the body is a determinant of its interactions with the broader environment. Yet, such bodily movements are facilitated or constrained by the socio-cultural markers of a society, such as pejorative and demeaning attitudes or insensitive design.

In particular, there is a recognition that impairment does not exist in a social vacuum, or that impairment is not pre-social but is socially defined and constructed. Who or what is defined as disabled depends, in part, on social and political processes in seeking to identify and categorise different types of impairment. Bio-social perspectives note that impairment is usually collapsed into a series of general and chaotic categories, such as vision, mobility and hard-of-hearing, which do little to reveal the complexities of impairment. Indeed, impairment is neither fixed nor static, or confined to any particular part of the population. It can be temporary or permanent, debilitating or not; in short, it is a contingent condition dependent on circumstances. Thus, while 1 million people in the UK are registered as blind or partially sighted, most have some sight, and yet all are varied in their capacity to see. There is, then, no singular form of vision impairment nor, arguably, any singular building or design response which would or could cater for the multiplicity of needs of vision-impaired, or other, impaired people.

This suggests that property professionals' responses to the design needs of disabled people have to be, by necessity, flexible and adaptable to the myriad of potential bodily interactions with(in) the built environment. However, as the next part of the chapter suggests, the property industry, like others, tends to perpetuate social and attitudinal barriers to the facilitation of disabled people's access, by virtue of operating with a reductionist understanding of impairment (as a form of mobility deficiency), while, often implicitly, augmenting the values of the medical conception of disability.

Social and attitudinal barriers in the development process

The debates outlined in the last part of the chapter are, we would argue, core to an understanding of the interrelationships between development, design and providing for the needs of disabled people in the built environment. Indeed, we wish to argue that the social relationships underpinning the design and development of the built environment are inscribed with disablist values and attitudes, or those characterised by, at best, paternalistic or patronising actions, and, at worst, by outright ignorance, wilful neglect and even conscious or deliberate evasion of disabled people's needs. While these statements may seem strong, they reflect the views of many disabled people interviewed by us, and also evidence provided by property professionals themselves. For instance, as a director of a property company argued: 'somebody needs to say, OK, we are very sorry, nobody wants to be prejudiced against the disabled but there are certain things they cannot do. They can't fly planes, they can't go hang gliding . . . you've got to be realistic and that's what I find frustrating'.

As subsequent chapters will show, pejorative attitudes of this type are not uncommon in the property industry or society in general. Indeed, professionals' lack of knowledge and awareness of disability is a significant barrier in inhibiting the development of appropriate design to meet the needs of disabled people. Thus, Greed (1999: 270), in referring to the education and training of people in the construction industry, suggests that the subcultures of design, property and construction professionals are resistant to change in not permitting 'much space for wider strategic and holistic approaches to . . . social factors'. Likewise, the education of designers and architects is more concerned with buildings' aesthetics than functions or, as an architect said in interview: 'I think we are all trying to pursue an idea, to design an aesthetic.' However, for Weisman (1996: 274), and others, 'it is professionally myopic and morally irresponsible to teach students to evaluate architectural work in terms of aesthetics, building performance, and cost without also teaching them to consider whether what they are designing is ecologically intelligent and socially just' (see also Bloomer and Moore, 1977; Ghirardo, 1991).

While a mixture of professional and institutional ignorance and inertia inhibit professionals' responses to the building needs of disabled people, a range of problematical attitudes and fallacies about disability continue to inhibit change. In the building and property professions, some 'taken-for-granted' assumptions are part of the prevailing wisdom. These include, amongst others, four contestable assumptions:

  i that there is insufficient demand expressed by disabled people for an accessible built environment;
 ii that the provision of accessible buildings and environments is prohibitively expensive;
iii that the provision of accessible design for the needs of wheelchair users is sufficient; and
 iv that accessible environments can be provided by recourse to (technical) design solutions without any corresponding change to socio-cultural attitudes and practices.

We discuss and evaluate each proposition in turn.

There is insufficient demand for an accessible built environment

A view often expressed by property professionals is that there is little or no effective demand for the provision of an accessible built environment. In interview, many professionals echoed these sentiments, with one developer noting that, 'what's the point of providing facilities for disabled people? We never see any here and it would be a waste of a resource'. Another developer commented that 'we provided a load of additional facilities but they never get used and all it's done has been a drain on the company's resources' (see also the testimonies in Chapters 4 and 5). Others concurred with a surveyor suggesting that 'disabled access is very important for hotels and may affect value but for pubs and restaurants disabled access, or its absence, makes little or no difference to the value because trade from disabled persons is negligible'. There is, then, the perception that access need not be provided for disabled people because there are too few of them able or willing to take advantage of such provisions and related goods and services.

However, the notion that disabled people constitute a 'deficient demand' for goods and services does not correspond with much of the evidence. For instance, in a context where populations in many countries are ageing, it is more than likely that the demand for accessible environments will increase. As Figure 2.2 shows, population projections for the UK estimate that, by 2030, the proportion of the population aged 65 years and over will have increased from 20 to 30 per cent. Likewise, it is estimated that the proportion of the population in the USA, aged 65 years and over, will increase from 34.9 million in 2000 to 51.6 million by 2030 (figures cited in Salmen and Ostroff, 1997: 4). Similarly, in places like Singapore, there is significant ageing. In 1990, 10 per cent of Singapore's population was aged 60 years and above, a proportion which will increase to 20 per cent by 2030 (Shantakumar, 1994). Such figures are important given that the likelihood of developing a physical and/or mental impairment increases with age (see, for example, Thompson *et al.*, 1990).

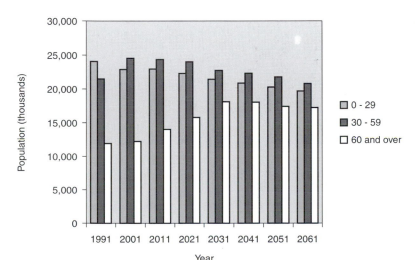

2.2 Projected population by age, 1991–2061, United Kingdom.

The demand for all sorts of accessible buildings, facilities and products is evident in a range of contrasting contexts. For instance, Thamesdown Borough Council (1994) estimated that in 1991 there were 2.4 million people in England and Wales in need of accessible housing. Likewise, Rowe (1990) noted that while there were 4.25 million people with mobility impairments in 1990, there were only 80,000 accessible homes in the UK. Pieda plc (1996: 1) have also commented on the UK's housing stock in that '1 in 4 households contain at least one person with some form of disability . . . the need for accessible housing is therefore substantial . . . the majority of the nation's existing housing is ill suited to the needs of disabled people, or of anyone whose mobility is impaired'. This is particularly the case given that, in a national UK survey of housing, only 29 per cent of disabled people living in private households thought they had all the necessary adaptations (see Barnes *et al.*, 1999: 120; Lamb and Layzell, 1994). Similarly, in relation to transport, 90,000 disabled people in London are eligible to use subsidised taxi services but, as Barnes *et al.* (1999: 121) note, 'there are so few vehicles that potential travellers cannot expect to make more than one trip per week' (see also Barnes, 1991; Heiser, 1995).

The deficient supply of goods and services to disabled people is, in part, because disabled people's expression of demand is often latent and suppressed. Such latency is often beyond the control of disabled people and related to broader societal attitudes and practices. For instance, disabled people tend to lead invisible lives, often within the confines of institutions and their rules, or bounded by dependence on the availability of carers, or other forms of support, to facilitate their mobility and movement. Quite often, the support to facilitate their movement and mobility is absent or infrequently available. Moreover, many disabled people feel emotionally uncomfortable or 'out-of-place' in shopping centres or other public places. Thus, while the provision of physically accessible places per se is a necessary ingredient of usage, it is not sufficient; the social and attitudinal context must be accommodating too. As a disabled person, in interview, recalled: 'I've gone into River Island [a clothes store] in my wheelchair and they've looked at me in a disgusting way as though "You can't wear our clothes". I just had to get out of my wheelchair to look around and try and blend in.' In this instance, demeaning attitudes, and (in)actions by staff, did everything to encourage this wheelchair user not to enter the premises (see also Imrie and Kumar, 1998).

Similar pejorative attitudes are evident in some parts of the property industry with the potential to suppress disabled people's demand for access to the built environment. For example, one of the more contested arenas in recent times in the UK relates to the extension of the building regulations to regulate for the provision of accessible housing (see Chapter 3). In responding to the Department of the Environment's (DoE, 1995a) proposal to extend access legislation to housing, the House Builders' Federation (HBF), the main lobbyist for house builders, objected on the basis that there was insufficient demand by disabled people to warrant the new regulations. The debate ranged around the DoE's 'visitability' standard or the recommendation that the ground floor of new dwellings be made accessible to wheelchairs by providing ease of entry and a downstairs toilet. However, the HBF (1995: 1) argued that:

It is highly improbable that most purchasers of new homes will ever be visited by anyone in a wheelchair and we consider that, given that visit-ability is the declared objective of these proposals, they therefore repre-sent a wholly disproportionate response to a very limited problem.

The HBF's solution to anyone visiting was to suggest that 'if a disabled person visits a home owner, it is to be expected that they can be assisted over the threshold'. This comment is problematical for reinforcing the view that disabled people have no objections to third-party assistance, or do not mind being made dependent on others. The logic is also self-fulfilling, in that without the provision of independent means of access to places, many disabled people will choose not to visit, so supporting many develop-ers' views that disabled people rarely frequent the facilities they provide.

 Disabled people are also inhibited from moving around because the fragmented nature of the development process (i.e. the divisions between professional roles and realms of expertise) sometimes results in a lack of connectivity from one place to another, thus rendering ineffective specific, project-based, initiatives to generate accessible places (see Imrie, 1996). Indeed, developer responses to access are piecemeal and usually one-off with little attempt to develop accessible environments beyond the immedi-acy of the specific project. The United Nations (1995: 2) have noted that:

> Even if public buildings are barrier-free, reaching them is often a problem. The problem of accessibility cannot be tackled piecemeal, but requires a holistic approach . . . there is a need for architects, engineers, and urban planners to realise that token provision of a few reserved parking lots, ramps, toilets and lifts is insufficient.

The implication is that if barriers are removed, disabled people, potentially, have the opportunity to move, unimpeded, from place to place. In this sense, disabled people constitute an untapped or hidden form of demand or market waiting to be cultivated. This was the underlying premise of the Americans with Disabilities Act (ADA, 1991) which was born out of a context which recognised the potential spending power of disabled people. As Kemp (quoted in Imrie, 1996: 64) said, in campaigning for the ADA:

> there are good dollar and cents reasons why business should be inter-ested in disabled people . . . disabled people purchase goods and services just like any other consumer . . . A smart business person would make sure that his or her business was accessible to and usable by disabled people . . . 36 million Americans can be a profitable market for you.

Others concur, with businesses increasingly seeking to target latent con-sumers or those that have been offered limited opportunities to gain access to goods and services. Thus, retailers are keen to attract disabled people. The UK retailer, Tesco (2000), present themselves as having intro-duced 'a number of initiatives and facilities designed to make shopping easier for customers with disabilities', including wide aisles and checkouts, customer escorts for vision-impaired people and adaptive trolleys for attachment to wheelchairs. The facilitation of disabled people's demands for access can have a dramatic impact on the business environment. For instance, Scott (1994) refers to sales in a pizza parlour in the USA whose sales increased by 80 per cent within a few months of introducing a TDD telephone system for customers with hearing impairments. Likewise, Touche Ross (1993) suggested that the potential market for disabled tourists in Europe in 1993 was worth £17 billion, but only if the built environment was made fully accessible.

The provision of accessible design is prohibitively expensive

The Disability Rights Task Force (1999: 7) in the UK have commented that 'there is a perception that the needs of disabled people and those of business are in conflict – that additional rights for one must be at the expense of the other'.[3] In particular, a common response by property professionals, as to why access facilities and features are not provided, is that 'it costs too much'. As one of our respondent developers argued, 'I think the problem is the built-in assumption that access costs more. It's one of those things that we're all indoctrinated with.' A surveyor concurred in suggesting that access 'does not really enhance value and saleability and it incurs additional costs' while, in interview, an architect noted that 'developers will do what they have to but they will be looking at the financial bottom line'. Likewise, the HBF (1995), in commenting on the cost implications of house-builders having to provide, as a legal requirement, lifetime homes, have suggested that 'as a result of the requirements to provide a ground floor WC in all new homes, the industry's starter homes will be a larger and more expensive product' (quoted in Hunt, 1998: 8).

Such views are more or less ubiquitous in the building and development professions.[4] For instance, Gleeson's (1997, 1999a) study, of access policies and politics in New Zealand, shows that cost arguments were core to transport providers' resistance to the possibilities of a legal ruling in favour of the provision of universal access to the bus system. A transport manager of one company said that he 'was concerned about costs being imposed on ratepayers to benefit a group of people of unknown size' (cited in Gleeson, 1999a: 191). For another provider, the provision of universal access was seen as analogous to the 'death' of the national bus system or, as was argued (*Otago Daily Times*, 1995, quoted in Gleeson, 1997: 387):

> If we accept [such a] decision and put the demands into place we would not have a public transport system: we just wouldn't be able to afford it . . . if we adhere to the Human Rights Act it will be at the peril of our efficient and well used system.

This affordability argument is, however, characterised more by hyperbole and invective than considered analysis underpinned by research (Gleeson, 1999a; Imrie, 1996, 1997). In interview, some property professionals, albeit a minority, were resistant to the idea of opposing the provision of access on cost grounds (see also the testimonies in Chapters 4 and 5). Thus, in commenting on professionals' resistance to access, an architect said:

it's not an argument. If you can't provide it you shouldn't be doing it, end of story. If you can't put in a new plumbing system or you can't put the heating in you don't omit the plumbing, you don't omit the roof insulation so why are you omitting the access? In fact it's bizarre, because if you can't give access to the building what's the point of having the facility?

Some research suggests that property professionals' views may well be misplaced in that the provision of access in new buildings does not generate much, if any, additional development costs (Council on Tall Buildings and Urban Habitat, 1992; Wilkoff and Abed, 1994). As de Jong (1983: 10) has commented, 'both public and private construction budgets should be able to meet the additional costs with little or no apparent hardship'. Others concur in estimating that additional costs for most new build costs should not exceed 1.5 per cent of the total construction costs (Council on Tall Buildings and Urban Habitat, 1992; Wilkoff and Abed, 1994). For instance, studies from the US General Accounting Office (1998, 1999) demonstrate that the inclusion of accessibility features in new site construction usually totals less than 0.5 per cent of construction costs.

Likewise, in relation to the provision of accessible homes, the Joseph Rowntree Foundation (JRF, 1997) suggest that the total additional costs of a lifetime home are £484 for a one-bedroom flat of 50.6 square metres and £747 for a two-bedroom house comprising 73.2 square metres. Similarly, Habinteg Housing Association (1999) have estimated that lifetime homes cost £300 to £400 more to build than conventional housing stock. As Donnelly (cited in Slavin, 1999: 8), a consultant to the JRF, has argued about lifetime homes, 'the special design features aren't expensive, and they aren't intrusive – many people don't even realise they are living in a lifetime home until disability strikes – they are just good, thoughtful features built in from the very start'. As the Access Committee for England (1995: 10) noted, 'the average cost of between £180 and £400 ... is a small price to pay for such large long-term benefits, but it is also insignificant compared to other factors affecting house prices, such as geographical location, land price and interest rates'.

The costs of making 'reasonable adjustments' to existing premises, to ensure their accessibility to disabled people, may also have been over estimated by employers and other parties (see also Chapter 3). For instance, the Department for Education and Employment's (2000) survey of 700 firms in England and Wales, found that the costs of making 'reasonable adjustment' were minor. Thus, 44 per cent of adjustments cost less than £49 and only 5 per cent were more than £5,000. As the Equal Opportunities Minister, Alan Howarth (cited in Hilpern, 2000: 9), has commented, 'the requirements under the Disability Discrimination Act to make reasonable adjustments has clearly not resulted in any undue costs [for employers]'.[5] Such views have been reinforced by others, with a spokesperson for the Royal National Institute for the Blind (quoted in Hilpern, 2000: 9) stating that, 'we have always argued that most adjustments employers have to make would be relatively cheap. The biggest barrier that disabled people have in terms of employment is the attitude of employers'.

However, while the provision of particular types of accessible environments will incur, potentially, additional costs, there are monetary, as well as human, costs associated with maintaining, and reproducing, an inaccessible built environment. Arguably, such costs ought to be 'factored-in' to any evaluation of the merits, or not, of pursuing policies to generate accessible environments. Thus, most governments regard inaccessibility to the built environment as generating a real cost in preventing disabled people from gaining access to employment and a wage. In the USA, only 26 per cent of disabled people are employed full time, with over 50 per cent dependent on various forms of government support programmes and social assistance. National expenditure in the USA, in supporting disabled people out of work, is $200 million per annum and £26 million in the UK (see Wilkoff and Abed, 1994). Such figures, in part, pre-empted the assent of the ADA in the USA, a statute which was as much about reducing Federal spending on disabled people as it was in seeking to promote their civil rights (see Chapter 3). As was argued at the time:

> some will argue that it costs too much to implement this bill [the ADA]. But I reply, it costs too much to go on without it. Four percent of American gross domestic product is spent on keeping disabled people dependent
>
> (Senator Edward Kennedy, 1989, quoted in Imrie, 1996: 64).

Other research indicates that significant cost savings can also accrue to public sector expenditure on adaptations to housing for disabled people (Pieda, 1996). As Pieda (1996) indicates, public sector adaptations to dwellings cost £200 million per annum (up to 1996) yet this does not come anywhere near meeting current needs. As Sangster (1997) suggests, the provision of lifetime homes will save £5.5 billion of government expenditure over 60 years, with savings accruing from reduced expenditure on adaptations and reduced need to move people to residential care.[6] Indeed, far from access provision being a cost, its absence may well detract from commercial profits. As the Arts Council for England (1998: 5) have noted:

> Denying disabled people access to the arts is not only a human rights issue, it is financial folly. Accessible venues, clear sign posting and information, affordable pricing policies, auxiliary aids such as induction loops or infrared systems, audio description, sign language interpretation and improved services will result in more customers, more ticket sales and higher profits. In 1993, it was estimated that the spending power of disabled people (14% of the population) was £33 billion. The economy suffers from excluding a market of 6.5 million people.

However, as some authors suggest, the attitudes of property and building professionals are unlikely to prioritise access because they focus on costs rather than the lifetime values of buildings (see, for example, Guy, 1998; Guy and Henneberry, 2000; Joseph Rowntree Foundation, 1997). Others concur, with Wylde *et al.* (1994: 32) suggesting that some property professionals resist accessible design features for a range of pragmatic and practical reasons. Foremost, access features and related products are often unfamiliar to designers, builders and other professionals, or as Wylde *et al.* (ibid.) note, they 'may be perceived as needlessly complex and costly'. Moreover, obtaining the necessary products is often not straightforward and 'suppliers often know little about accessible products and applications' (ibid.). For an architect, in interview, the problem is a lack of aesthetic appeal of access products or, as he suggested, 'we tried to improve the appearance of the disabled toilet but we couldn't find an economical solution that didn't look institutional'.

The majority of disabled people are wheelchair users

Disability, as the second part of the chapter suggests, is a highly contested and culturally fluid term in that there is no singular meaning or understanding of it which easily transcends time and place. Indeed, as Linton (1998: 10) notes, disability is 'an arbitrary designation, used erratically both by professionals who lay claim to naming such phenomena and by confused citizens'. In popular parlance, however, disability is associated with mobility impairments and, in particular, wheelchair users. Wheelchair-reductive models of disability dominate professionals' attitudes and responses to the needs of disabled people, yet very few registered disabled people are wheelchair users. In the UK, for instance, it is estimated that 4 per cent of registered disabled people are dependent upon a wheelchair and, of these, only 1 per cent are dependent on a wheelchair at all times (OPCS, 1987). Likewise, in Sweden, of the total numbers of registered disabled people, a minority, that is 3 per cent, are dependent on a wheelchair.

However, official government documents and directives have, over the years, tended to promote mobility impairment (related to wheelchair users) as the problem to be redressed rather than seeking to understand impairment as a myriad of possible, and often changing, bodily conditions. As Monahan *et al.* (1998: 5) have argued, the building regulations in the UK, despite criticisms, continue to have 'limited application, mainly to wheelchair users and those with reduced mobility largely ignoring the needs of people with a range of disabilities' (see also Chapters 3 and 4). Likewise, as Imrie's (1996, 1997, 2000a) research shows, local authority officials tend to categorise disabled people in ways which do little to reveal the complexities of their lives or their specific needs with regard to access in the built environment. In asking respondents whether or not they operated with a definition of disability and disabled people, those responding in the affirmative tended to reinforce the notion that disability is reducible to a specific type, that of wheelchair users (Imrie, 1996, 1997).

Thus, as one respondent said, 'disabled people have walking difficulties and disability is a condition that confines people to wheelchairs' (quoted in Imrie, 1997: 429). Others made comments like 'limited abilities', 'wheelchair-bound', and 'people with mobility impairments'. By responding primarily to the needs of wheelchair users, such professionals are reacting, in effect, to a minority of people with physical and mental impairments. Yet, disability is also associated with 'abnormality' or something which is not common and confined to specific cohorts of the population. Indeed, official, government definitions of disability regard it as a measurable deviation from a (bodily) state of normality. However, as Barnes *et al.* (1999: 23) note, the latter is underpinned by 'culturally generated criteria about what it is to be normal' or knowledge (about the body) which is 'heavily laden with able-bodied assumptions and prejudices'. For Barnes *et al.* (1999), the notion of a 'normal' body is a misnomer in that it assumes a fixity to the body which no-one ever attains or, as Lefebvre (1991: 196) notes, the complexity of the body undermines reductionist 'distinctions between normal and abnormal states, between health and pathology'.

In contrast, disabled people are characterised by a range of impairments which defy simplistic categorisations or definitions. Such impairments may be temporary or permanent, debilitating to bodily movements or not, and involve varying degrees of pain and discomfort. Bodily difference and diversity are core characteristics of the population, and most people, during their lives, will be affected by physical and/or mental impairments. Similarly, it is possible to experience a loss of bodily function or capacity because of the types of activities that one is engaged in, and the sorts of environments that one is exposed to. Thus, carrying heavy shopping bags, or pushing a pram along uneven surfaces, are sometimes cited as disabling activities insofar that the functional capacity to carry them out is often compromised by social and environmental barriers (i.e. the absence of a car to do the shopping with or the poor and cluttered state of the pavements in inhibiting the ease of movement of those with young children in prams). Likewise, heavy swing doors in public buildings, or out-of-order escalators, are other examples of disabling contexts, or where broader, social and structural phenomena potentially compromise people's functional capacities.

The term 'disability', then, is chaotic in the sense that it suggests that there are a commonality of types and experiences which can be defined in and through the term 'disabled'. The acceptance of this view is one which has the potential to lead to a series of standardised responses, by property professionals amongst others, to the needs of disabled people. This is too often the case in the context of the built environment, where it is seen as sufficient to provide ramped access and not much more. In contrast, a recognition and understanding of the multiplicity of bodily impairments, and the complexity of their interactions with broader social and environmental factors, ought to be the basis for professionals' responses to the access needs of disabled people.

Accessibility can be overcome by technical and design adaptations

The dominance of the medical model of disability, in influencing ways of thinking about disabled people and their lives, is all too apparent in relation to suggestions about how best to overcome the debilitating nature of the built environment. For Gleeson (1999b: 98), the medical view suggests that 'the development of ever more sophisticated (and increasingly computerised) adaptive technologies – in the form of aids, appliances and accessible urban design – will eventually liberate ever greater numbers of disabled people from the social and economic constraints imposed by their bodily impairments'. In noting this, Gleeson quotes a range of enthusiastic advocates of what he terms the 'techno-paradigm', including engineers interviewed by Scherer (1993). As Scherer's study (1993: 84; quoted in Gleeson, 1999b: 98) suggests, engineers 'see assistive technologies and environmental modifications as . . . the primary solutions to the functional limitations of a physical disability'. Likewise, advocates of universal design tend to prioritise the application of technological products as core to over-turning inaccessible environments (see also Chapter 1).

These perspectives emphasise the natural limitations of the impaired body and acknowledge the compensatory possibilities of specialised tech-nologies, like guidance systems for vision-impaired people and motorised wheelchairs. Such technologies, so it is argued, can reduce the 'deficits' disabled people have (or get rid of, or ameliorate, their impairment) and, potentially, enhance their abilities to move around the built environment. However, individual adaptations, such as the use of prosthetic devices, are a necessary, but not sufficient, response in enabling disabled people to gain access to the built environment. Too often such devices mark disabled people out as 'deviant' and serve to stigmatise and exclude. For instance, Imrie and Kumar (1998: 22) recount the experiences of a vision-impaired person: 'lots of vision-impaired people won't use a cane because they feel vulnerable with it – it is a sign and a signal. When you go around town you often get your cane kicked out from under your hand and you lose grip . . . so why go out?' This implies that, technically, such devices might enable disabled people to gain access to particular places, yet, in social and cultural terms, they may have the reverse effect.

Thus, technical devices, in and of themselves, might facilitate little or nothing if the broader societal value systems and relations, which serve to stigmatise, marginalise and discriminate against disabled people, or con-tinue to see them as less than worthy, are not overturned. For instance, while a place of employment may technically be accessible to a wheelchair, this is rendered meaningless if the employer has little regard for the pro-ductive or work potential of wheelchair users. Likewise, if an employer is negative about the productive potential of people with learning difficulties, technical adaptations, in and of themselves, can have little meaning or influence (Shakespeare, 1998). In such instances, the social values and atti-tudes which de-value disabled people are the issue. Facilitating access for disabled people, then, is more than providing fixtures or fittings or adapt-ing part of a building or the wider built environment. It is part of a broader process which, as Gleeson (1999b: 115) suggests, 'must be won through a lasting transformation of the political, economic, institutional and cultural forces that shape our cities and societies'.

Such transformations seem far away, particularly in a context where dis-abled people's experiences of technologies are often at odds with the promises held up by advocates of assistive, and other, devices. In particu-lar, the social relations of technological production are characterised by disabled people's lack of involvement in the conception and design of technologies made for their use (see Gleeson, 1999b; Imrie, 1996; Roul-stone, 1998). For Roulstone, an enabling technology policy requires a rights-based framework aimed at transforming the wider socio-attitudinal environment within which the development and use of new technology is framed. As one of our interviewees commented, in relation to the design of his wheelchair, 'for double amputees (like me) the ordinary wheelchair is a problem – no weight in the front and all at the back. So it can tip back ... it's very frightening and I have little involvement in designing these things ... I ought to as I'm the one who uses it.' Such views affirm Wajcman's (1991: 22) observation that (disabled people's) 'experience of existing technology is a pre-condition for the invention of new technology'.

Gleeson (1999b) also refers to the awkwardly titled 'thoughtless design' theory as another dominant, yet problematical, conception of the problems confronting disabled people in the built environment. As Gleeson suggests (1999b: 105), such theory conceives of the built environment as a physical obstacle course, comprising a plethora of what he terms 'problematical spatial arrangements' such as 'poor cartographic information, inaccessible transport systems, and low density urban form'. Such obstacles, in and of themselves, are, so the theory claims, the source of disabled people's inability to move with ease. The eradication of design barriers will, allegedly, generate accessible environments. These views underpin legal directives on accessibility (see Chapter 3 and Gooding, 1996). They also influence planners' approaches to access and provide property professionals with, arguably, 'easy-to-identify' solutions in redressing (physical) barriers in the built environment.

However, like technological adaptations, the reconfiguration of design is a necessary yet insufficient response to the (access) needs of disabled people. As Gleeson (1999b) and others suggest, the discriminatory design of buildings is the immediate source of disabled people's exclusion from buildings, yet 'the real source of disablement is the set of social forces that produce disabling workplaces and exclusionary technology' (Gleeson, 1999b: 110; see also Roulstone, 1998). Such perspectives note that only a transformation of social attitudes will enable the production of non-disabling design, in that design is a reflection of social relations (as well as constitutive of those relations). In this sense, design adaptations to buildings can only induce incremental change. Property professionals, in this scenario, need to re-appraise their attitudes towards, and understanding of, disabled people in ways which reject bio-medical conceptions of disability, and embrace perspectives which acknowledge disabled people's oppression by mainstream attitudes and institutions.

Conclusions

As Young (1990: 38) suggests, socio-institutional barriers are forms of injustice in inhibiting certain people 'from developing and exercising their capacities or expressing their experiences', while permitting others 'to determine without reciprocation the conditions of their action'. For disabled people, the inability to develop their capacities, or determine the conditions of their lives, is, as the chapter has indicated, connected to a history of institutional incarceration, and a dependence on welfare and care systems. Socio-cultural attitudes, of disabled people as somehow inadequate, inferior and abnormal, and ultimately to blame for their lowly status in society, have also been powerful in conditioning the broader knowledge bases (and prejudices) about disabled people. In turn, disabled people's lives are bounded and barriered, characterised by patterns and processes of socio-economic and political exclusion, especially in relation to what Madanipour (1998: 80) terms 'access to decision making, access to resources, and access to common narratives'.

Broader social and attitudinal barriers are core to the continuing exclusion of many disabled people from the built environment. Such barriers propagate the powerful idea that disability is a state of impairment which can be overturned by medical treatment and cure. There is, according to such views, little or no need to (re)adapt the environment except to cater for the more debilitating types of impairment. Providing for the building needs of disabled people is, then, conceived of as a form of 'special provision', even charity, over and beyond what is or ought to be required. Indeed, providing for disabled people's requirements is tempered by property professionals' general, and often unsubstantiated, belief that the provision of accessible environments may well impose unreasonable costs on the industry. These views, as Part II of the book shows, dominate property professionals' conceptions of disability and are core to (continuing) discrimination against disabled people in most spheres of their lives.

Such discussions are important in thinking about how the social relations and structures of the development process relate to disabled people's exclusion from the built environment. How do property professionals learn about the needs of disabled people, and with what effects upon the development process? In what ways do professionals interact with disabled people and with what influence upon the form and content of development projects? For instance, in what ways do different project cycles, and fiscal conditions, impinge on how access issues are considered and developed, or not, within the context of a development brief (see, especially, Chapter 6)? Similarly, how does the legislative context on access inform and influence professionals' attitudes and responses to the needs of disabled people, and how far is it a mechanism for challenging and overturning the debilitating nature of the medical conception of disability? These are themes we now turn to in Chapter 3.

Further reading

Many of the ideas referred to in this chapter have been extensively developed elsewhere. A good starting point is Shakespeare, T. (ed.) (1998) *Disability: A Reader*, Cassell, London; also, other books to consider are, Drake, R. (1999) *Understanding Disability Policies*, Macmillan, London; Barnes *et al.* (1999) *Exploring Disability: A Sociological Introduction*, Polity, Oxford; Marks, D. (1999) *Disability: Controversial Debates and Psychosocial Perspectives*, Routledge, London. The classic, and path-breaking, text is by Oliver, M. (1990) *The Politics of Disablement*, Macmillan, London. Gleeson, B. (1999) *Geographies of Disability*, London, Routledge, and Imrie, R. (1996) *Disability and the City*, Paul Chapman, London, provide useful insights into the spatial and temporal nature of disability. An engaging text, which deals with broader philosophical issues in relation to disability is by Bickenbach, J. (1993) *Physical Disability and Social Policy*, University of Toronto Press, Toronto.

3 Access directives in the development and design process

Introduction

Access statutes and codes of practice are becoming a feature in a number of countries, where developers are required to provide minimum standards of entry and access for disabled people to public and commercial buildings, and, more recently, residential dwellings. As Michailakis (1997) notes, 62 nations worldwide have accessibility standards or laws, although, as Imrie (1996) suggests, the majority of legal frameworks are vague and difficult to enforce (see also Gooding, 1994, 1996). In England and Wales, for example, Part M of the Building Regulations requires developers to provide access where 'reasonable and practical', a phrase which enables developers, potentially, to circumvent the legislation. In contrast, in New Zealand, developers are required to provide accessibility in ways which permit disabled people to 'carry out normal activities and processes in that building' (Building Act, 1991, section 47; see also Gleeson, 1997). Likewise, in the United States, section 303 (a), of the Americans with Disabilities Act (1991), requires developers of commercial and public buildings, constructed for first occupancy after 26 January 1993, to be 'accessible to and usable by individuals with disabilities'.

This chapter explores the role and significance of legislative and regulatory provisions concerning property development and providing for the building needs of disabled people. The discussion is placed into a broader exploratory framework showing, and seeking to explain, the rise and significance of access rules, codes and regulations worldwide, with a particular focus on the UK, Sweden, New Zealand, the United States and ASEAN countries (see also Gleeson, 1997, 1999a; Gooding, 1994, 1996; Imrie, 1996, 1997, 2000a; Scott, 1994; United Nations, 1995).[1] As the material indicates, access statutes are variable in form and content yet tend to privilege investor decisions over third-party interests, such as disabled people. The themes to be explored include: the types of access codes and statutes which exist in a range of countries and the socio-political forces which have pre-empted them; what the legislation is and what it implies for providing for disabled people's design needs; how the legislation operates in a range of different development contexts; how access legislation influences development attitudes and practices; and the relative strengths and weaknesses of contrasting access directives and statutes.

In discussing these themes we divide the chapter into four sections. The following section describes the development of access statutes and codes in a range of different countries. Then, we evaluate the role of access legislation in seeking to secure accessible environments. We develop the argument that the legal basis for securing access, while variable between nations, is generally weak and ineffectual with limited means of enforcement. In the third section, we explore the statutory environment in the UK and evaluate its strengths and weaknesses in seeking to regulate the attitudes and practices of property professionals. We conclude by commenting on the possibilities, problems and issues in seeking to strengthen legal frameworks in order to facilitate disabled people's access to the built environment.

Statutory frameworks and comparative legal systems: the broader context

Legislative, and other, policy responses in different countries to the needs of disabled people have a lengthy and varied history (see, for example, Albrecht, 1992; Barnes *et al.* 1999; Doyle, 1995; Drake, 1999; Gleeson, 1999a; Gooding, 1994, 1996; Michailakis, 1997; Stone, 1984). From formative frameworks of containment or segregation, to contemporary programmes of inclusion and the propagation of civil rights, disability policies have been developed through a series of discrete, yet interrelated, stages. In particular, many western countries have adopted policies and programmes which seek to redress the lack of social and economic opportunities available to disabled people. The United Nations Declaration on the Rights of Disabled Persons (1975) is regarded as an important moment in seeking to develop equal rights for disabled people and forge anti-discrimination principles. As the Declaration (1975: 1) notes, 'disabled persons have the inherent right to respect for their human dignity . . . and have the same fundamental rights as their fellow citizens'. However, by 1987, an evaluation by the UN, of how far such principles had been developed and adhered to, concluded that:

> very little progress has been made throughout the world, especially in the least developed countries where disabled people are doubly disadvantaged by economic and social conditions. The situation of disabled people may indeed have deteriorated in the last five years.
>
> (UN, 1987: 2)

Partly in response to such observations, the UN has pursued a range of equal opportunities policy measures for disabled people including the development of its Standard Rules (United Nations, 1996).[2] These have established broad principles for nation states to adopt domestic anti-discrimination and equal opportunities legislation. As the UN (1996: 3): has stated:

the purpose of the Rules is to ensure that girls, boys, women and men with disabilities ... may exercise the same rights and obligations as others. In all societies of the world there are still obstacles preventing persons with disabilities from exercising their rights and ... it is the responsibility of States to take appropriate action to remove such obstacles.

As Drake (1999) suggests, however, there is no singular trajectory or philosophy underpinning policy programmes and practices worldwide. Instead, there is much policy diversity and complexity conditioned by country-specific social, institutional and political attitudes and values.[3] For instance, Drake (ibid.) refers to the laissez-faire or minimalist policy model, characteristic of a range of countries including China. As Drake (ibid.) recounts, disabled people have few civil rights in China with less than 6 per cent of five million disabled children enrolled in schools (see also Boylan, 1991). Likewise, Potts (1989) refers to China's absence of a social security system for disabled people: disabled people either have to be cared for by their families or, as Drake (1999: 97) observes, be referred to a 'social welfare institution operated by the local Bureau of Civil Affairs'. Other countries are not dissimilar to China in propagating a punitive and dependency-based culture which denies disabled people the range of civil rights. For instance, in Malaysia, disabled people are permitted to vote in a general election only if they are in the presence of an immediate relative or the presiding officer (United Nations, 1995).

Other countries have adopted welfare policies and programmes designed to provide state support for disabled people. As Drake (1999) notes, there is much variability in welfare policies ranging from the maximal programmes in Sweden to minimal welfare support in countries such as Portugal, the UK and Italy (see also Michailakis, 1997). What they share in common is a commitment towards programmes to enable individual adjustment (to circumstances) or the provision of some compensation to disabled people for their exclusion from different spheres of society. Thus, in Portugal, policy is paternalistic in revolving around 'pedagogic methods whereby society may be made aware of the duty to respect and assist the disabled' (Article 71 of the Constitution of the Portuguese Republic, 1990). In contrast, Sweden's model of disability policy is organised around medical rehabilitation, although underpinned by a welfare system which provides a wide range of support services for individuals unable to work. Thus, if medical rehabilitation is ineffective or inappropriate, additional measures include various (compensatory) types of disability pensions, annuities from employment injury insurance and special employment programmes.[4]

In contrast, there are some countries which seek to place disability issues into a broader civil or human rights framework underpinned by legislation. Disability statutes and policy frameworks around a civil rights agenda are of recent origin and reflect, in part, the emergence of a politics of disability in specific countries (Barnes *et al.*, 1999; Scotch, 1989; Shakespeare, 1993; Stone, 1984). This is especially so in places like Canada, New Zealand, Australia and, particularly, the USA with the passing of the Americans with Disabilities Act (ADA, 1991). The ADA's provisions include anti-discrimination measures which permit the federal government to initiate litigations against transgressions of the statute (Gooding, 1994; Imrie, 1996; Scott, 1994). As the ADA (1991: 2) suggests, the intention is to provide 'a clear and comprehensive national mandate for the elimination of discrimination against individuals with disabilities'. The legislation seeks to propagate disabled people's rights to have access to the full range of goods, services and other life opportunities, although, as Higgens (1992) suggests, the ADA is essentially conservative while wedded to a market welfare ideology (see also Gooding, 1994, 1996; Scott, 1994).

The variety of legal frameworks concerning the needs of disabled people are broadly reflected and reproduced in access legislation and related policies and practices. In particular, the majority of statutory responses world-wide seek, as a priority, to regulate for access in buildings used by the public with fewer or no controls over private dwellings or public transport. Regulatory systems concerning access can be divided into at least three types. Foremost are those countries which do nothing or encourage little more than voluntary codes of conduct and statutes which are vague and rarely implemented. Such directives tend to reinforce the power of private property owners to determine the contours of the built environment. Thus, in countries like the Philippines, access legislation has been framed in a context where, as the UN (1995: 3) argue, the 'awareness of the needs of disabled and the elderly at the local level is minimal'. As Lazoro Jr (cited in the United Nations, 1995: 7) notes, the ineffectiveness of access codes and statutes in the Philippines is due to their disregard by those 'in the private sector and government'.

Similarly, in Malaysia, a code of practice on access for disabled people to public places provides little more than guidance to developers on how they ought to respond to the building needs of disabled people. As the United Nations (1995) have said, very little monitoring takes place to evaluate how far guidelines are adhered to, while there is no legislation to ensure the accessibility of public transport. Likewise, in Indonesia there are no national building regulations on access. As the UN (1995: 24) have commented about Indonesia, 'there is an overall lack of awareness [about access] among local-level decision makers, consequently, access issues are given low priority; budget restrictions, lack of adequate planning, and the absence of a monitoring and evaluation system impede progress towards the achievement of a barrier-free environment' (see also Imrie, 1997). Moreover, the UN have characterised property professionals' attitudes in Hong Kong as 'negative' in a context where the building code is regarded by architects 'as further constraints on their creativity' (UN, 1995: 8). As the UN suggest (ibid.), 'the hope of a barrier-free environment for Hong Kong remains distant'.

These comments could be equally applied to a second category of countries which have similar types of prescribed building codes or regulations relating to access. While such countries prioritise the investment decisions of developers, they do so within an overall framework which seeks to secure, through statute, minimum levels of provision for disabled people (see Table 3.1). There is often a presumption that disabled people ought to be given equal treatment and that redistributive, welfare measures, based on special needs, are an appropriate response. However, legislation tends

Table 3.1 Access standards in Sweden, the USA, the UK and Japan

Description	Sweden	United States	United Kingdom	Japan
Entrances and exits	In entrance doors, lift doors and corridor doors or in openings along passageways, the clear passage dimension should not be less than 800 mm.	A minimum clear width of 815 mm will provide adequate clearance. When an opening or a restriction in a passageway is more than 610 mm long, it is essentially a passageway and must be at least 915 mm wide.	A minimum clear opening width of not less than 800 mm.	One exit/entrance in a building should be wide enough for wheelchairs to pass through. Its width shall be 800 mm or more. At least one doorway to each room shall be constructed so that wheelchair users can pass through it, and its width shall be 800 mm or more.
Corridors	A corridor or similar should not be less than 1300 mm wide.	The minimum clear width of an accessible route (corridor) shall be 915 mm.	An unobstructed width of 1200 mm for wheelchair access.	Corridors, etc., shall have a width of 1200 mm or more.
Stairs	Unobstructed widths of at least 1200 mm.	Each stairway . . . shall have a minimum clear width of 1220 mm between handrails.	Unobstructed widths are at least 1000mm . . . and (the provision of) a suitable continuous handrail on each side of flights and landings if the rise of the stair comprises two or more rises.	Handrails shall be installed.
Lavatories	A WC should have the dimensions of at least 1500 mm by 2000 mm and room for a complete turn of a wheelchair.	A WC should have the dimensions of at least 1525 mm by 1220 mm.	A WC suitable for wheelchair users should have at least the dimensions of 1500 mm by 2000 mm.	Where lavatories are provided in a building, at least one toilet stall for wheelchair users shall be provided in the building.

Sources: DETR, 1999b; ADA, 1991; Boverket, 1987; United Nations, 1995.

to be weak because of voluntarist frameworks which are designed to educate and persuade, rather than coerce, providers of goods and services to be sensitised to the needs of disabled people. Statutes also tend to distinguish between public and private spaces, generally regulating for access in the former but often not the latter. For instance, in countries like the UK, access, and related, legislation is underpinned by codes of practice and a voluntarist context which seeks to maintain governments' commitment to ensure that access requirements do not impose 'unnecessary burdens on employers which may prohibit job growth' (Department of Employment, 1990: 16; see also the next section of the chapter).

Likewise in Sweden, developers were, until recently, regulated by the Planning and Building Act (Boverket, 1987), and prescribed design guidance and specifications enforceable by building permits departments. On 1 July 1995, however, a 'self regulating' system emerged in that the detailed specifications of projects were no longer subject to scrutiny by building permits officers. Instead, the onus is on developers to produce a control plan or details of how a development will conform with the statutory framework.[5] This, potentially, is leading to a weakening of legal controls and public scrutiny of developers, and is seen by some as a retrograde change. As a building control officer, in interview, said, 'if you can prove a ramp is accessible at less than 1:12 then this is OK and so the standards are not binding and legal . . . if a developer can prove it works it is accessible.' Other property professionals in Sweden were sceptical of the system which, as an architect said, 'is like asking a thief to take self responsibility for not stealing again and asking them to come back again in a month and to tell you that they haven't stolen anything. It's so naïve. I don't believe it. Control has to be separated from the development companies that themselves have to be controlled.'

A third category of regulation relates to countries, such as New Zealand and the United States, which have sought to underpin their access codes and statutes with civil rights or anti-discrimination legislation. For instance, in New Zealand, the Human Rights Act (HRA, 1993), which has superseded the Building Act (1991), is a form of anti-discrimination legislation which seeks to guarantee the access of disabled people to places, facilities and vehicles (specified in sections 42 and 43 of the Act). As Gleeson (1997: 375) notes, the HRA has outlawed the refusal 'to allow anyone access to or use of places or vehicles which the public is entitled to use'. Similarly, in the United States, the ADA (1991) stipulates that the provision of barrier-freedom in all new public buildings is compulsory while any renovations and redevelopments of existing buildings require access to be provided for all categories of disabled people. The ADA (1991: 4) also permits individuals to file complaints of transgression to federal district courts while injunctions can be served prior to the construction of a building if an individual complains that they are about 'to be discriminated against' (see also Doyle, 1995; Gooding, 1994, 1996).

Gleeson (1997: 372), in referring to access legislation in New Zealand, notes how the 'accumulation of laws and codes concerning different aspects of access has certainly created a complex and labyrinthine area of state regulation'. However, the main thrust of the legislation is not dissimilar to the UK or other countries which broadly seek to minimise regulatory controls over private sector investment decisions. Thus, in New Zealand, the Building Act (1991) states that accessibility ought to be gauged in a number of ways, in relation to new buildings and where substantial alterations occur to existing structures. Foremost, a building is to provide 'reasonable and adequate provision by way of access' which permits a disabled person 'to visit or work' in that building in ways which enables them to 'carry out normal activities and processes'. Likewise, in the USA, the ADA requires existing structures (i.e. buildings) to be made accessible but only where 'readily achievable'; that is, where expense is not prohibitive to a provider of goods and services. Such statements, however, provide wide scope for interpretation with the notion of 'reasonableness' or 'readily achievable' being a potential source of debate and disputation (Doyle, 1995; Gooding, 1994).[6]

Evaluating access directives and statutes

The UN's (1995) critical appraisal of access legislation in ASEAN nations reflects some of the major shortcomings in access policies and practices worldwide (see also Gleeson, 1997, 1999a; Imrie, 1996, 1997; Michailakis, 1997). For the UN, most countries fail to incorporate access considerations into urban and rural development projects, while the formulation of legislation occurs without considering the needs of all disabled people. Policies tend to be targeted at the needs only of mobility-impaired people (Goldsmith, 1997; Imrie, 1996). Local authorities are often bereft of specially-trained staff, and human or material resources, to enable them to develop and implement access directives. For instance, constraints to implementation of access legislation in the Philippines are related to 'insufficient support from a broad range of participants' and a 'shortage of technically-trained workers to expedite proper implementation' (UN, 1995: 4). Likewise, in the study of local authorities in the UK, Imrie (1996, 1997, 2000a) discovered an absence of officer knowledge about access issues, and high levels of ignorance about how and when to use the building regulations in seeking to secure access in building projects (see also Gleeson, 1997, 1999a).

Most access legislation, worldwide, is also problematical for reproducing medical and reductive conceptions of disability. For instance, the Canadian Human Rights Act (Canadian Human Rights Commission, 1983: 2) defines disability as, 'any previous or existing mental or physical disability including disfigurement and previous or existing dependence on alcohol or a drug'. Likewise, the Australian Disability Discrimination Act (1992) notes that discrimination is prohibited on the ground of 'impairment' or against a 'handicapped person'. Similarly, the ADA covers all sorts of physical impairments, including Acquired Immunity Deficiency Syndrome (AIDS) and facial disfigurements. As the ADA states (1991: 2), a physical impairment is 'any physiological disorder or condition, cosmetic disfigurement or anatomical loss'. Such definitions are, in part, problematical for they 'adhere to the view that the plight of disabled workers is the result of the limitations of disability and of disabled persons themselves, and the notion that disability is often a social construct is implicitly rejected' (Doyle, 1995: 335). These values are unlikely to bring strong forms of regulation to bear against broader social forces such as the development industry.[7]

Whatever the definitional limitations and scope of the legislation, evidence suggests that the use and enforcement of access law, worldwide, is inconsistent and uneven within and between regulatory authorities (Doyle, 1995; Gleeson, 1997; Goldsmith, 1997; Gooding, 1994, 1996; Imrie, 1996, 1997; United Nations, 1995). The inability to enforce legislation is a feature highlighted by the United Nations (1995). As the UN has observed (1995: 8), in relation to the access statutes in countries of the Asian and Pacific region: 'the enforcement of such legislation is weak. Very few countries and territories have identified regular courts of law as the main enforcement mechanism for their respective legislation.' However, the lack of enforcement mechanisms is not confined to ASEAN countries and, as Gleeson (1997: 386) observes, in relation to a survey investigating the enforcement of access legislation in a local council in New Zealand, 'nearly 40 percent of buildings were found to be in violation of the access code. A separate set of surveys carried out in New Zealand's largest city, Auckland, in 1993 indicated similar compliance problems in several of the city's major hotels' (see also Gleeson, 1999a).

Ambiguities, exemptions and 'get-out clauses' are also a core characteristic of access statutes, thus diminishing their coverage and effectiveness. For instance, in Australia, the Building Code (1990) exempts offices and shops smaller than 500 square metres in area from the requirement to provide access, while access is not required to upper levels of any buildings (see McAuley, 1996). Assistive listening devices in auditoria are also exempt from the legislation. Likewise, section 42 of New Zealand's Human Rights Act (HRA) specifies a range of 'exception clauses' including, as Gleeson (1999a: 179) notes, 'privately owned domestic dwellings, small industrial buildings, various agricultural buildings and other minor structures'. This is not dissimilar to the UK's Disability Discrimination Act (DDA, 1996) which originally permitted a range of exclusions from access compliance, including educational establishments, crown lands or estates, and military bases (see the next section of the chapter for a fuller discussion of this point).

The ADA also permits 'get-out clauses' like 'undue hardship' to be used in deciding whether or not commercial operators have to remove barriers or facilitate better levels of accessibility to their buildings (see Gooding, 1994; Scott, 1994). Employers are also exempt from the ADA when to meet its provisions would entail 'unreasonable financial costs' or where they have fewer than fifteen employees. Operators of public facilities, like transport authorities, have 30 years, from the date of assent of the ADA, to make existing stock accessible (see Imrie, 1996, for an amplification of these points). Moreover, the United Nations (1995) documents a number of exclusions premised around the prioritisation of investor decisions, or seeking to let markets determine the supply (or not) of access facilities for disabled people. In particular, most ASEAN nations, like countries elsewhere, provide exemptions from compliance with access legislation on the basis of physical constraints imposed by the structure of existing buildings, as well as in relation to a building's historical significance (see United Nations, 1995).

Access legislation is problematical in seeking to regulate, primarily, for access into buildings rather than taking into account the broader infrastructure which characterises the built environment as a whole. Thus, most access legislation has little to say about routeways, pavements, street lighting, or any other facets of the built environment which might make a difference to the mobility and movement of disabled people. Access is reduced to a specific feature, the building, and usually only to public, not residential, buildings. There is little sense of the connectivity of environments or of the need to generate connected routeways for accessibility to be meaningful to disabled people. Legislation tends to promote one-off, ad hoc, design responses related to a specific building or design project. For instance, the UN (1995: 10) have reported that elevated footbridges in Hong Kong are a common sight, yet few escalators or ramps are provided 'because it is felt that they would take up prime commercial space'. There are, however, some exceptions. For instance, the National Building Code of Australia (1992) states that a continuous accessible path of travel must be available to and within all public buildings and facilities.[8]

The interpretation and implementation of access legislation is also a matter of concern, and there is some evidence to suggest that legislation is often used by regulators in selective and partial ways (see, for example, Gleeson, 1997, 1999a; Imrie, 1996, 1997, 2000a). For instance, Gleeson's (1997) study of access in the city of Dunedin, New Zealand, demonstrates the often arbitrary application of access statutes by regulatory authorities. In one instance, the council did not ask a commercial operator to install a lift during a major refurbishment, despite the legislation requiring this to be done. Likewise, Imrie's (1996, 1997) research reveals variable and sometimes illegal practices by local authorities in the UK. In one instance, a local planning authority was acting illegally by referring all applicants to the 1987 version of Part M of the building regulations, despite these having been superseded by the revised and updated 1991 version. Regulators are also often reluctant to use statutory instruments where access is concerned. Refusals of planning permission, on grounds of non-compliance with access, are rare and the use of planning conditions, to specify what developers have to adhere to with regards to access, is underpinned by cautious practice (Imrie, 1996, 1997).

Some authorities justify their limited use of the building regulations, or other access statutes, on the grounds of the legislation scaring away much needed investments. As a planning officer in the UK, in interview, said (quoted in Imrie, 1997: 440), 'any additional costs to an applicant can kill development stone-dead', while another commented that developers 'are only interested in profit' and 'consider the requirements in terms of cost/benefits to themselves . . . access is hardly a consideration' (quoted in Imrie, 1997: 441). Similarly, Gleeson's (1997, 1999a) study of Dunedin identifies an economic or investment rationale underpinning the reluctance of officers to fully use the raft of access legislation. Thus, as a building controls officer commented, in a letter to a Disability Coordinator at Otago University, 'all owners are not sympathetic to the requirements of the disabled code and some projects have not gone ahead because of these requirements' (quoted in Gleeson, 1997: 379).

Such findings suggest that the use of financial or economic incentives, to persuade developers or building owners to respond to the needs of disabled people, may be appropriate. For instance, in December 1989 the

Ministry of Finance in Singapore introduced fiscal measures to encourage owners of places of employment to modify their premises to facilitate access for disabled employees. The scheme permitted owners to incur tax-deductible expenditure of up to $100,000 on building works. Consultative services, concerning building design for access, were also provided by a voluntary team of architects, with the first meeting free of charge. In Japan there are minimum and recommended standards on access to public buildings. The latter specifies more generous space standards than the former and seeks to facilitate 'best practice' in relation to building access. While developers need not adhere to the recommended standards, those that do are able to apply for special financial assistance, such as loans at special interest rates, from the Government to offset (the anticipated) higher development costs.[9]

Despite the weaknesses of access legislation and its enforcement, it does provide disabled people with some legal, and often moral, means of influence. Evidence from the USA, for instance, shows that the ADA has transformed aspects of provision of services to disabled people. Thus, research by the National Council on Disability (1993: 31) concluded 'that so much has been achieved in so little time'. Likewise, Scott (1994: 26) notes that the 'ADA has also had an impact on the visibility of disabled people within society' (see also Gooding, 1994). Media reports also convey an impression of positive and far-reaching changes. For instance, a news report in the national newspaper, *USA Today* (1993; cited in Gooding, 1994: 95–6) suggests that, 'braille dots are popping up next to numbers on automatic teller machines. Phones for the deaf are being established in sports arenas . . . From office to movie theaters, the impact of the most sweeping piece of civil rights legislation ever enacted is being seen, heard, and felt.'

However, while a legal approach to disability and discrimination is important in helping to redress injustices against disabled people, we concur with Doyle (1995: 337) who notes that 'the limitations of legal formulae must be recognised' in that 'legislation cannot hope completely to redress the vulnerability of disabled people' (see also Gooding, 1994). For Doyle (1995), legislation, particularly anti-discrimination law, is capable of containing overt discrimination but not of eradicating it. Rather, political and economic power needs to be redressed to provide disabled people with the means to influence both government and corporate behaviour in relation to the provision of goods and services. This is a theme we return to in later chapters.

Access and statutory regulations in the United Kingdom

Property professionals' responses to the access needs of disabled people in the UK are framed, in part, by a range of statutory and legal instruments. In England and Wales, the mechanism for securing access is Part M of the building regulations (the now disbanded Part T of the building standard regulation in Scotland, Part R in Northern Ireland). Part M was introduced in 1987, extended in 1992 and 1998, and seemed to be a radical breakthrough in access legislation in the way it widened the scope of control to all public and commercial buildings and, latterly, to residential dwellings (see Goldsmith, 1997). Yet, Part M, and related legislation, is weak and, as some observers have noted, it couches regulations in a vague and ambiguous manner which does little to define clearly what is possible (Barnes, 1991; Goldsmith, 1997; Imrie, 1996, 1997; Imrie and Wells, 1993). It encourages developers to adhere to minimum standards of provision, while reducing definitions of disability to three (medicalised) types of impairment, that is mobility, hard-of-hearing and vision.

The legislation, including the DDA, seeks to minimise developer costs and to retain a voluntaristic system which prioritises the rights of developers to determine, in large part, what will be provided for disabled people. For instance, the Minister for Local Government in 1993, David Curry, in commenting on a proposal to extend the remit of Part M, noted that: 'whilst committed to creating an environment more accessible to people with disabilities we must ensure that any additional costs do not bear unreasonably heavy on those who provide and use buildings or on the community which ultimately pays the price for goods and services' (Curry, 1993). Similar views have been expressed by other politicians reluctant to legislate on matters of disability and discrimination. Thus in 1993, John Major, the then Prime Minister, argued that 'we are continuing to work to eliminate unjustified discrimination against people on the grounds of their disability. We believe that this is best achieved by education and persuasion backed up by targeted legislation to address special problems' (Major, 1993).

Regulations relating to disabled people's access needs have their origins in the Chronically Sick and Disabled People's Act (CSDP, 1970). Section 4 of this legislation requires developers to provide access where 'practicable and reasonable' in new buildings and where 'substantial improvements are made to existing ones'. Such directives have been supplemented with planning legislation requesting local planning authorities to inform developers of access standards (see Goldsmith, 1997; Gooding, 1994, 1996; Imrie, 1996, 1997). Thus, the 1971 Town and Country Planning Act (as amended by the 1981 Disabled Persons Act) states that 'planning authorities should draw the attention of developers to the provisions of the 1970 Act and to the BS5810 Code of Practice for access of the disabled to buildings'. Formative legislation, such as the CSDP Act, was seen as weak, with CORAD (1982) noting that statutory frameworks were doing little to 'address the issues'. As the Silver Jubilee Committee (1979: 2) commented, 'there is no way of compelling a developer to make reasonable provisions if they choose not to do so'.

Likewise, additional directives, such as Development Control Policy Note 16 (DoE, 1985: 3), did little more than insist that 'when a new building is proposed, or when planning permission is required for the alteration or change of use of an existing building, it will be desirable for the developer to consider the needs of disabled people who might use the building'. Other planning guidance reinforces the weak status of planning in access matters. Thus, Planning Policy Guidance 1 (entitled General Principles and Policies, DoE, 1992, revised 1997), sets out general ground rules on procedures in planning. However, wording in the document is vague and lacks any sense of how access provisions might be enforced. Moreover, the Access Committee for England (1994) have argued that the 1992 version of

Planning Policy Guidance 1 is 'confusing and misleading' while noting that phrases like 'might use', 'are encouraged to' and 'should consider' do little to specify what is permissible from what is not. As MacDonald (1995: 5) concludes, 'the negative and vague tone of Planning Policy Guidance 1 (1992) is a disappointing start to an examination of disability and planning'.

Other government guidance on the planning system, such as Planning Policy Guidance 12 (Department of the Environment, Transport, and the Regions, 1999a) notes that the development plan should consider social need, including the needs of disabled people.[10] Guidance also encourages planners to use the range of policy instruments including setting conditions on planning permissions in relation to access.[11] Thus, Circular 11/95 (Department of the Environment, 1995b) notes that 'where there is a clear planning need, it may be appropriate to impose a condition to ensure adequate access for disabled people'. However, as the previous section intimated, research indicates that planners are circumspect in their use of planning instruments in relation to access, or as a planning officer noted, in relation to the dearth of legislation, 'there is insufficient policy back-up and a lack of political commitment – access is not a high priority' (quoted in Imrie, 1997: 437). Others were equally circumspect about the use of conditions. As a planning officer commented, 'planning conditions imposed on planning decisions requiring disabled access are often overturned on appeal', while another said that 'we could never make a planning condition on access stick ... so why bother in the first place?' (quoted in Imrie, 1997: 436).

Notwithstanding planning guidance and legislation, Part M of the building regulations is centre-stage as the main mechanism for seeking to secure accessible environments (Goldsmith, 1997; Imrie, 1996). It provides general guidance to developers on access standards, and information as to how these standards can be met (see Goldsmith, 1997). However, as Table 3.2 indicates, Part M is restricted to a limited range of building contexts. Thus, while the regulations apply to new buildings and extensions including a ground storey, they do not apply to alterations, change of use or to extensions to dwellings. Moreover, exemptions include Crown buildings, schools and statutory undertakers, while there is no design advice about how decoration or signage might enhance access. Buildings constructed prior to 1992 are exempt from Part M, unless they have been extended. Even here, as Barnes (1991) suggests, the requirement is that access should not be made worse. The regulations, as the previous section intimated, also revolve around a medicalised conception of disability and refer to a narrow range of impairments (compared with, for example, similar building regulations in the United States).

The provisions of Part M fall far below what the Disability Rights Task Force (DRTF, 1999: 76) regard as adequate disability access standards. In a thorough-going review of disability legislation, in relation to disabled people's civil rights, the DRTF have questioned whether or not there is a case for access requirements to apply equally to all categories of buildings. They have also queried how far Part M ought to apply to existing buildings and the extent to which a change of building use should fall within the ambit of the building regulations. Others have questioned the workability of parts of the building regulations, in that they lack direction and clarity in

Table 3.2 The current (1998) Part M Building Regulation

Requirement	Limits on application
Interpretation M1: In this part 'disabled people' means people who have: (a) an impairment which limits their ability to walk or which requires them to use a wheelchair for mobility; or (b) impaired hearing or sight.	1. The requirements of this Part do not apply to: (a) a material alteration; (b) an extension to a dwelling, or any other extension which does not include a ground storey; (c) any part of a building which is used solely to enable the building or any service or fitting in the building to be inspected, repaired or maintained.
Access and use M2 Reasonable provision shall be made for disabled people to gain access to and use the building.	
Sanitary conveniences M3:(1) Reasonable provision shall be made in the entrance storey of a dwelling for sanitary conveniences, or where the entrance storey contains no habitable rooms, reasonable provision for sanitary conveniences shall be made in either the entrance storey or a principal storey. (2) In this paragraph 'entrance storey' means the storey which contains the principal entrance to the dwelling, and 'principal storey' means the storey nearest to the entrance storey which contains a habitable room, or if there are two such storeys equally near, either such storey. (3) If sanitary conveniences are provided in a building which is not a dwelling, reasonable provision shall be made for disabled people.	
Audience or spectator seating M4: If the building contains audience or spectator seating, reasonable provision shall be made to accommodate disabled people.	2. Part M4 does not apply to dwellings.

Source: Department of the Environment, Transport and the Regions, 1999b.

requiring that 'reasonable provision' be made for disabled people's access needs (Barnes, 1991; Goldsmith, 1997). This term, so some contend, provides too much discretion and latitude to developers to determine their responses to the building regulations (Barnes, 1991). For others, it provides the latitude and discretion to local authorities (Goldsmith, 1997). This implies that developers cannot approach a building project with any certainty about regulators' understanding and interpretation of Part M and what, subsequently, they will be asked to adhere to.

However, as Chapters 4 and 6 will show, some developers may well be using access standards beyond those of the building regulations. In part, this is related to, as Chapter 2 indicated, more competitive property markets and higher specifications in building design and construction (Ball, 1998; Cadman and Topping, 1997; Guy, 1998). It is also related to a greater awareness, especially by retail companies, of the need to get disabled people into premises in order to encourage them to spend on goods and services. In addition, a range of, mainly government funded, organisations, have been encouraging the development of access standards well in excess of Part M. Thus, as the Arts Council for England (1998: 4) have commented about Part M, 'although a valuable tool, it is not comprehensive and only provides access to facilities and not to all spaces'. In contrast, as Table 3.3 shows, the Arts Council for England and other funding bodies, as a condition of their ethos of 'access for all', specify standards of access at a level which are more generous than Part M (and to be adhered to by those that they fund). This is significant given that the Arts Council for England, in 1999–2000, funded 156 Capital projects at a cost of £110 million (Arts Council for England, 2000).[12]

While Part M remains the main mechanism for regulating developers' responses to the access needs of disabled people, the DDA (1996) has introduced a raft of regulations which have significant implications for property professionals. The Act is essentially a Code of Practice which does not, in and of itself, impose legal obligations. However, as the Code of Practice (DDA, 1996: 1) states, 'the Code can be used in evidence in any legal proceedings under the Act. Courts must take into account any part of the Code that appears relevant to any question arising.' The relevance of the Code (1996: 1), for the development industry, is primarily in relation to Part III of the DDA which 'is based on the principle that disabled people should not be treated less favourably, simply because of their disability, by those providing goods, facilities or services to the public or by those selling, letting or managing premises'. This, then, implies that service providers will be required to make 'reasonable adjustments' to ensure compliance, either by removing physical impediments (to access) or by changing the place from where the service is delivered.

The DDA is viewed from a number of other countries, such as Sweden, as a progressive piece of legislation in providing disabled people with possibilities to pursue court actions against developers transgressing access directives (Imrie and Hall, 1999).[13] However, a range of commentators are less than enthusiastic about the DDA (Barnes *et al.*, 1999; Gooding, 1996; Hawkesworth, 2001). As Gooding (1996: 1) notes, Lord Lester, a prominent civil liberties lawyer, referred to the DDA as 'riddled with vague, slippery and elusive exceptions making it so full of holes that it is more like a

Table 3.3 Building regulations and guidelines from funding bodies in the UK: a comparison of access requirements and recommendations

	Part M	Arts Council for England	Scottish Arts Council	English Sports Council*
Ramped approach	Not steeper than 1 in 15 if individual flights are not longer than 10 m, or not steeper than 1 in 12 if individual flights are not longer than 5 m. Surface widths are at least 1.2 m and whose unobstructed widths are at least 1.0 m.	Any new or refurbished ramps should aim to be at a gradient of between 1 in 15 and 1 in 20 and have level resting places (1500 mm deep) every 5 m. Do all ramps have an unobstructed minimum surface width of 1200 mm?	1:12 with a length of ramp at 5000 mm maximum: 1:12 is the maximum pitch. A ramp at 1:15 is preferred, with 10,000 mm maximum length before the introduction of intermediate platforms. The minimum width is 1200 mm with the preferred dimension as 1800 mm.	The maximum gradient for 10 m lengths of ramp is 1 in 15; but if the sloping sections are shortened to 5 m they can be slightly steeper – up to 1 in 12. No ramp must ever be steeper than 1 in 12. 1 m minimum clear width; 1.2 m minimum unobstructed.
Entrance doors	Minimum clear opening width of not less than 800 mm.	At least 900 mm (between door stops) wide.	900 mm clear opening minimum.	A clear opening width of at least 800 mm.
Internal doors	Minimum clear opening width of not less than 750 mm.	Minimum width of 900 mm (between door stops).	750 mm clear opening, with 800 mm the preferred minimum.	All doors should ideally have clear, unobstructed openings of at least 800 mm (a minimum of 750 mm is required by the building regulations).
Corridors and passageways	An unobstructed width of 1200 mm for wheelchair access.	Do all routes and corridors used have an unobstructed minimum width of 1200 mm?	A width of 1200 mm is the minimum for a corridor with 1600 mm the preferred dimension.	Corridors must be at least 1.2 m wide, and preferably 1.5 m … clear width.

Passenger lifts	Has a car whose width is at least 1100 mm and whose length is at least 1400 mm.	Are the internal dimensions of new lifts a minimum of 1400 mm deep by 1600 mm wide?	The minimum size is 1100 mm by 1400 mm as the internal dimensions of the car. If there is a high level of traffic then a lift car with an internal size of 1400 mm by 1600 mm could be considered, so that two wheelchair users can be accommodated.	The internal lift space must be at least 1.1 by 1.4 m.
	Has landing and car controls which are not less than 900 mm and not more than 1200 mm above the landing and car floor.	Are the lift control buttons and emergency telephone/alarm button set at a suitable height for wheelchair users (i.e. between 750 mm and 1200 mm from the lift floor)?	Controls need to be easily operated at a level between 900 mm and 1200 mm above floor level.	Controls set at 900 mm minimum height and 1.2 m maximum height.
WC compartment for wheelchair users	A WC suitable for wheelchair users should have at least the dimensions of 1500 mm by 2000 mm.	Do the toilets meet the minimum standard dimensions of 1500 mm wide by 2000 mm long?	A standard unisex toilet is 1500 mm by 2000 mm minimum, which allows a single side transfer onto the WC. A peninsular WC allows transfer from both sides and requires an overall size of 2000 mm by 2500 mm.	The peninsular layout cubicle (minimum size 2 by 2.5 m) is the preferred design wherever space allows. The standard layout cubicle (minimum size 1.5 by 2 m) takes up less room. Some wheelchair users will find it less convenient than the more generous peninsular type, but it is acceptable where space is tight.
WC compartment for ambulant disabled people	Minimum dimensions of 800 mm by 1500 mm.		The minimum size of a toilet able to be used by an ambulant disabled person is 800 mm by 1500 mm.	Minimum dimensions of 800 mm by 1500 mm.

* The English Sports Council is now known as Sport England.

Source: Appleton, 1996; Arts Council for England, 1998; DETR, 1999b; Appleton, 1998.

colander than a binding code' (Hansard, 22 May 1995: 813; quoted in Gooding, 1996: 1). Gooding (ibid.) also observes that:

> The DDA is indeed a confusing, contorted and unsatisfactory piece of legislation. It fails to establish a clear principle of equal treatment which should be the essence of a law countering discrimination . . . the Act's fatal equivocation towards the principle of equality for disabled people has produced an extremely complicated and unclear law, hedged around with exceptions and justifications.

In particular, the DDA permits service providers not to make reasonable adjustments if they believe health and safety standards are at risk. This, though, places too much emphasis on the opinions of the service provider and has led the DRTF (1999: 58) to declare that this aspect of the legislation potentially lends itself to endorsing stereotypes and prejudices (e.g. the inability of disabled people to fend for themselves or their presence being a fire risk). Like Part M, the DDA also reinforces medical and individualising conceptions of disability, while perpetuating an understanding of disability as something which is abnormal. As the DDA (1996: section 1, 2) says, 'a person has a disability for the purposes of this act if he [sic] has a physical or mental impairment which has a substantial and long term adverse effect on his ability to carry out normal day-to-day activities'. There is, then, a pathological conception of disability underpinning the DDA or, as Gooding (1996: 9) comments, the DDA 'does not reflect any fundamentally new understanding of disability' (see also Doyle, 1995).

There are potential points of conflict and confusion between the DDA and other pieces of building and planning legislation (see DRFT, 1999; Gooding, 1996). In relation to historic buildings, the Planning (Listed Buildings and Conservation Areas) Act (1990: section 16 (2), quoted in Gooding, 1996: 43) has established the standard that 'special regard' shall be given to the 'desirability of preserving the building or its setting or any feature of special architectural or historic interest'. How, then, might this conflict with the DDA's objective of seeking to provide goods and services to disabled people? As Gooding (1996: 43) suggests, while the Planning Act takes precedence over the DDA, 'this will not mean that an organisation operating from a listed building will be exempt from the DDA requirements. Providers must attempt to meet both sets of requirements.' Likewise, there is some confusion about the relationship between the DDA and Part M of the Building Regulations. Which one takes precedence, if any, and what are the possibilities of 'double jeopardy' arising, or where service providers are required to respond to contrasting, and potentially conflicting, legal directives?

Moreover, the DDA was set up with no strategic enforcement agency and, until recently, was overseen by an advisory body, the National Disability Council (NDC). For Gooding (1996), this was problematical because the NDC was only empowered to advise the Secretary of State on the operations of the Act. For its enforcement, the Act was, and probably still is, dependent on the ad hoc process of individuals bringing forward cases. As the DRTF (1999: 3) note, 'the lack of an enforceable body, responsible for ensuring compliance with disability rights legislation was, perhaps, one of the greatest flaws in the DDA'. However, some of these limitations and problems are, at the time of writing, being addressed by the DRTF. One recommendation, recently incorporated into a White Paper, was the setting up of a Disability Rights Commission (DRC) in April 2000, with the remit to eliminate discrimination against disabled people and, in particular, to enforce the DDA. As the DRTF (1999: 54) have said, the DRC ought to work with government and business 'to promote the benefits of design for all products and encourage manufacturers to supply information accompanying their goods in accessible formats'. In particular, the DRTF (1999: 59) have stressed that 'it is right that the benefits of integrated services for customers and service providers alike should be promoted'.

The changing legislative frameworks on disability generally point towards a more positive and knowledgeable societal understanding of disabled people and their needs. As the DRTF (1999: 2) have noted about UK statutes, 'whilst legislation in itself cannot force a change in attitudes, it can provide certain rights and lay down a framework that will encourage and hasten a change in culture'. Indeed, for the property industry, the next few years, particularly in the UK, would seem likely to lead to significant changes to legislation on access. Thus, the DRTF's observations about accessibility are, potentially, far reaching for property professionals in seeking to extend legal duties to those involved in the selling, letting and management of properties. As the DRTF (1999: 66) have observed, in relation to a disabled person seeking to make adjustments to a privately rented dwelling, 'they [the landlord] should not be allowed to withhold consent unreasonably for a disabled person making changes to the physical features of the premises'. Likewise, the DRTF (ibid.) have suggested that estate agents be brought within the ambit of revisions to legislation in requiring them 'to promote the inclusion of access information in sales and letting material'.[14]

Conclusions

Access directives and statutes are a feature of most countries, yet they tend to be underpinned by an economic rationale that prioritises the profits of corporations over the needs of disabled people. For instance, in relation to extending access legislation to manufacturers in the UK, requiring them to design their products to accessible standards, the DRTF (1999: 61) have said that this would be unfair, placing UK manufacturers at a competitive disadvantage. In the majority of countries, particularly those without civil rights legislation, disabled people and their organisations are not generally entitled to initiate legal action to ensure the implementation and enforcement of access legislation. This depends on the administrative authorities yet, for them, access tends to be a minor concern (Gleeson, 1997, 1999a; Imrie, 1999b). Evidence also suggests that the enforcement of access directives is weak, with few countries having developed adequate monitoring and evaluation mechanisms and procedures. As Doyle (1995: 336) comments, in relation to disability law, its failure 'can largely, albeit not entirely, be explained by a lack of commitment to and weakness in the policing of such special legislation'.

While the volume and scope of access legislation is increasing, attitudes towards disabled people are predominantly framed by conceptions of the 'undeserving poor', or seeking to provide minimum standards of access. Thus, in the UK, Part M of the Building Regulations is premised upon the provision of a 'minimum standard', rather than legislating for the highest possible quality of accessibility. As Doyle (1995: 335) notes, it is still the case that 'legislators adhere to the view that the plight of disabled [people] is the result of the limitations of disability and of disabled persons themselves'. Moreover, while legislation, such as the DDA, has the potential to counter some aspects of discrimination against disabled people, it tends to operate, what Gooding (1994) characterises as, 'leisurely timetables' without, as Doyle (1995: 345) suggests, the 'commitment of public funding that will be necessary to bring about the structural changes needed to promote disabled equal opportunity'. Given that most of the built environment, in the UK context, falls outside the regulatory powers of the Building Regulations, it is clear that much more has to be done to bring equality of opportunity to bear upon the movement and mobility of disabled people.

Nonetheless, the development of anti-discrimination legislation has a number of noteworthy implications. Foremost, as McAuley (1996: 10) suggests, there has been an increase in community awareness about the needs of disabled people and, in Australia, 'many government departments and large organisations in the private sector are busy doing access audits'. Likewise, in the UK, access audits have proliferated in a context whereby providers of goods and services are seeking to work out the implications of the DDA for their operations (see Gooding, 1996). New benchmarks of design and planning are beginning to emerge, while disabled people have had expectations raised that the DDA will be a powerful mechanism for change (DRFT, 1999; Gooding, 1996). In these, and related senses legal directives ought to be a focal point for disabled people's efforts to (re)shape the processes underpinning much of the development process.

Further reading

There are no comprehensive texts about international differences and similarities in access legislation and related policies and programmes. A superficial overview, although a useful starting point, of access legislation in different countries, is provided by Michailakis, D. (1997). The publication by the United Nations (1995) *Promotion of Non-Handicapping Physical Environments for Disabled Persons: Case Studies*, UN, New York, is one of the better publications although it also suffers for its brevity of treatment of the subject matter. The publications by Gooding (1994, 1996) are excellent in relation to the ADA and the UK. Other studies worth perusing include Gleeson's (1997) article on environmental access and regulation in New Zealand, and the book by Brian Doyle (1995) *Disability, Discrimination and Equal Opportunities: a Comparative Study of the Employment Rights of Disabled Persons*, Mansell, London.

PART II
Illustrations

4 Developers' responses to the building needs of disabled people

Introduction

In general I think the industry is not sufficiently sympathetic to these problems

(Developer interview)

This chapter is an exploration of one facet of the development process, that is, the attitudes, values and practices of developers in facilitating and/or constraining disabled people's access in the built environment. As Chapter 1 indicated, the production of the built environment is shaped by what Guy (1998: 267) terms 'profit seeking development agents' or those that seek to maximise rental returns on the sale of lettable space. For many developers, and related agents, the supply of ancillary infrastructure, such as accessible toilets, is not necessarily congruent with their economic interests. In particular, the development process is characterised by a range of socio-institutional structures and relations which are insensitive to, and ignorant of, the needs of disabled people. However, while acknowledging this, we develop the proposition that developers' responses to disabled people are not necessarily invariant, predictable, or reducible to a cost calculus. Rather, our evidence is illustrative of a heterogeneity of developers' attitudes, values and responses to the needs of disabled people.

We develop and discuss this proposition in the rest of the chapter, by referring to information generated by twenty-four interviews with property companies located primarily in London, and ten case studies of development projects located in Birmingham, Brighton, Dartford, Glasgow and London (see Appendix 1 for further details). Interviews with property companies were derived by a random sample taken from company listings in the property journal *Estates Gazette*, *Estates Gazette Interactive* (a web site), and Dun and Bradstreet's *Key British Enterprises* (1997). Sample companies differed by size, scale and type of operations, ranging from specialist operators (such as retail developers) to those with wide-ranging property portfolios and operations. A standardised questionnaire, with open-ended questions, was used for this part of the research. The total number of interviews is, in one sense, arbitrary, yet it reflects a certain exhaustion to the process in that, after about twenty interviews, we were hearing similar stories and tales about developers' responses to disabled people and diminishing returns were setting in.

The case studies were chosen to reflect a diversity of project and development contexts, including offices, theatres, leisure centres, retailing and art galleries. The cases comprise new build projects, such as the Armadillo Conference Centre in Glasgow and the Bluewater retail park in Dartford, and refurbishments of historic buildings, such as the Lighthouse, Scotland's Centre for Architecture, Design and the City in Glasgow and Ikon Gallery in Birmingham. The cases span a range of procurement or contractual arrangements including design and build and speculative and client-commissioned schemes. Each case is characterised by a range of different approaches to identifying and tackling the building needs of disabled people. Such diversity was important to the research in order to respond to 'the structures of building provision' or, as Chapter 1 suggested, to document the particularities of development contexts in shaping professionals' responses to the needs of disabled people. Thus, in each of the cases, specific factors, such as the attitudes of the client, or the financial nature of the project (e.g. whether lottery finance was attached or not), were important in fashioning the approaches to access.[1]

The case research was based on a mixture of participant observation, depth interviews, attendance at local authority meetings and the inspection of key documents and records such as project plans, development control case files and minutes from planning committee and development project meetings. Interviews were conducted with the full range of professionals involved in the case projects, including project managers, clients, contractors, surveyors, architects, building control officers, planning officers, local politicians, access consultants, etc. In addition, interviews were conducted with disabled people in the project areas about the level of their involvement in the case projects (and their involvement in development processes more generally). The data generated were primarily qualitative or based on the testimonies of key actors in the development process. In total, 112 case interviews, or an average of 11 interviews per case, were carried out in the period from March 1998 until April 1999.

Interviewees gave permission for interviews to take place on the understanding that their comments would not be used in a manner likely to identify them (unless they authorised otherwise). The quotations used here have been organised into themes raised by professionals who were part of a user network that we set up to guide the research (see Appendix 1 for further details about the user network). However, such themes, revolving around issues such as defining the subject (i.e. disabled people and their needs) or developers' means of responding to access directives, were of core concern to the interviewees too. The material reflects particular views of key actors and it is used to indicate feelings, ideas and opinions of those involved in the design and construction of the built environment. Obviously our choice of quotes, and the order and form in which they are presented, reflects our own biases yet they do, we believe, portray an accurate account of how developers and related professionals felt at the time of the interviews. Indeed, in the context of the cases, the validity of accounts could, in part, be checked against documents, such as minutes of meetings and through triangulation.

In using this diverse material, we divide the discussion into four. First, we discuss property developers' knowledge of, and attitudes towards, disability and disabled people's building needs. Second, we consider property developers' responses to the building and access needs of disabled people. Third, the significance of statutory and regulatory controls, and their interpretation, is evaluated as a factor in developers' responses to the building needs of disabled people. Finally, we seek to evaluate the importance of consultative and participative processes in influencing developers' responses to the building needs of disabled people.

Developers' knowledge of, and attitudes towards, disabled people

Societal knowledge of, and attitudes towards, disabled people have their roots in a complex history (Barnes, 1991). In the UK, disabled people have always been socially and economically marginalised, with opportunities denied to them. As Chapter 2 indicated, their history is a contradictory fusion of society's denial of their existence, countered by a vigorous charitable ethos seeking to provide disabled people with a basic means of sustenance and welfare. Disabled people are variously the objects of pity and derision, while medicalised conceptions are the dominant discourses of disability in reducing societal understanding of disabled people to the limitations imposed upon them by their physical and mental impairments. For disabled people, such discourses are problematical in perpetuating an understanding of disability which conceives of the impairment as the problem to be cured. This, in turn, denies the multiplicity of ways in which social structures operate to disadvantage disabled people and absolves society from necessarily articulating or developing moral standpoints about disability (and a disabling society).

Property developers tend to reflect and reproduce these broader societal knowledge bases, with few respondents connecting disabled people's status to moral questions or, indeed, to broader issues about citizenship and rights. In particular, most developers have little knowledge of the extent of physical and mental impairments in society. As one developer, in interview, said, 'an access officer quoted me an amazing statistic that something like 10 per cent of the population of this country are disabled in some way'. Others were sceptical about providing for what were seen to be a minority of building needs and requirements. As a respondent commented, 'disabled people are a minority of the population, therefore by providing facilities specifically designed for them we are discriminating against able-bodied people which is also unfair'. Such respondents had little notion of inclusive design or of the possibilities for sensitising buildings to all users. Indeed, some were concerned about what was perceived to be the inferior nature of building designs based on access. As a respondent said, 'architects should resist "overkill" . . . and avoid designs which satisfy minority groups to the detriment of the majority and the architectural integrity of the building itself'.

Such responses seem to reflect Young's (1990) observation that mainstream institutions seek to normalise and cater for a limited range of (bodily) differences (see also Imrie, 1996). Likewise, developers' definitions of disability, and disabled people, shows a limited notion of what disability is, or alternatively, a broad-based conception relating to an exclusive set of, usually mobility, impairments (which, we would argue, does little to reveal the complexities of the body's physiology). One developer noted that 'from my experience, when people are referring to buildings being designed for disabled people they immediately think of people in wheelchairs, someone who can't get around too easily'. These views were repeated by a range of interviewees, with another noting that 'people's minds do concentrate on people in wheelchairs . . . I think there has been an overconcentration [on wheelchairs]'. In concurring, one developer was critical of the provision of facilities for wheelchair users to the detriment of others. As he said:

> I suspect that buildings are probably designed with a picture of a wheelchair user as the model for a disabled person rather than a person who has a hip problem or arthritis or who can't open door handles. A circular doorknob is elegant but it's bloody difficult to open if you've got arthritic hands.

A number of developers were aware of the need to define disability in much broader terms than mobility impairment. As one developer remarked:

> hearing impaired you don't think about, to be honest. Because you don't see it [the disability] you're not aware of it. We would put braille on a lift but hearing is something that, well, perhaps you don't need to cater for. I can't think of an immediate incidence.

For another respondent, disability was also seen as much more than a mobility impairment. As he said:

> everybody at some stage in their life goes through a stage when they're not in A1 condition so that's the way you play it. It's not just the percentage of the population who are blind, or whatever, it's all the population whether you're a small child, somebody elderly or pregnant . . . it's too easy to think that you just deal with people in wheelchairs . . . it's general access for the wider population.

However, simplified and reductive understandings of disability tend to be more prevalent than not, a situation not confined to the UK. In Sweden, for instance, reductive views were also expressed. In interview, one developer said that, 'the term we use is restrictive movement (rörelsehinder)', while another said, 'I mainly refer to impairments of movement – a person dependent on a wheelchair'. Others, while acknowledging the definition of disability as primarily 'rörelsehinder', were attentive to alternative possibilities with some referring to vision-impairment and the debilitating effects of temporary impairments, like a broken arm. However, these were in a minority. Swedish developers intimated that access, while a standard building requirement and not unimportant, is a minor issue; or, as a developer argued, 'we respond to it as a matter of routine but it is one of the least important considerations in a project'.

Likewise, developers in the UK tend to regard access for disabled people as a minor consideration in building projects (see Imrie, 1996). As a developer, in interview, said, in referring to access, 'when we have a tenant the last thing they'll ask us is that sort of thing'. Others concurred, with the director of a large development company noting that, 'I would say, looking at the sort of perspectives of my co-directors, in scale of importance, relative to all the difficulties we have to overcome in getting these projects to go, this [access] is a relatively minor issue, so people aren't focused on it'. Developers also intimated that access is a disposable item if other, more important factors intervene, or as a respondent said, 'if the overall development can't be made cost effective it won't happen and a lot of these things, like creches and shopmobility, take away space and, therefore, take away revenue'.

Few developers dissented from the view that the property industry ought to be more responsive, and responsible, in providing accessible environments for disabled people. As one developer said, 'I think we as a company are anxious to be seen as user friendly and there are certain emotive things that one does want to contribute to'. Similarly, key property professionals, such as chartered surveyors, concurred with such views. For instance, a postal survey of UK surveyors shows that 90 per cent (or 108 practices) of the respondents believe that the property market should provide more accessible buildings (see Appendix 1 for details of this survey). As a respondent said, 'there is now a more general awareness amongst the public of problems caused by lack of access and these features should be promoted in new developments'. Another commented that, 'as providers of property, we have a duty of care morally, if not in law, to consider the needs of all users of buildings we produce'. However, few practices (14 per cent, or 17 firms) have any stated policy (written or otherwise) or procedures for dealing with the access and building requirements of disabled people.

Part of the difficulty for property professionals, in responding to disabled people's access needs, is that access is seen as contributing little or nothing to a building's valuation and marketability. As a developer said, 'I don't think that it helps in any form of letting to be honest . . . there is no real commercial gain, it's just doing what is right'. Others concurred, with another developer noting that an accessible building is no more likely to be lettable than one that is not. As he said, 'it doesn't make the slightest bit of difference because the occupiers look at so many factors and I think that [access] comes way down the list'. The survey of UK chartered surveyors confirms such opinions with very few of the respondents (18, or 15 per cent) feeling that access provisions would enhance the market valuation of buildings. Typically, the feature where valuations are likely to increase is the provision of lifts to all floors. Other features, such as tactile floors and paving, induction loops for hard-of-hearing and colour contrasts for vision-impaired people, will, according to the majority of respondents, make no difference to market valuations. Some even consider the provision of wheelchair ramps as likely to diminish a building's market value.

Developers also argue that there is little demand from tenants and clients for accessible buildings. As a construction director of a development company noted, 'The tenants' expectations are that we'll have solved it in the base building plans. They'll have thought that we've thought through the process and quite rightly so in that sense.' For instance, some see access features, such as stair lifts, as an irrelevance in that few people will either want, or need, to use them. As a respondent said, 'you rarely see disabled people using the lifts that we put in, or people in wheelchairs'. For developers of speculative office schemes, such features are regarded as additional cost factors which consume lettable space without providing demonstrable benefits to their clients. For one London-based office developer, access directives are problematical in that 'the core is getting bigger, therefore the offices are getting smaller and, obviously, from a developer's point of view, that's where my money is. The core, with the lift, stairs and lavatories is a necessity, but I don't make money out of it.'

The heterogeneity of developer responses to disabled people's needs

As Chapter 1 suggested, the economics of real estate are broadly driven by considerations of cost minimisation and profit maximisation. Mainstream economics assumes that developers will seek to supply property which does not compromise this underlying equation. The research indicates that cost considerations were a recurrent theme, with many developers referring to cost limitations in seeking to facilitate access. As a UK developer noted, 'additional facilities always cost money . . . they are not huge sums of money but they do become large sums if you start trying to apply it everywhere here in the building. It can become – for a very small percentage of the population – quite an investment.' Others concurred, with an access consultant noting how developers will seek to contain costs by not exceeding legal minimum requirements. As he commented, 'what they tend to pull it back to is the building regulations and that's where it always comes back to the cost'.[2]

However, the attitudes and responses of property professionals to disabled people's access needs are not invariant, predictable, or reducible, as mainstream economics would argue, to a cost calculus or a series of prescriptive responses. As one developer said, 'the cost thing is a load of nonsense because in terms of percentage of total cost, it makes no difference at all'. Another agreed, suggesting that, 'if you're designing from scratch, then to design those items [access features] in at the beginning is pretty minimal. If, in fact, it's more expensive.' In distinction, the evidence suggests that developers respond in a complexity of ways, and to a variety of stimuli, to the building and access needs of disabled people. In this, we concur with Rydin (1997: 6) who notes that 'while the prevailing ethos [of surveyors and related professions] may suggest an economic goal of maximising returns when taking these decisions, this is not inevitable. As with almost all professions, there is an ethical basis to their operation and self-justification.'

Such attitudes, and related responses, depend in part on the conjuncture of specific social and institutional relations, including the type of development company and development. Developer-interview, and case material, suggests that there are a range of important developer/development categories. Foremost, speculative developers, who probably will not own the building for more than a year, or alternatively, will sell onto a pension fund, are usually, in the words of an interviewee, 'interested in initial capital costs and not in anything beyond that ... they will only provide what legislation requires ... a short term view'. Another respondent concurred, suggesting that:

all that they [funders] want to know is what the financial return is and is it going to be an improving return. If it is and they like the project then that's it. All they want to know from that point on is that it meets the building regulations. They certainly wouldn't impose conditions at that level of detail because it's of no interest to them.

Case evidence confirms this, with developers of speculative office schemes particularly interested in minimising the loss of what they regard as lettable space to 'non-productive' uses such as lifts for disabled people. As a developer suggested, 'we need to make a profit at the end of the day. We need to consider the viability of an office development on the gross to net area. Wasted space equals decreased rent.' Another suggested that 'one problem, as a developer, has always been that you are constructing a building usually with no tenant, so you are trying to predict the range of uses'. Other interviewees agreed, with one explaining that 'on office buildings local authorities want us to have wider corridors ... it's all about loss of space. That's not space you can use commercially and therefore we use narrow corridors, we reduce staircases but still within the legislation.' Another commented that, 'I imagine that when you're building a commercial office development then the inclination may well be to try and cut corners and keep it as cheap as possible'.

Some respondents noted that speculative developments were being tempered by a 'new realism' or, as the director of an international property firm said: 'if we're developing a new building it needs to be marketable and the market now expects accessibility for disabled people, together with the fact that local authorities will expect us, and encourage us, to provide facilities for access'. However, for most developers of speculative schemes, there are constraints in seeking to respond to the range of access and other directives. Thus, for one developer, 'you don't want to go too far towards the end-user's requirements because after a few years if they leave, it's still got to be marketable to other people. So, unless you're an actual owner-occupier, most developers will actually amend or tweak things towards a particular client but they won't actually design towards the client.' Other professionals concurred with an architect, in commenting on his clients, suggesting that: 'generally, private sector clients are only interested in the initial capital costs and not in anything beyond that ... they will only provide what legislation provides'.

In contrast, Figure 4.1 suggests that, in schemes that cater for the general public, such as shopping and leisure centres, developers show a greater awareness of access issues, and more of a willingness to provide access features than is apparent in office schemes. In retail and leisure schemes, the cost/economic factor includes the spending potential of disabled people but also developers' perception of the need to be inclusive. As one developer noted, 'clearly there is a by-product of getting disabled

4.1 Commercial office space and retail development: contrasting attitudes to access.
Source: Tim Partington, Chapman Taylor Partners, 1999.

'The retail shopping centre market is totally dependent on footfall and getting the public to use the building. Therefore, the buildings need to be user-friendly to enable that to happen. If you get the toilet provision wrong, for example, and people have a bad experience they don't go back to a building. You know, they might have enjoyed their shopping but then they had to queue for half an hour to go to the toilet, well, they don't go back. The same applies very much in the leisure and cinema sector, possibly more so, because the competition is ever increasing. The operators are always looking at what we can provide that just gives us an edge over our competition. You know, can the screen be bigger, can the sound system be better, can the seats be more comfortable? So, again, access is an important issue. How do we allow disabled customers to use the building as any other person? Not to have to be accompanied by a member of staff is a very important issue. [But] commercial office space, I think, has to catch up if you like. It's seen as less of an issue for the developer there because he's letting space to someone. Yes, there may be one or two disabled people using that building but they [developers] tend to take a much tougher view on it and if you have to provide, say, three disabled toilets on a floor that's taking up what they call valuable lettable office space and the net-to-gross ratio in office buildings is absolutely critical in today's market place. So, if that has a detrimental effect on the net-to-gross then they're much tougher about it.'

people into centres. There is a spend and we want to accommodate that spend. But, clearly, we are also very much in the public domain.' Others made similar comments, with another developer saying that 'we don't want to alienate groups and we want to provide a quality facility . . . we're looking at whatever facilities we can provide to go way beyond [the building regulations]'. Others concurred, with a major international retail developer expressing a broadly held view:

It's difficult to quantify access costs. You can put in X amounts to just cover the bottom line . . . but you don't do that. You're creating a total environment. You've got to make it right for everybody. You could say that the environment you're creating at the end of the day will enhance the retailer in the end because it will increase the number of people and it will enhance the perception of the centre. So, potentially, we could actually charge higher rents because we know the quality of the product we're giving is much more than people expect down the road. So you can say it costs more but it generates more too.

Moreover, public developers and/or clients, such as local authorities or utilities or public service providers, such as railway companies, have, in the words of a UK interviewee, 'a direct role in it, they've a more social, caring attitude about the buildings they put up'. They also have to respond to critical public opinion, scrutiny and viewpoints. For instance, in the case of the Armadillo Conference Centre, largely funded and developed by the local authority, Glasgow City Council was keen to ensure that access issues were addressed by all concerned. The building control officer said, 'we identified the disability issue and got into negotiation with the architect and owner of the building. From a PR point of view the council had to look as if they were producing a building with good disabled access' (see also Figure 6.1). Other public authorities are rigorous in ensuring access for disabled people to public spaces and, as one developer noted about the Sports Council, 'they are strongly influential about any leisure or lottery [funded] buildings now. You'll find that most sports buildings are pretty good as far as disabled access is concerned and their guidelines tend to be slightly more than the regulations.'

In particular, one of the more significant elements in changing client and/or developer's perspectives on access for disabled people relates to projects where access provisions are a condition of funding (see also Chapter 6). In the UK, for instance, the funding of commercial development projects, by the National Lottery and other groups, such as the Arts Council for England and English Heritage, are often conditional on developers building beyond the building regulations.[3] Indeed, architects commented that much of their work was being changed by the particular conditions stipulated by such funding organisations. Thus, for one respondent, the access requirements to ensure lottery funding for a particular project, The Lighthouse, ensured that the client was 'very willing' to have total accessibility within that development (see Figure 4.2).

Developers' attitudes to access also depend on whether a project is new build or a refurbishment of an existing building. As a developer said, 'if you went over-prescriptive with Part M it would cause huge difficulties with the refurbishment of existing buildings'. This is particularly the case with historic buildings or those with listed status. Thus, an architect, in interview, commented: 'a large proportion of building projects involve conversion or adaptation of existing buildings. Sometimes, especially in the case of listed buildings, it is necessary to moderate the provision for people with disabilities for reasons which have nothing to do with attitudes, no matter how committed the participants are to access for all.' The building regulations also provide 'get-out clauses' for developers in refurbishing buildings. As a building control officer noted, 'while the building regulations do have an underpinning on new buildings a lot of planners' work is on refurbished buildings and in those areas the building regulations have not got a lot of teeth'. This is a theme we now turn to.

The significance of statutory and regulatory controls and their interpretation

In general, developers are supportive of the building regulations and many see them, as one stated, as 'a starting point, and that's how they should be treated'. Others concurred, with one developer stating that 'I think it's become a standard part of what we provide and I think that by and large it represents a reasonable provision'. Developers like the 'open-ended' nature of the regulations and are generally happy to negotiate access into their schemes, although, as a developer said, 'I can't recall anybody saying, well we want to do more than the building regulations'. The regulations,

4.2 The Lighthouse, Glasgow.

The Lighthouse, Scotland's Centre for Architecture, Design and the City, opened in July 1999. The building, originally designed by Charles Rennie Mackintosh, is the former home of *The Herald* newspaper. After lying empty for about 15 years, it was refurbished and redeveloped with £12 million funding from sources such as Glasgow City Council (£1.5 million), the European Union (£4.2 million), the Scottish Arts Council (£2.1 million), the National Heritage Lottery (£3.5 million), and the Glasgow Development Agency (£0.5 million). As the project director said about the Lottery funders, 'they are hugely important, because they are the biggest free money'. A stipulation of Lottery funding was the appointment of an access consultant. In conjunction with the consultant, designers paid much attention to the needs of vision-impaired people, in particular the positioning of signs, heights of lettering and typefaces. An infrared audio system, at three points, throughout the building, is a particular feature. As the consultant said, 'they're putting in audible signs and that is programmed in and that will be one of the first buildings that I know of that's got a complete system of audible signs in the building'.

for some developers, have been vital in raising their awareness of disabled people and their needs. As a developer noted:

> Part M has been the catalyst for raising the profile of access issues and I think that is only right because for those of us who are fortunate enough to be able-bodied, unless there's actually something there in statute that makes you think and consider these things, then you don't naturally think about all the issues relating to the disabled.

Most respondents were in agreement that their responses to access were conditioned by the legislation, or as one person in interview said, 'is it driven by legislation or will companies take it on because they feel they've got a social role to play? At the moment I feel that it's only legislation-driven.' Others agreed, with one developer suggesting that, 'ultimately it's up to the government to direct the industry and then for the industry to comply with that' (see also Gooding, 1994).

This suggests that developers passively respond to access directives rather than seeking to influence or transform them. However, some respondents felt that the attitudes of developers were informed by social and ethical considerations and a willingness to be pro-active rather than merely react to legislative requirements. As one respondent said, 'it's always the carrot and the stick, isn't it? I think the argument that should carry more weight is the moral issues. You know, it's the right thing to do.' Others felt likewise, with some commenting on what they saw as progressive social forces seeking to mould the legislative directives. For one developer, for example, a duty is to facilitate access for all to his retail developments, if only to ensure the expansion of the market to all possible types of consumers. As he suggested, 'government legislation has had an impact but coupled with that I think there has been a general desire within the industry – architects, surveyors, and others – to want to accommodate, within reason, the disabled shopper'.

Some developers also seek to design well beyond the minimum standards and to anticipate the cost and other implications of the changing regulatory frameworks. The more astute development companies and institutional investors are aware of the potential financial implications of the DDA which, from October 1999, required service providers to adhere to a revised Code of Practice on the provision of accessible facilities, services and premises (see also Chapter 3). As one developer argued, 'one or two institutional investors are smart enough to realise that legislation is imminent and therefore think that if you don't put that [access] in that we're going to have to come back in a year's time and put it in and in that respect it's going to cost us £100,000'. Others agreed with one developer noting that the minimum standards are less than adequate, and might well work against the development of a broad customer base. As he suggested, 'on a day to day basis we're dealing with people and we want to supply them with a wonderful experience when they come to the centre. Therefore, you want to move from the purely legislative approach to trying to provide the best that you possibly can to cater for the needs of everybody within there.'

Thus, while Part M emphasises the provision of minimum standards, it would be problematical to assume that developers necessarily adhere to them. Indeed, the research is revealing in demonstrating some developers' antipathy to minimum standards, with one interviewee arguing that, 'you can pick up Part M and they tell you how to deal with disabled access but it's about taking it one stage further, what is best practice'. Others concurred, with another developer stating that, 'where possible we do more than merely comply, we would always seek to provide maximum access'. The more progressive development companies regard Part M as dated and largely irrelevant in producing sensitive and quality products. As the director of a retailing development company argued, 'although our design manual is Part M compliant we're about best practice requirements and that's what we've set down'.

In influencing developer responses to access issues, it is not so much the regulations per se which are determinate but their interpretation. The discretionary nature of the building regulations is, we would argue, a potential strength in permitting the possibilities for local authorities to negotiate with developers to attain access beyond the prescribed minimum standards. For one developer, interpretation of the regulations 'varies tremendously with the different authorities. Some are quite stringent and have a high standard on behalf of disabled people whereas other authorities are more lenient.' For some developers, this is an issue given that, as a respondent argued, 'I'd just like them [local authorities] to be more commercially flexible. I would like the regulations to have a commercial insight, particularly when you're down at the bottom end, whether it be a small office or shop.'

However, the evidence suggests that many developers are attuned to local authority variations in legal interpretation and usage, and prepared to bargain around the minimum provisions. As one developer said, 'the internal side is really just a case of what building regulations dictate and there's a certain amount of negotiation as to the precise implementation of them'. In one local authority, for example, knowledgeable officers, sympathetic to commercial imperatives and the needs of disabled people, drew the developer's attention to access issues at an early stage. As one of the building control officers commented:

> the way you control it is to take an agenda to the applicant themselves and we did a lot of work with the local access group to come up with a wish list beyond Part M. We've tried to push the developer up the good practice curve really and basically using the disability legislation and making them aware that it's not just Part M in isolation.

The developer, in turn, was responsive to the local authority and willing to respond to the local political environment. In another case, an access consultant was introduced to a city council-sponsored project nearly a year after it had moved from its design conception to implementation stages. For the project manager, this was problematical because 'we'd already costed everything and then we were being told to make changes which changed the costing of the project'. Likewise, the access consultant felt that the timing was less than satisfactory, while commenting on the indifference of the development team to access issues. As he said, 'it's down to chance that something on access is actually developed and I've then commented on it rather than actually been included in the design process, which is not to our liking'.

The role of consultative and participative processes

The design and development of the built environment occurs through a myriad of specialist tasks dominated by professionals deploying expert knowledge. However, as Monahan *et al.* (1998: 1) note, 'it is not common practice for architects and designers to consult disabled people when creating buildings. Their clients do not have disabled access needs as a priority in the competitive, cost conscious nineties.' This is reaffirmed by our research which indicates that disabled people's participation in development and design processes is usually absent or never much more than 'arms-length' consultation (also, see the relevant parts of Chapters 5 and 6). In particular, property development and related building processes are, for Ventriss (1987: 281), dominated by neo-conservative thinkers or those who argue that 'the virtues of participation have been taken too far'. As Ventriss (ibid.: 282) notes, a popular viewpoint is that modern society is 'suffering not from a paucity of participation but from too much' or what he terms an 'overloading of government'.

Our research evidence suggests that, more often than not, disabled people's views are not sought by developers. When their views are solicited, they tend to be incorporated as an after-thought rather than as an integral element in informing development schemes. There are few instances of developers talking with disabled people prior to the submission of a planning application, while a recurrent issue is that there are no formal mechanisms for them to meet developers or their agents. As one developer said, 'I have to try and farm that [consultation] down the line, so it would be dealt with by the architect. It [consultation] does happen but not all that often.' Such views tallied with the experiences of access groups and, as a member of a group commented:[4]

> time and again planning applications seem to get through the system even though we don't like a lot of the design details. We never ever meet the developers or architects or anyone for that matter who might be important. The chair of the access group says there's no need because it will all be handled by the planners and the system. Well, it isn't from what we can see.

Other groups cited similar experiences, with most noting that developers do little to facilitate access and usually ignore their views. For some, consultative processes between developers (or their agents) and disabled people were little more than public relations exercises. The views of the chair of an access group, with regard to a recently completed retail development, were typical:

> The developers seemed to take on some of what we said but not much. One or two things did change in the scheme but others didn't – we didn't want a shining floor but they left it. We complained about the steepness of the ramp but they said they couldn't do anything about it –

we wanted a rest area halfway up it rather than a continuous slope. We didn't really get any reason from them for not doing anything. So, they ignored some of our recommendations. We suggested a chairlift at the bottom of the stairs but got nothing on this.

Others felt that developers would listen to their views but only within the financial strictures of the project. As the chair of an access group commented, 'I would certainly say that they [developers] have been prepared to listen, but there has been a feeling that their primary concern is a financial one'. Similar views were expressed by others, with an access officer noting that discussions were rarely able to challenge developers seeking to pursue their objective of securing maximum lettable space.[5] As she suggested:

> the difficulties [in discussions] come when you are asking for more than lifts or more space or a better arrangement of toilets and it's going to take up lettable office floor space. They might be quite amenable to begin with and then they'll go back to the client who will say 'Do I have to do this?' They will come back and say that the client will only do the absolute minimum because he's losing another foot of lettable space and if you multiply that up through the building that's where there can be difficulties.

For developers, consultative processes are often regarded as unnecessary in that, for them, the regulatory or statutory parameters, such as the Building Regulations and the DDA, are themselves the legitimate results of consultations with the relevant groups and that no more is required to take disabled people's views into account. For instance, as one developer commented, 'I believe that mandatory requirements incorporated into legislation are the result of extensive consultation and that they are constantly evolving. I do not, therefore, see the need for additional such consultation.' Others concurred while expressing the problems of delay as a result of consultation. For one respondent, 'it's more the delay . . . the clients just want to get it sorted because most of the time, it's not a big issue for them'.

Others felt that disabled people's lack of understanding of the commercial imperatives and pressures of the development process worked against the possibilities of consensual outcomes. As a developer of a retail scheme commented, about consultative processes with the local access group:

> if we'd left it more open it would have dragged on and the access group didn't understand the pressures we were under . . . we know we have to make the building accessible and if we had had fuller involvement we would have got bogged down. There's no reason to think that fuller involvement by the access group would have made the end product any better.

Another voiced similar sentiments and added that consultations are counter-productive in that 'what you do find when you've got a diversity of groups is that sometimes one person's aspirations are in conflict with how somebody else sees the space working'. Other respondents felt likewise in that consultation is not time effective and that client funding does not allow for time to consult. In this sense, even if developers or their agents wish to consult with disabled people and their organisations, they may very well be constrained by wider imperatives and pressures within the development process.

Such attitudes and practices are widespread with evidence from Sweden, for instance, showing that developers rarely have direct engagement with disabled people. Like their UK counterparts, Swedish developers feel little need for consultation over specific project details because they regard the building regulations as being the end result of prior consultative processes between disabled people's organisations, government and the building industry. As a Swedish developer said about consultations, 'I have never been in any . . . the handicapped organisations work closely with Boverket [the Swedish Board of Housing, Building and Planning] and consult with them when they are writing the rules'. Such attitudes, in part, relate to the programmatic nature of Swedish society which regards the formal consultative process as sufficient in fulfilling the objectives of a democratic society (see Cousins, 1998). Thus, for one developer, 'I have never been in discussion with disability organisations . . . there are no problems with the regulatory system'.

Others felt little need to consider access beyond advice contained in design manuals. Thus, a Swedish developer justified his lack of consultation with disabled people: 'I have found answers to my questions in the regulations, official publications and in publications from the disability organisations'. Others argued that disabled people's lack of knowledge of the development process was a hindrance to the pursuit of quality in urban design. As one developer argued, 'I think it's because they're not builders. They know about the difficulties for disabled people, but some of these people, they want everything.' Others concurred, with another Swedish developer suggesting that they do little more than consult with access consultants to avoid conflict with diverse parties. As he suggested, 'it's better with an expert I think. I suppose they [disabled people] have a lot of wishes and we don't have time to solve all of their problems. It's better to have one person to talk to.'

However, many developers acknowledge experiential knowledge, and its potential importance, in feeding into development projects. As a UK developer said, in relation to a recently completed shopping centre, 'on the one that we've just finished and sold we had a number of meetings with the access group. It brought it all down to earth; you know you talk to these people and the fact the light is two inches too high makes life impossible for them and you think "bloody hell" . . . so yeah, it's humbling and always worth doing. It's always useful to listen.' In this sense, consultative and participative processes have the potential to develop shared understanding, while contributing to a better quality of product. As a developer said: 'on our second square here we actually met up with the people who were expressing concerns and I think when you do, and when you say what you're trying to do and achieve, then, I think there's much more of an empathy coming back from them as to why you're doing what you're doing.'

Conclusions

Property developers have limited knowledge of disabled people and their needs, and regard them as a minor consideration in building projects. The evidence suggests that the needs of disabled people are poorly understood by developers and their agents, partly because potential tenants and clients rarely express a demand for accessible buildings. Statutes reinforce minimal developer responses, while there is little or no requirement for developers to consult with disabled people about the content of building projects. However, property developers, and the development industry, are not necessarily averse to responding to the needs of disabled people nor are they unaware of their legal and, sometimes, moral obligations. In this sense, the strategies of property developers, and related agents, are not wholly reducible to what Luithlen (1994: 125) terms 'rent relations', and there is some evidence of a heterogeneity of motives, attitudes and responses by developers towards disabled people's building requirements.

Seeking to reorientate aspects of the social relations of the development process is important if the building needs of disabled people are to be addressed and implemented in the context of development projects. We concur with Guy (1998: 266) who, in referring to developers' responses to environmental issues, argues that research 'should stress opportunities for property professionals to put their knowledge and concerns into effect' (see also Guy and Shove, 1993). Part of this relates to the changing contexts and opportunities for property development, including, for instance, the influence of National Lottery funding. There is also a need to understand how and why the motives and responses of developers differ with regards to responding to the needs of disabled people. While all developers operate to maximise (rental) profits, some are more likely than others to respond to access issues, even within the same spheres of operation (such as retail development). To understand such diversity one needs to develop, after Guy (1998: 279), 'a more heterogeneous portrait of the social organisation of the development industry'.

This heterogeneity is influenced by a complexity of factors surrounding the building or project context, including, amongst others, client attitudes, knowledgeability of key participants in the project team of disabled people's needs, the interpretation and implementation of access regulations by local planning authorities and the disposition of disabled people, locally, to influence development projects (and the willingness or not of project managers to permit disabled people or their representatives to participate in the development process). For instance, as the research suggests, the social relations of the local political environment is a critical factor in influencing developer strategy (see also Imrie, 2000c). Thus, in places where local officers are committed to meeting the needs of disabled people, and where the local political system is supportive of officer directives, developers are unlikely to resist meeting requests for access provisions in projects. In this sense, where a development takes place is often crucial in influencing how far developers are likely to respond to the needs of disabled people.

While such understanding is important, a number of practical and political issues have to be addressed. Foremost is the argument that access provision is a prohibitable cost. This maxim has become a more or less unchallengable part of developers' reactions against providing for disabled people's needs, yet, as Chapter 2 notes, there is little or no evidence to suggest that providing for disabled people's design requirements is any more expensive than providing for all building users. Access statutes are also weak because they define disability in reductionist terms, while requiring minimal developer responses to disabled people's building needs. This surely requires some redress, particularly in a context where the more innovative and progressive developers are seeking to build far in excess of the provisions laid down in Part M. Likewise, the planning process needs to think about how to interlink, more effectively, user views of development projects with those of developers, or at least consider how best to establish mechanisms for communicative and interactive dialogue. Ultimately, policy and political strategies must recognise that developers' commercial concerns and actions have moral and ethical implications (for disabled people).

Further reading

To gain a broader understanding of the attitudes and motives of property developers, readers should refer to Cadman, D. and Topping, R. (1997), *Property Development*, published by E & FN Spon. The articles by Ball, M. (1998) and Guy, S. (1998) provide excellent insights into ways of thinking about how and why developers operate as they do. While there is little or nothing published about the interrelationships between disabled people and developers, Gleeson, B.'s (1997) study of the development process in New Zealand is useful. Likewise, readers should refer to the Centre for Accessible Environment's journal, *Access by Design*, which regularly publishes short articles and reports about how far the development process is responding to the needs of disabled people.

Case study:
Bluewater, Dartford, UK

Long sweeping entrance into one of
Bluewater's malls, featuring a gentle
gradient for ease of wheelchair access

An important aspect of designing for disabled people's needs are the attitudes and values of property developers and their clients, and their underlying motivations in pursuing particular courses of action. Such motivations, and their influences on the development process, are well highlighted by the Bluewater retail development in Dartford, Kent. Bluewater is a 100 hectare out-of-town retail development comprising 154,000 square metres of retail floorspace and attracting up to 30,000 consumers on a typical Saturday. Started back in 1994, and opened in March 1999, Bluewater is the largest retail development in Europe with 320 stores in three interconnected shopping malls. The project had a construction value of £350 million and, as Eric Kuhne, the concept architect, said in interview, the aim is to make Bluewater 'one of the finest retail experiences in Europe . . . a place where everyone can come to and feel at home'.

The project was initiated and implemented by the Australian company Lend Lease, who was both the developer and client of the scheme. At the outset, a client ethos, or specific set of attitudes and values, was brought to bear on the project. This set the broad parameters within which specific design details were developed and implemented. As the project manager said, 'we're not claiming that we're going to get everything right. We started off with a set of aspirations . . . we regard disabled people as an important part of our customer base, and it was always the intention to provide the best for them.' He amplified by noting that the needs of disabled people are paramount at Bluewater. As he suggested, the developers have provided an attractive environment for disabled people with 'wider car park spaces, increasing sight lines, and slopes never greater than 1:15'. One of Bluewater's architects concurred in noting that 'we have done our best to ensure that we have easy access . . . we try to provide an uncluttered environment and avoid having ramps'.

These statements reflect, in part, Lend Lease's objective for Bluewater; that is, social inclusivity by seeking to design for the diverse needs of everyone visiting the centre. As Bluewater's project manager noted: 'we, as a company, are very, very customer driven. A huge amount of work was done in the early days of the project in talking to focus groups . . . actually analysing what people want.' He qualified this comment by referring to the contents of the company's mission statement which states that Bluewater 'should be established and operated as the market leader in accessibility among regional shopping centres'. The local authority concurred, with a building control officer noting that, 'You've got to take your hat off to Lend Lease, they have a different approach and they're very keen to be good corporate neighbours and they see it as a partnership with the local authority and the local community.'

Bluewater is unusual in that most development practices tend to minimise design features that reduce lettable space. As the developer of a recently refurbished retail centre, Churchill Square in Brighton, said: 'floor space is money and rent. We need to give the client the most efficient layout. Circulation, toilets, and back-house areas often get forgotten and are seen as not that important . . . we need to go with the minimum requirements.' Such views formed the broad remit for the architects' approach to the development which, as he admitted, 'paid more attention to our client's requirements than to disabled people's and we were driven by the commercial needs of the clients. We had a programme to keep to and it was a concern to us and our client.' A representative of the client concurred in suggesting that there was very little demand for accessible design features or, as he said, 'it's frustrating to put things in when you know they won't serve a function'. He qualified this by stating that, 'why should we provide more than the minimum? You rarely see disabled people using the facilities we provide.'

The main entrance to Churchill Square
Shopping Centre

Such views were accompanied by
tentative and ambivalent remarks about
accessible design. As the client's
representative said, 'at the end of the
day you can only, sort of, strike a
balance and take a middle line and
hope that you're actually providing
something that benefits the majority of
people . . . you really can't design for
every single disability'. The architects
qualified this by suggesting that a
reductionist definition of disability, that
of mobility impairment, was adequate
for responding to the needs of disabled
people. As the lead architect commented, 'the main definition of disability is wheelchair access and it is this that
mainly influences the design of a building. It has the biggest impact in terms
of provision of lifts, changing the levels
of floors and eating into commercial
space.' This, as the local building control
officer noted, limited the design process
from the outset. As he said, 'discussions
with the architects rarely mentioned

much more than the needs of wheelchair users. We felt this was too narrow
a focus and likely to lead to a limited
range of provisions.'

In contrast, Bluewater's architects
were instructed by the client to, in the
words of the project manager, 'make
the place right for everybody. Anybody
could create a shopping centre that
works for 90 per cent of the people 90
per cent of the time but the idea is that
we've set ourselves apart from that and
actually think [about everyone].' To this
end, Bluewater provides tenants with
advice and information about compliance with the DDA. Such actions
underpin Lend Lease's commitment to
an inclusive approach concerned not
just with the buildings, but the spaces
around them, the attitudes of prospective tenants and their staff, and 'after-
care' management systems to ensure
that access to the centre is maintained
at all times. For instance, the project
manager noted that prospective tenants

have to conform with Lend Lease's access standards. As he commented:

> the whole design philosophy with the retailers is that we don't want them to come down and give us their standard high street store. The idea is that you come to Bluewater and this is our philosophy, this is what we do in public spaces, this is the kind of environment we are creating, what are you going to do now?

In contrast, many developers provide little advice, guidance, or encouragement to prospective tenants about responding to the needs of disabled people. As a project manager of Churchill Square commented: 'they [the tenants] know their business, they are aware of the regulations and they will design their shop to that. As soon as we've agreed terms we send them a copy of the tenant's manual which governs how they design their shop and other things.' This manual is not a legal agreement however, and prospective tenants have discretion in how they interpret and implement it. The developer also assumed that prospective tenants will comply with the legislation and do not seek design standards beyond the statutory minimum. As he suggested, 'it's not up to us to tell the tenants what to do'. In contrast, Lend Lease regards tenants' attitudes and practices as needing to reflect the corporate ethos of the shopping centre or, as the project manager said:

> it's no good us producing some of the public spaces and somebody goes into a store [and can't get access], because we'll all be tarred with the same brush because Bluewater is an entity to a degree and the idea is that what we provide is followed through everywhere.

The development of Bluewater comprised much more than just exchanges between professionals in that members of a newly established access group were involved and regular attenders at meetings. As the head of building control noted: 'the access group go up to the site and there is a general update so they're just not hearing what's happening from us but directly from the developer'. For one of the access group members, the meetings were working because Lend Lease 'have listened. It's been quite satisfying that some of the ideas we've had they've actually taken on board.' Others concurred in noting how Lend Lease adopted an inclusive style of engagement or, as a member of the access group said, 'I would certainly say they've been prepared to listen'. Indeed, disabled people's involvement, at the crucial stages of the development, was called upon by Lend Lease.

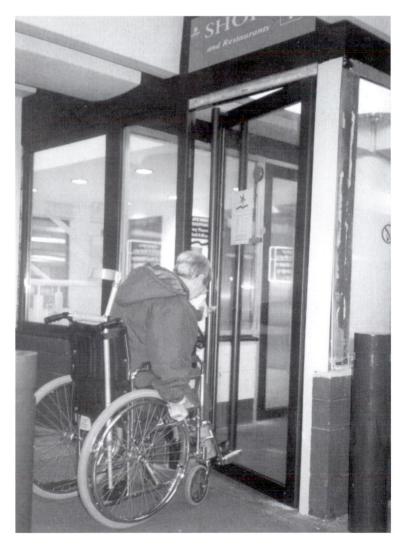

Obstructive swing doors at Churchill Square

As the manager of a disabled person's resource centre commented, 'we have responded to what's going on. So we looked at the external arrangements, the car park, the layout, drop off points. There's been some really effective spin offs.'

Collaborative and consensual processes of this type are the exception rather than the rule. For instance, in Churchill Square, the consultative process was characterised by conflicts of interest and poor channels of communication, dialogue and interaction. No formal channels of communication were established between disabled people, the local authority and the development team. As a planning

Non segregrated public toilets at Bluewater

officer stated, 'the developer changed their minds several times about what was happening, so I could understand how the access group might have felt that they weren't being kept informed, or misinformed on some things. They weren't sure who was saying what.' As a minute from a meeting of the local access group noted, 'the issues appear un-negotiable with the other party [the developer] who appear most unhelpful and seem unable to fully understand the concerns of the disabled'. This view was to appear prophetic over the next 18 months during which, as the head of building control said, 'the architects didn't go far enough relating to the disabled. They started out negotiating and it ended up as a war really.'

Contrasts in attitudes, values and practices, between development teams, are also pronounced in relation to Part M of the building regulations. Thus, as the project manager for the Bluewater development said about Part M, 'it's woeful ... any architect or designer can pick up Part M and build a structure that complies with that and some of the stuff in that is 20 or 30 years out of date. We're going well beyond the building regulations here.' Others in the company felt likewise, with a Lend Lease consultant noting that the minimum standards are less than adequate, and might well work against the development of a broad customer base. As she commented, the developer 'was very keen to appraise design, to do more than the minimum, and also not to do it in terms of lip service ... they've shown willingness'. In particular, Lend Lease was keen in moving beyond providing just for wheelchair users. As the project manager said, 'things like colour tone contrasts, floor materials, reducing glare ... it's these kinds of issues, not just ramps having to be 1 in 12. That's the easy stuff to do.'

Unlike Bluewater, many developers tend to accept Part M as a necessary piece of legislation which has to be adhered to (for legal reasons). As the project manager of Churchill Square noted, 'it's a good piece of legislation which provides the appropriate level of regulation. We're happy to fall in line with it and have no objections to its provisions.' Likewise, his appointed architects expressed no disquiet with the provisions of the building regulations and equated a fully accessible environment with compliance with the provisions of the building regulations. As he commented, 'the proposals for the development are fully accessible to disabled people and are designed to comply with current building legislation'. Such attitudes were prevalent throughout this company's development team, with the head of building control noting that, 'once they'd set their stall out they only did the bare minimum to satisfy what we can enforce. Unfortunately, I couldn't say they'd gone beyond Part M.'

Contrasts in attitudes, between this company and Bluewater, are evident in relation to the provision of sites for shopmobility schemes. Whereas Bluewater's shopmobility site is up and running and an integral part of the shopping centre, the other company's, at the time of writing, is an empty shell in a basement car park still awaiting funding. The developer was reluctant to respond to disabled people's requests to site the shopmobility in the centre of the car parking area, or, as the project manager said, 'it wasn't commercial sense to put it where they wanted'. He amplified this concern: 'I couldn't tell you the revenue per car per parking space to the shopping centre, but you've halved the revenue, so I mean it is actually quite a big concession'. After protracted discussions, and much disagreement, a site was provided in the car park in the basement of the development. However, the shopmobility site is less than satisfactory in requiring users to share the internal roads with motor vehicles. The site is also positioned at some distance from the entrance to the shopping centre.

An understanding of the contrasts between developers' and/or clients'

Shopmobility site at Churchill Square

reactions to the needs of disabled people, while not wholly reducible to the attitudes and values of the clients, reflects Guy's (1998) observation that clients are core to design and development processes. While Lend Lease has sought to interconnect an inclusive design philosophy with the pursuit of a profitable venture, this is in marked contrast with the many developers and clients who tend to equate designing for disabled people's needs with additional cost and loss of profits (see Chapter 6).

The Shopmobility centre at Bluewater

5 Architects and disabling design practices

Introduction

> There can be no dichotomy between good design and usable design or between beauty and function in architecture. To look beyond the physical structure of a building to its social consequences, to the sort of people and activity it contains, and to its effects upon the surrounding community is a necessary aspect of good design.
>
> (Sommer, 1972: 4)

Disabled people's design needs seem to feature rarely in architects' consciousness, with Willis (1990: 18) suggesting, perhaps unfairly, that 'the architect and architectural student no longer cares how a thing works any more – only how it looks'.[1] Likewise, Bloomer and Moore (1977: ix) castigate architects for their pre-occupation with architecture as an abstract visual art and the consequent failure to develop body-centred design; that is, an architecture sensitised to the three-dimensionality, or diversity, of bodily movements and needs. Architects' conceptions of the body have tended to see it as pre-formed, fixed and known, leading some to refer to the ideas and practices of architects as necessarily producing 'standard-fit' design, that is, decontextualised, one-dimensional architecture (Colomina, 1994; Grosz, 1994; Tschumi, 1996). Others, however, note that architects' values and attitudes towards their subject matter are varied and complex; their actions are constrained by the economics of the building process towards the (inevitable) production of 'fixed spaces, not fluid ones, in a predictable and permanent relationship to each other' (Knox, 1987: 388).

In developing, and engaging with such ideas, this chapter seeks to understand the interrelationship between architects' values and attitudes, and the construction of built environments which are broadly insensitive to the diverse needs of disabled people. It is based on the premise that the ideologies, values and attitudes of architects, as key agents in the development process, are important in influencing the particular design and building experiences of building users (see also Knesl, 1984; Knox, 1987). In particular, the chapter focuses on architects' understanding of disability and disabled people's building and design needs. It seeks to reveal the contrasting ways in which architects define, and design for, disability, the types of competencies that they have acquired to do so and the range of problematical assumptions and attitudes that they bring to bear upon processes of architectural production and designing for disabled people's needs.

However, we wish to stress that there is no necessary relationship between architects' attitudes or values, and the design and construction of a disablist, or any other type of built environment. Indeed, architects are one of many actors and institutions involved and implicated in the development of the built environment, and a fuller understanding of the architect's role requires a broader contextualisation of design processes (see, for example, Dickens, 1980, and the arguments in Chapter 6). We concur with Knox (1987) in that there is a danger of trivialising the role of the architect as passive, as an instrument of the client, or elevating them to a position of supreme control, able to fashion the built environment as though it were purely a product of design. Yet, neither conception is adequate because they either understate 'the broader context of social and economic forces . . . or overplay the roles of architects' (Knox, 1987: 371). As Knesl (1984) suggests, for example, architecture is pre-determined by political and economic power, including laws, statutes, codes and corporate clients. In this sense, the socio-economic, political and ideological relations of architectural theories and practices are critical to consider in order to gain some understanding of processes of social exclusion in the built environment.

In addressing such themes, we divide the chapter into three. First, we provide a brief overview of debates concerning architects' relationships with building users, where we seek to qualify and develop the observation by Bloomer and Moore (1977) that the attitudes and values of architects is an important site and source of building users' estrangement from the built environment. Second, using data from a postal survey of architectural firms in the United Kingdom, we evaluate architects' understanding of disabled people's building needs and their attitudes and responses to the diverse requirements that disabled people have in seeking to use the built environment. Finally, we conclude by considering how the disablist attitudes, values and practices of most architects and architectural practices might be changed.

Architects, buildings and users: some preliminary comments

As McGlynn and Murrain (1994) note, it has never been a feature of the culture, social ethics and practices of design professionals to see themselves as part of wider political processes. As they comment, architects seem to have limited understanding of the relationships between values, design objectives and the design intentions derived from them. Design theory tends to concentrate on the technocratic and technological, reducing questions of access and form to the functional aspects of the subject, yet ignoring what Davies and Lifchez (1987) have termed the social psychology of design or trying to understand what it is that people really want. In this sense, as Davies and Lifchez (ibid.) argue, the popularisation of architecture as 'high art', or pure design, is underpinned by a capacity to perpetuate an impersonal, often alienating practice, given that the focus is about the aesthetic, or the building form, not the user or the pragmatics of the functioning of the building. Buildings, then, in this interpretation, are treated as an abstraction, something over and beyond, somehow able to transcend, the socio-political contexts within which they are produced.

Such discussions are illustrative of architects as purveyors of their own pretensions rather than the needs of the people or communities that they seek to serve. As Jackson (1996: 3) suggests, in a highly controversial text, architectural discourses and practices are elitist and protected by monopoly, or what he terms the 'ethics of a social contract' which underpins architects' professional status. In turn, the vanity of the architect is paramount and preserved, or, as Knesl (1984: 7) notes, there is tacit acceptance by the architectural profession that buildings are the creative vision of architects and 'belong to' those that design them (see also the critique by Wolfe, 1981). Indeed, architects, such as Le Corbusier, 'suggested that people would have to be re-educated to appreciate his visions' (quoted in Knox, 1987: 364). Likewise, Mies Van der Rohe, in commenting on clients' capacities to choose between alternate schemes, noted that 'He doesn't have to choose. How can he choose? He hasn't the capacity to choose' (quoted in Prak, 1984: 95).

Moreover, the design features of many modernist, and other schemes, particularly in the post-war period, gave vent to those who saw a crisis in architecture in its inability to develop a humanistic focus (Pawley, 1983; Sennett, 1990; Venturi, 1966; Wolfe, 1981). As Knox (1987) suggests, post-war architecture was characterised by unfulfilled promises with practical failures in design which were often inattentive to differences in people's building needs. This, coupled with the seemingly untouchable status of architects, led many commentators towards what Dickens (1980: 107) terms the 'fetishising of design', or focussing attention on buildings and architects rather than the broader social processes and relations 'that surround the production and meaning of the built environment'. Indeed, there was, and still is, a tendency to blame architects for building failures or, as Knesl (1984: 7) notes, it 'is an adage that if architects lived in or used the buildings they designed they would not design them as they do'.

Such observations, while supported, in part, by elements of design theory and practice, seem to us to be reductionist and generalised, with the potential to scapegoat architects for failings, and failures, in architectural and building design. For Rabinowitz (1996: 35), for example, changes in the building and development industry have removed many of the architect's powers whereby 'the most significant design decisions are made before the project ever reaches the architect'. Increasingly, the development and construction of buildings is focussed on design management and teams, with architects only one of many players in the conception and implementation of building design (see Chapter 6). Indeed, far from design processes being coherent and bounded within the architect's ambit, as some suggest, they tend to take shape within a complex nexus of institutional and agency-level interests (Jackson, 1996). What seems critical, then, is less to develop a critique of architects per se, but to position their attitudes, values and actions within broader networks of social interactions and contexts.

Yet, while concurring with this, we seek to develop Knox's (1987: 367) observation that architects should be regarded as urban managers who 'exercise a degree of autonomy and control over patterns of urban development in ways that reflect their distinctive professional ideologies and career structures'. In this, we agree with Knesl (1984: 3), that the operational and communicative demands of clients never determine spatial order completely and 'leave room for lacunae of freedom'. This, amongst others, is a theme we now turn to.

Evaluating architects' attitudes and practices towards disabled people's needs in the built environment

In investigating architects' attitudes and practices towards disabled people's building needs, we conducted a postal survey of a 10 per cent sample of architectural practices operating in the UK at the beginning of February 1998. An eight-page questionnaire, comprising a series of both open-ended and closed questions, was sent to 770 architectural practices registered with the Royal Institute of British Architects (RIBA). In each instance, the questionnaire was sent to a named individual within the sample practices. In seeking to attain country-wide coverage, the sample was derived from a proportional selection of practices in every county in the UK by using the RIBA computer database. After a postal and telephone reminder, a response rate of 207 (or 27 per cent) practices was attained.[2] The questionnaire results provide a mixture of both numerical and qualitative, or non-numerical, responses whereby respondents have often added their written opinions or testimonies to a range of open-ended questions. In seeking to provide insights into architects' views of designing for disabled people's access requirements, we particularly draw on their (self) testimonies as illustrations of attitudes, values and practices (see Appendix 1 for more details about the survey).

In discussing the diverse material in the postal survey, we divide the discussion into four. First, we consider architects' definitions and conceptions of disability in order to develop some understanding of how disabled people's building needs are incorporated, if at all, into design considerations. Second, we document and discuss the role and importance of educating and training architects in relation to disability and design matters. Third, we explore user involvement and the extent to which architects seek to draw in the views of disabled people into design processes. Finally, we comment on the interrelationships between statutory regulations and architects' perceptions of how they ought to respond to legislative directives on access in the built environment.

Architects' attitudes towards disability and disabled people

A number of observers note that non-disabling design can only be inclusive if it seeks to facilitate access for people with a wide range of physiological and mental impairments (Hayden, 1985; Imrie, 1996; Lifchez and Winslow, 1979). Indeed, inclusivity is premised on some sensitivity by architects, and others, to fluid and shifting definitions of disability. Yet, as Matrix (1984: 3) notes, there is an assumption by architects of 'sameness', of normality, amongst the population, 'that all sections of the community want the environment to do the same things for them'. Moreover, Imrie (1999a) indicates that ableist bodily conceptions underpin architectural discourses and practices with evidence to suggest that the specific mobility and access needs of disabled people rarely feature in the theories and practices of designers or architects (Davies and Lifchez, 1987; Hayden, 1985; Weisman, 1992). As an architect, in interview, said, 'the consideration of disability issues is not in the mind of architects as a general rule. It just isn't. It's not part of our culture.'

Not surprisingly, the survey of architects' definition of disability shows that disabled people are rarely thought about in architectural practices. For instance, only 55 respondents (26 per cent of the sample) provided a definition of disability which is used to inform their working practices.[3] Of these, the emphasis, like that of developers, was on the stereotypical image of the physically impaired or wheelchair user. One respondent, for example, felt that disability covered those 'people with [a] physical impairment which limits their ability to walk about within the built environment'. For others, disability was defined as 'providing access for physically impaired', while some stated that disability is reducible to 'wheelchair requirements' and the status of 'paraplegic'. Such definitions, however, tend to reinforce a generic, and stereotypical, conception of what disability is (i.e. a form of mobility impairment).

Reducing disability to users of wheelchairs has the potential to orientate architects towards specific design types and solutions (for disabled people) which will fail to cater for the multiplicity of physical and mental impairments which are not wheelchair dependent. As Table 5.1 shows, in the design of a building, architects take into account the needs of specific types of disabled people, usually those with mobility or physical (ambulant) impairments. Of particular significance is that 125 (60 per cent) of the respondents rarely or never take into account the building requirements of people with learning difficulties. This is partly connected to the absence of societal understanding of what learning difficulties are (see, for example, Atkinson, 1993; Bruner, J., 1986). Architects, and other professionals, are taught nothing about, for example, dyslexia, yet contrasting mental or

Table 5.1 The types of disabled people that architects account for in designing a building (by numbers of respondents)

	Always (%)	Sometimes (%)	Rarely (%)	Never (%)
Vision impaired	44 (21)	86 (42)	44 (21)	14 (7)
Hard of hearing	25 (12)	71 (34)	58 (28)	29 (14)
Physical/mobility impaired	166 (80)	26 (13)	3 (1)	0 (0)
Learning difficulties	17 (8)	44 (21)	67 (32)	58 (28)

Source: Authors' survey, 1998.
$n = 207$
NB: where numbers across the columns do not equal 207 the shortfall is due to non-respondance.

	Always (%)	Sometimes (%)	Rarely (%)	Never (%)
Colour contrasts	32 (15)	79 (38)	45 (22)	23 (12)
Accessible toilets	174 (84)	18 (9)	0 (0)	0 (0)
Induction loops	15 (7)	67 (32)	51 (25)	37 (18)
Tactile paving	39 (19)	91 (44)	30 (14)	18 (9)
Ramps	128 (62)	59 (29)	2 (1)	0 (0)
Lifts to all levels	89 (43)	78 (38)	15 (7)	2 (1)
Lighting	88 (43)	48 (23)	30 (14)	18 (9)
One entry point	48 (23)	81 (39)	22 (11)	10 (5)
Level entry/access	128 (62)	57 (28)	2 (1)	0 (0)

Table 5.2 Design features that architects routinely seek to incorporate in to buildings (by numbers of respondents)

Source: Authors' survey, 1998.

n = 207

NB: where numbers across the columns do not equal 207 the shortfall is due to non–respondance.

cognitive capabilities require adaptive environments (and design solutions) to enable individuals with learning difficulties to recognise places and orientate themselves from one locale to another.

Biases against particular types of disabled people are reinforced by the practices of architects and the design features that they routinely seek to incorporate into building design. As Table 5.2 indicates, the types of design features for disabled people which tend to be incorporated into buildings include accessible toilets, ramps and level entry or access points. In contrast, induction loops, tactile paving and colour contrasts are seen as secondary considerations. Little or nothing which addresses the needs of people with learning difficulties is incorporated into much contemporary building and design processes although, as the Newhaven example below suggests, some architectural practices are sensitised to such concerns. However, the general ignorance of little more than mobility impairments reflects, in part, the paucity of the Building Regulations which, as Chapter 3 documented, emphasise wheelchair entry and access above other considerations.

Other groups of respondents took a broader approach towards disability. One commented, for example, that their definition would encompass 'any person with physical, mental, visual or audio impairment of any form', while, for another, disability covered 'people with some degree of impairment, whether physical, sensory or mental'. Some definitions were problematical in reinforcing demeaning and pejorative conceptions of disabled people, such as 'designing for the non-standard' and 'disadvantaged in comparison with the average able bodied person in any way'. Likewise, another respondent noted that a disabled person is 'someone who is unable to respond to the environment as an able-bodied person'. Others reinforced the idea of disability as somehow being abnormal, that is, generating a demand for what is not normally required, and, consequentially, of less relevance to them and their practices. For instance, one respondent saw disability as akin to a special need or, as he commented, 'we generally design for wheelchair users as a standard requirement for all building types. Other disabilities are only considered if the building is required for additional specific disabilities.'

Example 5.1 Responding to the design needs of elderly, frail and mentally infirm people

Newhaven Downs House

Newhaven Downs House

Newhaven Downs House in Sussex is a fifty-bed nursing home for elderly frail and mentally infirm people, with day care facilities for both residents and local people. The £3.2 million building, which opened in 1996, is a replacement for a small hospital that was providing in-patient care for elderly people in Newhaven. The client was the South Down Health NHS Trust and Newhaven Downs was the second of a number of capital projects they had undertaken since they were formed. The home was designed by Penoyre & Prasad Architects, who were appointed after winning a two-stage design competition in 1994. This was the second nursing home that the architects had worked on, the first being for West Lambeth Community Care Trust in south London. They have subsequently designed two other buildings for South Down Health NHS Trust.

The architects brought with them a broad awareness and understanding of disability based on their professional and personal experiences, in particular their work with people with learning disabilities and autism. The architects enhanced this knowledge and experience through working with elderly and infirm people at Tooting Bec hospital in London. This practical experience enabled them to develop design ideas for Newhaven Downs to assist residents who experience disorientation in their movement and mobility. Penoyre and Prasad was established in 1987, and the practice has worked on a number of projects for disabled people. However, this is not seen as a specialism, nor, suggests Greg Penoyre, should it be. As he explained, 'if you can design buildings which are available to anybody then you make ordinary the specialness of disability. The idea of making little of disability, by making the demands on the disabled person the same as the demands on anybody else, is quite a levelling device in a way and one which we feel quite strongly about.' With particular reference to people with learning disabilities, he suggests that:

A naturally lit corridor

> people are remarkably capable of adapting and there are times when it's actually a very good thing if they are challenged with the need to adapt, like it's good for any of us. The issue is whether you can challenge people in a way that is creative and giving to them, rather than oppressive to them. It's quite good if there are three steps for somebody to think about getting up because after a while they don't think about getting up them any more; they just get up them.

Given that the client, South Down Health NHS Trust, provides a distinct service, they were clearer than many as to their requirements for the building. As Penoyre said, 'there was a very good, clear brief in terms of the service that was going to be provided and in terms of the spaces they needed'. However, the architects had to be proactive or, as Penoyre suggested, 'clients tend to enshrine what they understand around them rather than what they don't know might be possible; our input is always to show them, to say, well shall we do it this way or what about this?' Indeed, one of their strengths as a practice, Penoyre suggests, is their ability to openly explore designs with clients and building users:

> As early as the competition we took the brief requirement that there be a central sitting area and a dining area and said wouldn't it be better if there were several sitting and dining areas? We made the dining areas destinations at the ends of corridors so that you never came to a dead end – you always came to a light, bright public room. So in that sense we changed the brief and then developed that idea. One of the things that we tend to do with new clients, if we can, is go and visit other places with them so that we can learn together.

Change in texture of handrails

Consultation took place through exhibitions at which the scheme was presented to patients and the local community. However, the detailed development of the project was mainly undertaken with the client and the staff user group. As Penoyre said:

> one doesn't want to be too romantic about working with the would-be patients or residents of a building who are either not well enough to communicate and understand, or their mind is not on the same matters. Newhaven is typical of these schemes where we will talk to the residents and they will appreciate that. In fact, they were very involved in choosing colour and things like that.

As many residents have impaired senses, the interior has elements that stimulate the senses using colour, surface or spatial variation and tactile references to aid orientation and to create an environment which caters for residents' clinical and therapeutic needs (see also Hall, J., 1999). Colours have been chosen carefully 'to activate and calm the space – blues in the quiet rooms, yellow in the entrance' (Niesewand, 1999: 7). Wherever possible, corridors are naturally lit using clerestorey windows so that circulation spaces are light and spacious. Corridors are wide enough to accommodate two wheelchairs and have been broken up into shorter distances through designing the bedroom areas in L-shaped blocks around the gardens. As Penoyre commented, 'wherever possible one avoids frustrating or confusing people and always ensuring that there are places to visit rather than just routes to things'.

Floor finishes have also been used to assist residents' recognition and awareness of spaces with carpeted areas, vinyl and wooden floored areas helping them to distinguish between different rooms and spaces. Likewise, tactile suggestions were also used throughout the building. Handrails, for example, feel different in different parts of the building. Residents know that they are in a public corridor because the handrail has a smooth groove in it, that they are where they live because the handrails are bumpy, and that they had come to a corner because the handrail goes from wood to steel. Similarly, different types of door handles have been used to help distinguish between bedrooms and bathrooms.

One of the ideas underpinning the design was that of passive stimulation and signalling rather than a direct, noisy kind of signalling. The architects encouraged the client not to put too many signs up, 'which is difficult with a health authority because they're used to putting signs on every door'. Signs were put on toilet doors, for example, but there are no arrows pointing to departments, so avoiding an institutionalised feel more typical of many health care buildings. The architects were also able to utilise the landscape through the fall in the site to provide a two-storey building with ways out into the garden on either level. The building provides level access from both ground and first floor into gardens, terraces and courtyards, integrating both the inside and outside of the building.

Bedroom door handles

Such definitions, whether wheelchair and mobility-based, or premised upon a particular physical or mental impairment, are problematical because, in Oliver's (1990) terms, they reduce disability to the physiology of the body or the specific (bodily) impairment. As Chapter 2 suggested, this is akin to reducing disability to an individual, or pathological, medical condition which can be cured through treatment and rehabilitation (see also Abberley, 1993; Imrie, 1996). In turn, a disabling state is conceived of as less to do with the insensitive practices of, for example, architects, and more to do with the individual impairment (of a disabled person). Most of our survey respondents were, implicitly, reproducing a pathologising or a 'blame-the-victim' definition of disability. Only a single respondent defined disability beyond the reductionist and pathologising framework, or, as the respondent said, 'disability is a function of a disabling environment, not of the individual. By promoting inclusive design the environment can be made more accessible for all.'

Other respondents were also aware of the fluid and complex nature of disability, or as one person said, 'there are umpteen forms of disability. We are probably all disabled in some way or another. We may not be aware of it even . . . there's no such thing as somebody being normal'. Others concurred, with one architect noting that disability is impairment-based or it 'may be temporary and it may be part of an ageing process but we will all struggle at some point'. For another, 'I don't think there is a stereotyped disabled body because human beings have different levels of ability or disability . . . any environment can be disabling for anyone if it's badly designed'. In noting this, the respondent referred to wheelchair accessible toilets which, as he suggested, often comprised design elements which were disabling. As he said: 'an ordinary toilet seat [of the type used in wheelchair accessible toilets] is impossible to use if you've got a dodgy hip'. However, one person summed up a general feeling, that architects' ability to address access issues, by providing appropriate design, is compromised by broader structural changes in the development industry. As this respondent said, 'it's written in the *Architects Guide to Running an Office* that you had a role to your client, to your practice and to society. That's gone completely in market forces now. You look after your client.'

While a minority of respondents said that they had a definition of disability, 113 (56 per cent) commented that their company had specific policies to address access for disabled people. Most of these referred to Part M of the Building Regulations and compliance with current legislation. This, then, conforms to a stereotypical approach with, as one respondent said, 'wheelchair use as standard for all designs', while, for another, 'all designs are tested for wheelchair access for full compliance with building regulations'. However, a number of respondents said that their policies went beyond the legislation. For one architect, for example, 'requirements for disabled access are considered on all projects irrespective of whether it is a statutory requirement'. Likewise, another respondent commented that, 'we generally consider accessibility to all buildings and promote consideration by our clients'. However, for many practices, the costs of providing access into buildings is paramount, a feeling expressed by one firm who said that, '[we] discuss options with clients and inform them of statutory obligations. Non-statutory we look at the financial viability.'

Such findings from the UK are paralleled by experiences in other countries such as Sweden. For instance, our survey of Swedish architects' attitudes towards disabled people indicates that their definitions of disability are similar to those used by their UK counterparts (see Appendix 1 for details of this survey). As a Swedish architect said, disability refers to a person 'with a physical impairment which limits their ability to walk about within the built environment'. For another, 'there is an unspoken definition that basically involves impairments of movement and vision. The considerations concerning hearing and mental disabilities are not very extensive.' Others concurred, or as an architect said, 'we don't think too much about those without a walking difficulty . . . most of our design effort is aimed at building a ramp or something to let the wheelchair get around.'

Developing architects' awareness of disability and disabled people and the role of education and training

Architects' definitions of disability and disabled people are not surprising in a context where their training and education barely relates to the design needs of disabled people (Milner, 1995). Indeed, the RIBA's (1998) curricula briefly mentions disability in Parts 1 and 2 of the Design Studies examinations. Students are told that examiners will be looking at the ways in which they have 'interpreted and worked within the brief' which includes taking account of 'disabled movement within the building' (RIBA, 1998: 23). In interview, a respondent from the RIBA's education department noted that 'part of the problem is that so few disabled people do our courses and present no direct challenge to the system. It's easy to ignore their concerns.' Such exclusions are also reinforced by the fragmentary nature of the architectural profession, a situation which is epitomised by the inability of the RIBA to exercise corporate regulation or controls over the practices of its members. As a RIBA spokesperson commented, 'a lot of our practitioners are sole practitioners, it's all private and self regulating . . . the only regulatory body is the Professional Standards Committee but they're weak and only interested in financial irregularities'.

Moreover, while the RIBA stipulate that their members are required to take Continuing Professional Development (CPD) courses, equivalent to 35 hours per year, the respondent admitted that they 'don't need to declare to us that they've done it and we don't actually monitor the system'. The weaknesses of the formal education and training systems were made evident by respondents to the postal questionnaire, with most saying that their learning is acquired 'on the job' or through direct experience. Indeed, only 62 respondents (30 per cent of the sample) said that they had received any training in relation to disabled people's access needs. Training appears to occur on an ad hoc basis and from a variety of sources. Of the 62 respondents, 28 said that their training was provided by an architectural school, 15 by a private consultancy, 14 by local authorities while 28 said they had received training from a variety of 'one-off' sources, such as attending seminars, CPD sessions, and lectures.[4] Most were positive about training or, as one respondent commented, 'the full spectrum of disability is difficult to comprehend from the able person's point of view. There are many areas overlooked without training.'

Such views are evident in other countries. In Sweden, for instance, a postal survey of architectural firms revealed that 46 (44 per cent), a minority of the sample, had received some training in accessible design, mainly in architectural school. Training included instructions and guidance about access legislation, technical requirements and raising awareness of issues relating to disability. Most found the training to be useful, with one respondent commenting how 'it increased the consciousness that there are numerous needs and solutions and that making accessibility for everybody – everywhere if possible – is an important democratic issue'. The majority of Swedish respondents (62, or 59 per cent) also felt that architects require specific training for access issues. As one commented, 'students of architecture have very little experience of the conditions of the disabled. In the new buildings that are constructed one can see many examples of architects' ignorance of this issue.' Others suggested that training should not overemphasise technical issues and should 'be complemented with more insight into the life of disabled people'.

In the UK, while few architects have received any form of formal training, the majority of respondents (150, or 72 per cent) feel that architects do require some training to design buildings which take into account disabled people's needs. As one respondent said, 'schools of architecture pay only lip service to building standards, and access for disabled people is generally thought of as providing ramps'. Another concurred, adding that access issues are 'either not part of the current curriculum or have little emphasis'. Such views are supported, in part, by Milner (1995) who notes that more than half of British architectural schools, in 1994, were unable to address access issues adequately, primarily due to staff resistance. A number of our respondents also commented on the inherent problem of architects' personal make-up as limiting their understanding of disabled people's building needs. Echoing the critiques of Hayden (1985), Matrix (1984), and Weisman (1992), concerning a gender bias in architectural theories and practices, one respondent remarked on the impossibilities for architects in designing for disabled people's needs given that 'most architects are white, middle class, able-bodied males and consequently design from that perspective'.

However, a number of respondents questioned such sentiments, particularly the minority (49, or 24 per cent) who feel that architects do not require training to design buildings for disabled people's access needs.[5] As one architect commented, 'architects are trained to design for the entire range of human needs, types, circumstances, etc. . . . disabled people fall within this. There is sufficient advice available.' Another respondent noted that architects have the capacity of insight to know how to design for all, or, as he suggested, 'if they are good architects they are trained to know how to find answers to problems they haven't encountered'. Another concurred in suggesting that designing for disabled people's needs should involve a minimum response and be no more than following the building regulations (see also pages 109–11). Thus, for this respondent, 'compliance with approved document Part M should be sufficient'.

Likewise, others feel that legislation and regulations are likely to compromise architectural standards and innovation, flair and what some perceive to be the integrity of the architect. Others were particularly dismissive of special training to enable architects to design for disabled people's needs given that, as one respondent argued, 'there is a wealth of publication/documentation on this matter which is readily available ... the wide variety of literature available is more than adequate'. In particular, most of the sceptics about training felt that awareness was needed as opposed to training, or that information as opposed to training would suffice. As one respondent argued, 'common sense and traditional architectural skills together with a knowledge of Part M would suffice'. Others repeated such sentiments, with an architect adding that 'there are only relatively few relevant factors and these are mostly a matter of common sense'. However, another respondent, who feels that architects do require training, rebutted the 'common sense' view espoused by others:

> It is easy to think that one can anticipate disabled people's needs by a combination of common sense and applying the Building Regulations. However, I think that the topic is more complex than people imagine and needs to be dealt with in a more detailed way in architectural training.

User involvement in the production of non-disabling design

A range of critiques, of architectural traditions and practices, claim that architects and their ideologies are woven into myopic pre-occupations with aesthetics, while deploying a series of technical discourses and practices which are coercive and exclusionary (Jackson, 1996; Knesl, 1984; Knox, 1987; Wolfe, 1981). As Knox (1987: 368) has commented, for example, the mainstream architectural journals and schools 'have always stressed the aesthetic over the practical' and, consequentially, have sought to discourage architects from diluting their visions by including the views and experiences of clients, other professionals and users. Indeed, architects such as Walter Gropius felt it to be undesirable to talk to building users because 'they were intellectually undeveloped' (quoted in Knox, 1987: 366). Moreover, Darke's (1984b: 415) study of architects, and the design of public sector housing, indicates that they have 'an overwhelming reliance on their own experience as a basis for assessing the needs of others, with a relatively minor contribution being made from other sources such as information from clients or direct information from users'.

However, as Table 5.3 indicates, a majority of the surveyed architects (130, or 65 per cent) said that they had consulted with disabled people and disability organisations about design or building matters. Of these,

Access groups	76
Vision impaired	23
Hard-of-hearing	18
Physical/mobility impaired	69
Learning difficulties	14
Other	42

Table 5.3 Disabled people and/or their organisations that architects consult with (by numbers of responses)

Source: Authors' survey, 1998.

n = 207

NB: some respondents had more than one response so numbers do not add up to 207.

76 (58 per cent) had undertaken consultations with the local access group and access officer. For one respondent, consultation was a matter of routine or 'access groups are generally a consultee in the planning application process and we often consult with them direct on accessibility matters'. Such consultations are entirely voluntary and architects do not need to take into account the views expressed. Indeed, this tends to be the case with the evidence, reflecting that of developer practices, suggesting that architects pay no more than lip service to the views of access groups (Barnes, 1991; Imrie, 1999b). For instance, the conclusions of an access group in an English coastal town, after dealings with architects and their client over a proposed shopping centre refurbishment, were that:

> it is disgraceful that all that voluntary input should have been ignored. It may well be true that you only get respect for what has to be paid for. The access group, as an advisory body, lacks any authority to take positive decisions and regretfully has been largely ignored for this fundamental reason.

Moreover, as other research highlights, access groups tend to be dominated by wheelchair users, and, far from providing wide-ranging advice, are more likely than not to reinforce architects' pre-conceptions of disability (as wheelchair use) (Barnes, 1991; Imrie, 1996; Goldsmith, 1997). For instance, as Table 5.3 shows, architects rarely consult with vision-impaired or hard-of-hearing individuals and their organisations, likewise with people with learning difficulties. In part, this is because such individuals, particularly hard-of-hearing individuals, are minor, or non-existent, players in access groups. However, survey respondents gave no indication of actively seeking out people with a diversity of physical and mental impairments beyond access groups or organisations with some official, local authority remit.

Some architects feel that access groups, and other disability organisations, have their own agendas and fail to take into consideration wider issues and implications of the design and building process. In particular, architects referred to the narrow-minded nature of disabled people's groups as being caught up in their very specific concerns, often to the detriment of other building users. Thus, as one respondent commented, 'most of these organisations are unlikely to accept that their own interests are only one part of designing a building. There are many other considerations.' Other respondents argued likewise, with one person, who had some consultative experiences with disabled people, suggesting that 'sometimes disabled groups have very rigid ideas on appropriate provision and some provisions exclude other groups of disabled people'. In particular, part of the problem for architects, expressed by a number of respondents, is the perception of an inability for access groups, and their members, to comment with any competence on the technical aspects of design, or as a respondent remarked, 'some groups do not have the technical information that I require at the moment'.

The role of the access officer, as an intermediary, was seen as being of particular importance in the consultative process. Indeed, some architects had little knowledge of how to find disabled people to consult with and, in this context, the local authority, as intermediary, was seen as crucial in facilitating consultative procedures. For instance, a respondent architect noted how 'some local authorities assist in making contact between such consultees [access groups] and designers at the planning stage – this is very helpful'. In addition, another commented on how 'most planning and building warrant applications are given to the access officer who consults the local disability advisory group and observations and recommendations are made'. Others, as the City of London Access Group example illustrates, felt that the access officer, and local authority more generally, could be a means of developing architects' knowledge of disabled people and their building needs. A testimony from one architect described a common situation. As she recounted:

> The way that we access a lot of information is actually to sit down working very closely with access officers in local authorities or access consultants. When we were working up in Nottingham on the Nottingham Media Centre, the access officer at the council was brilliant in terms of pointing us to source documents and gave us a very good document that the RNIB produced on signage which very clearly set out all the principles of colour contrast and contrast between backgrounds to signs and surfaces against which they are viewed and letter size relevant to viewing distance and stuff about tactile signs. I mean, where can you get embossed plans of buildings produced so that a blind person comes to a building, and you can have a plan of the floor levels of the cinema or theatre so that somebody could run their hand over it and feel the route to the toilets or the café or the bar. That seems like a really good thing for building users to be providing.

For others, however, disabled people remain hidden and non-vocal, difficult to detect or to find. This, in part, reinforces observations by Barnes (1991), and others, whose research shows that disabled people tend to lead hidden lives, often in institutions or as individuals dependent on carers to organise much of their daily lives (Morris, 1993). A significant minority of respondents (71, or 35 per cent) said that they had not consulted with disabled people, or their organisations, about any aspect of building design, nor had they any plans to do so. For a number of respondents, there was the assumption, similar to that held by developers, that the regulatory or statutory parameters, such as the Building Regulations and the DDA, were themselves the legitimate results of consultations with the relevant groups. Consequentially, most argue that no more is required in taking disabled people's views into account. For instance, as one architect commented:

> I believe that mandatory requirements incorporated into legislation are the result of extensive consultation and that they are constantly evolving. I do not, therefore, see the need for additional consultation.

Another architect voiced similar sentiments and added that consultations are counter-productive in that 'if architects tried to satisfy all parties at all times then nothing would be built'. Other respondents felt likewise in that

Example 5.2 The City of
London Access Group

The City of London Access Group was established in February 1988, shortly after the City Corporation appointed its first Access Officer, and following consultation between the Social Services Department, Occupational Therapists and registered disabled people within the City. The group currently has 40 members on its mailing list, meets in the Guildhall once a month, with the exceptions of August and September. The Group is structured around the Chairman, Vice-Chairman, Secretary and Management Committee members. All officers are elected at the AGM to serve for one year and must be disabled people, as must the majority of the Management Committee members. The majority of members are involved in the group in an individual capacity, as opposed to representing particular organisations, and are mostly City residents or ex-City workers. Given the unique demographics of the City of London – 7,900 residents and 270,000 workers – the Corporation aims to attract more members from the City workforce. Meetings take place on Wednesday lunchtimes between 12.30 and 2pm, as this allows those members who are working to attend. Typically, meetings feature guest speakers, either from within the Corporation or externally, such as service providers and researchers, along with the regular business. Occasional presentations by developers and architects are made at the monthly meetings and separate meetings may be called in the case of major development proposals.

Aside from the main Access Group, there are three Sub-Groups: the Management Committee, which meets every two months; the Planning Sub-Group, which meets monthly; and the Highways and Transport Sub-Group, which meets on a quarterly basis. Access Group members volunteer to join one of the sub-groups, each of which is chaired by a member of the Management Group. The Access Group is supported by the Corporation of London through the services of the Access Officer (at the time of writing, Julie Fleck) and her staff, an Assistant Access Officer and a secretary. This includes undertaking the administrative work for the monthly meetings and attending Management Committee and Sub-Group meetings. Julie Fleck has been in this post since December 1988 and both she and group members feel that this consistency has helped them to establish a clear organisational structure and a legitimacy, both within the Corporation and externally, amongst developers and their agents. As one of the members said:

I think that one of the strengths of the way that the City handles it is that our [amateurish, non-employee] comments get filtered through Corporation employees to the Planning department and onto the developers through the mouth of the Corporation, as it were. I think in that sense they have more clout or are seen as part of the Corporation's official response to the planning application.

The main duties of the Planning Sub Group, as set out in the Constitution, are:

- to examine planning applications with a view to ensuring safe and easy access to and within all new developments;
- to help the Corporation's Access Officer to provide the City Planning Officer and District Surveyor with comments on planning applications and advising them on access;
- to meet new architects and developers to discuss the accessibility of their planning proposals.

Typically, the group will look at four or five planning applications per meeting, these being schemes which the Access Officers and the Chair of the sub-group feel would benefit from being commented on. Given the particular nature of the City, planning applications tend to be office development, although these increasingly incorporate retail and leisure facilities, and refurbishments and conversions, including hotel and residential schemes. The planning sub-group comprises five or six regular attendees, which most people felt to be a suitable and manageable number. While none of those involved have professional experience of architecture and planning, members felt that this was not a major problem as the Assistant Access Officer attended all meetings and could offer practical advice as and when required. However, the Corporation does assist members who wish to extend their practical knowledge of access and planning issues through funding attendance at seminars in access auditing and reading plans. Nevertheless, the notion of access group members as experts, due to their personal experience of disability, underpins the ethos of the group and the Corporation. Group members also commented on how they had gained an understanding of the issues concerning others with different impairments to themselves and felt able to comment on issues and problems which may not affect them personally. Members were also aware of how the Corporation is keen to emphasise access for all, or inclusive design, as opposed to 'disabled access'. One member commented on how officials emphasise that it is not only disabled people who benefit but 'it's people struggling with luggage or with children and buggies. They all benefit from not having to put their own energy into moving around.'

The group meets with architects, submitting plans on behalf of developers, about five times a year, either at the behest of the access officer or the sub-group. The group members felt that, on the whole, architects were supportive and took on board the issues and concerns raised, although they were aware that their clients may be less accommodating and that the Corporation only has legal powers to enforce the building regulations and planning policies as set out in the Unitary Development Plan. Comments raised by the group are included in the Corporation's official response to applications, although the group tend not to consider revised applications unless there are further issues. Nevertheless, some members suggested that subsequent applications for different schemes by the same architects tended to have far fewer problems. Thus, as one of the members said:

I've always found meetings with architects and developers to be most fruitful. The architects have almost without exception been very receptive. And it's been a two-way thing where we've asked about points we're not clear about, which is illuminating for us. Sometimes there are site constraints – they don't often say financial constraints – but just for understanding their project and their approach to it, I've always found it most illuminating to sit in on the discussions.

Most of the members felt that it would be useful to follow through more of the development schemes they consider, although they realised that this is clearly difficult during the construction process itself. They have undertaken one or two site visits upon completion, including the Guildhall Art Gallery and Peters Hill, an office development with public spaces. Of particular concern at Peters Hill was the ramped access and provision of handrails on the site. Discussions had already taken place at planning application stage regarding the provision of handrails, with the planning department raising concerns regarding the visual impact of handrails (the site runs from St Paul's down to the new Millennium Bridge). However, as the ramp has a gradient of 1:20, handrails are not required under building regulations. At planning application, it was agreed that handrails would be provided on the stepped areas of the site, adjacent to one of the office developments. As one of the group members said, 'the handrail can be used all the way from the top down. I would have

Example 5.2 Continued

Peters Hill

thought that they would, or should, answer anybody with a walking disability like myself. I wouldn't use the ramp because I feel that if it was just slightly slippery I might fall over, so I'd head for the handrail and the steps.' Members also raised the possibility of alterations to the handrails to deter their use by skateboarders and, following this, small circles of stainless steel were bolted on top of the handrail at regular intervals.

The close working relationship between the Access Group and the Corporation is seen by those involved as a key factor in its effectiveness. As one member said, 'one of the enormous strengths [of the group] is the very close relationship with the Corporation's staff as I know that some Access Groups are held at arm's length and seen as a sort of pressure group'. Another member concurred, adding that, 'I'm sure we're not seen as a pressure group by the Corporation but our views are taken seriously'. Clearly the unique size and structure of the Corporation of London offers benefits for the effective running of the group and the consultative process. One of the group members **attends** access meetings in a neighbouring London borough and noted that while there was a good set-up there, you could tell that 'it's a little bit more difficult because of the size of the borough [compared to the City]'. The Access Officer feels that one of the reasons for the fact that the group works well is due to the size of the City of London and the lack of potentially conflicting groups which may be found in larger authorities. As such, while the City Access Group can, in some ways, be seen as a model organisation, it may not necessarily be possible to apply its approach elsewhere. Nevertheless, the Access Officer felt that other local authorities could follow the Corporation's example of facilitating the formation of access groups through setting up initial meetings, inviting members in and offering financial support.

Handrail at Peters Hill

consultation is not time effective and that client funding does not allow for time to consult. In this sense, even if architects wish to consult with disabled people and/or their organisations, they may very well be constrained by wider imperatives and pressures within the development process.

Such views are also evident in places such as New Zealand and Sweden. In New Zealand, Gleeson (1997, 1999a) shows that the inability to enforce access legislation is due, in part, to a lack of consultation between enforcement agencies (i.e. local councils) and disability advocacy groups. Similarly, in Sweden, architects suggest that consultations with disabled people are brief and tokenistic, with most of the consultative work occurring through the local municipality. Thus, for one person, their plans are discussed 'at a meeting with the municipal representative of disabled people', while, for another, 'the literature and stipulations contain an adequate foundation for decisions ... we don't need to consult beyond this'. Others were unsure about who to consult and a recurring response, highlighted by one person, is that 'it is hard to know who to look for [for consultative purposes]'.

Responding to statutory regulations

Architects are constrained and/or enabled by a range of wider institutional structures and processes and, in particular, by legal or statutory provisions which seek to regulate the development of accessible environments (Knesl, 1984; Knox, 1987). As Chapter 3 suggests, the legalistic provisions in the UK, concerning access for disabled people, are premised on a voluntaristic ethos which retain the prerogatives (and rights) of developers to produce more or less what they would like to. However, whatever the limitations of the building regulations, the majority of respondents (130, or 65 per cent), like developers documented in the last chapter, consider them to be sufficient in providing for the access needs of disabled people. A typical remark was made by one respondent who commented that 'this is a very satisfactory basic standard. There was really no legislation prior to the Disabled Persons Act 1981.' Another architect suggested that 'Part M sets a minimum standard which I believe is a marked improvement on the past and adequately caters for the great majority of people'. Thus, a number of respondents feel that the Building Regulations represent a shift in attitude towards ensuring greater access, that they are effective inasmuch as they set minimum standards. As one respondent noted:

> building regulations are, by their very nature, general standards. As a general safety net they are adequate. They should not be used as a design tool to create anything more than the minimum standards.

Another added how 'no legislation will cover all remits but it helps provide basics and makes the designer aware of issues'. A further respondent felt that 'it covers the subject as a minimum requirement but inevitably the decision to provide greater provision rests with the client'. However, another respondent suggested that, while Part M 'could be better it provides a starting point and gives me power in my negotiations with clients'. Others felt that Part M's specification of a 'minimum standard' is retrograde in enabling clients to design or 'dumb down' standards rather than aspiring to fully accessible buildings.[6]

In particular, a range of respondents feel that the building regulations are weak and fail to take into account the diverse and changing needs of disabled people. Thus, as a respondent noted, 'the regulations are in themselves a blunt instrument and require careful interpretation and thought'. Some architects feel that matters of legalistic interpretation, about what should be provided for disabled people, are inconsistent from one local authority to another, and are a source of confusion about what standards that they, as designers, ought to be attaining. For one respondent, for example, while Part M does, in part, provide for disabled people's access needs, 'in all such matters interpretation is crucial . . . unfortunately Building Control departments vary enormously in the quality of staff and the quality of their judgement'. Respondents are also concerned with the vagueness of legislation and the lack of specification of what architects can or cannot do to attain measures of access for disabled people (see also Imrie, 1996, 1997). One respondent, for instance, commented that the legislation is 'too reliant on the use of the term reasonable and there are many grey areas'.

Not surprisingly, a significant minority of respondents (45, or 22 per cent) feel that Part M does not provide for the access needs of disabled people. In particular, architects are frustrated by Part M's limited, and limiting, view of disability which, as we intimated earlier, mainly focusses on wheelchair access and the needs of mobility-impaired people. As a respondent said, 'there is no consensus on a minimum standard of provision for a range of disabilities other than mobility at its most basic'. This was one of the primary criticisms of Part M when it was initially introduced in 1987 and, while such criticisms led to Part M being revised in 1992, to cover a wider range of impairments, the amendments, according to a number of our respondents, do not go far enough and still miss out on some aspects of disability. As one respondent commented, 'it does little for disabled groups other than those with impaired mobility', while, for another, the regulations have a 'limited view of disability with no consensus on minimum standards or of standards for a range of disabilities other than mobility at its most basic'.

A number of other respondents feel that the legislation is particularly weak with regard to the majority of development projects, that is, those which are refurbishments and alterations to existing buildings (see also Foster, 1997; Imrie, 1996). Indeed, one architect noted that 'most access problems occur in the conversion/refurbishment of existing buildings where Part M is either unworkable or does not apply', while another commented that 'most of the built environment consists of existing buildings which are inaccessible and if not part of a construction project are then outside the remit of the regulations'. Others feel that relaxations of the regulations are too easily obtained from building control departments. Indeed, as an architect commented, developers will sometimes start a project without Part M approval and, consequentially, 'where work is started before approval is secured under the regulations, and is found not to comply, there is too much leeway in giving retrospective relaxation when the cost of rectification is high'.

For some, albeit a minority of architects, the importance of statutes and legislation is in strengthening their bargaining power with clients and developers in seeking to provide accessible buildings for disabled people.[7] In particular, the assent of the DDA led some of the respondents to suggest that it has the potential to transform attitudes and practices. As one respondent said, 'it is a powerful instrument in persuading clients of their obligations towards disabled staff and visitors'. For others, the DDA is providing greater power to architects to exert their influence over other agents, especially developers and institutional investors. For instance, one respondent sees the DDA as providing them with the power to 'inform our clients that in the absence of a demur we will design for optimum accessibility'. Others concurred, with one practice commenting that the DDA is 'a vehicle by which we can persuade clients to provide better buildings. Hopefully there will be a high profile case in law to focus attention on this issue.'

Conclusions

Architects are key actors or agents in the production of the built environment and their conceptions of different user groups are important, we would argue, in contributing to the content of design processes. In particular, architects are not dissimilar to other actors and institutions in tending to define disability in reductionist or impairment-specific terms. For instance, planners also conceive of disabled people as mobility impaired and 'wheelchair-bound', so too chartered surveyors, developers and society more generally (Barnes, 1991; Hall and Imrie, 1998; Imrie, 1997; Oliver, 1990). Such limited, and limiting, conceptions of (disabled) user groups confirm, in part, Darke's (1984a: 403) broader point about architects' conceptions of households, where the 'increasing variety in types of household is not given consideration'. Likewise, architects are rarely involved in the design of buildings and environments which take account of the multitude of physical and mental impairments which underpin disability.

Such estrangement is, in part, related to the absence of consultative and participative mechanisms between architects, design teams and disabled people. Indeed, there is some evidence to suggest that where architects do attempt to consult with disabled people, that such exercises are limited by the selective representations which are made. These tend to be by mobility-impaired people and wheelchair users with the potential to reinforce, rather than challenge, pre-conceived values which architects might bring to the consultative process. Moreover, evidence from our survey suggests that architects sometimes feel frustrated by broader, structural constraints operating on their abilities to facilitate accessible buildings, including clients' concerns with cost savings (which are not always justifiable or justified), the legal strictures of Part M, and what architects perceive to be the ignorance of clients, and other agents in the development process, about disability and disabled people's building requirements.

However, while situational or structural conditions stymie architects' abilities to respond to disabled people's building requirements, the survey also reveals professional resistance to responding to the needs of disabled people. This is particularly evident in the training and education of architects with little or nothing provided through RIBA accredited courses, and where the majority of the sample had not received training of any kind concerning disabled people's access requirements. In particular, architectural education and training is implicated in producing professionals defined by technical and specialist skills, seeking to draw tight boundaries around themselves and their practices. Many of the respondents felt that their architectural skills would suffice in dealing with access issues without the need for special training. Where professional resistance is breaking down, it tends to be caused by external factors, such as access criteria connected to National Lottery funding, than to internal critiques or reflection on values and practices.

As Davies and Lifchez (1987: 49; quoted in Imrie, 1996: 96) suggest, access for disabled people should not be viewed by architects as a constraint on architectural design, but should be conceived of as a 'major perceptual orientation to humanity'. Design matters cannot be closed-off to specific domains of expertise, nor can the heterogeneity of human building requirements be understood through the lens of a particular discipline or related set of ideas. Following Sandercock (1998: 229), it is important to (re)connect architects and their practices with broader social and political issues, and to provide the means for connectivity to be made 'between the built environment, and individual and collective human well-being'. The design and development of buildings, and the built environment, has the capacity, for example, to facilitate or to hinder people's movement and mobility, while particular designs, such as shopping malls and other quasi public–private spaces, are infused with powers of demarcation and exclusion. For disabled people, the built environment, and the processes which give it shape, remain disablist by design.

Further reading

The broader themes of the chapter are well developed in articles by Dickens, P. (1980), Knesl, J. (1984) and Knox, P. (1987). Readers should refer to the arguments developed in the excellent book by Weisman, L. (1992) *Discrimination by Design*, University of Illinois Press, Illinois and Bloomer, K. and Moore, C. (1977) *Body, Memory, and Architecture*, Yale University Press, Yale. The latter is a beautifully written and illustrated book. Goldsmith's (1997) book, *Designing for the Disabled*, is a well crafted and useful reference. With reference to designing for people with learning difficulties, two publications are worth considering: a report by the Royal Institute of British Architects (1999) on therapeutic environments, and an article by Smith (1999) on design and mental health care.

Case study
Ikon Gallery, Birmingham, UK

Ikon Gallery

Ikon's display board

Ikon is a contemporary art gallery situated in a refurbished Grade II listed Victorian school in Birmingham. Founded in 1963 by a group of artists, and originally situated in a kiosk in the Bull Ring, Ikon relocated three times, finishing up in the 1970s in a converted warehouse in John Bright Street. By the early 1990s, the lease was up on this building and it was deemed to be no longer suitable in terms of location and visitor facilities. The gallery, therefore, began looking for new premises. The former Oozells Street School, set within Brindleyplace, a 17-acre city centre office and mixed-use development, was identified as a potential new site (for details of the site, see the maps, below). As a listed building, occupying a prime location within the development site,

the school posed problems for the developers, Argent, in finding a suitable use for it. Ikon negotiated a lease with Argent, whereby they would pay a peppercorn rent for the building, subject to the scheme getting sufficient funding. The leasing agreement required Argent to pay for the external refurbishment of the building while Ikon was responsible for obtaining funding for, and redeveloping, the interior.

The development was awarded a total of £4.3 million of Lottery money in 1995, which was match-funded with European Regional Development Funding, the Argent contribution and contributions from some trusts and foundations.* Ikon was responsible for employing the architects, the London-based practice Levitt Bernstein, and

* Ikon Gallery was one of the first grant-aided-Lottery schemes. The initial grant was to the value of £3.7 million and a supplementary grant of £600,000 for the fit-out followed.

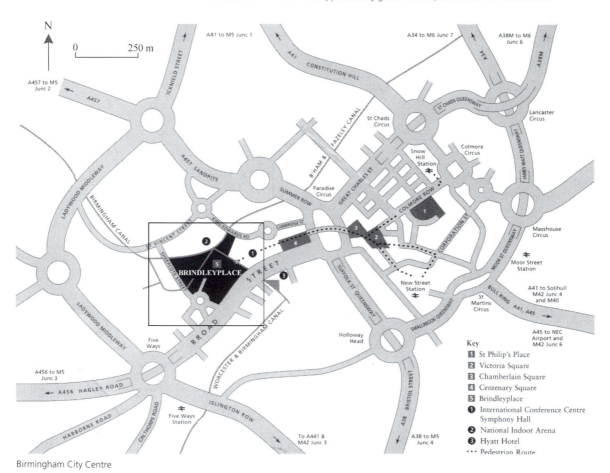

Birmingham City Centre

the contractors. The contractors, Tarmac, were employed under an amended JCT80 contract with contractor design portion, with some of the specialist packages – the glass stairs, the lifts and the mechanical and electrical parts – being their responsibility under separate sub-contracts.* Ikon and the architects were responsible for the design of the scheme, with the architects providing the flow of information to the contractors. This form of procurement allowed the architects to retain control over the building work; they were appointed to administer the contract and to inspect the works and were empowered to condemn work which did not comply with the drawings and specifications.†

From the beginning, access issues were to the fore. For Elizabeth Ann Macgregor, the gallery director, providing

---

* A 'JCT 1980 With Contractors Design' is, as Cadman and Topping (1997: 211) note, 'based upon the production of a performance specification by or on behalf of the developer'. Responsibility for the preparation of the design, and for its compliance with the various statutory requirements, rests with the contractor (see Chapter 6 for an extended discussion of such contracts, and also refer to Chapter 6 of Cadman and Topping).

† Under this contract the architects could inspect the works on a regular basis and all instructions to the contractor came from them. As Paul Clark said, 'The contract obliges the contractor to adhere to the drawings and specification. Should he wish to change anything specified, it must be with our approval. If work is not carried out in accordance with the drawings and specification we are empowered to condemn such work. In short, this form of contract gives us – and therefore, effectively and more importantly, the client – more control.'

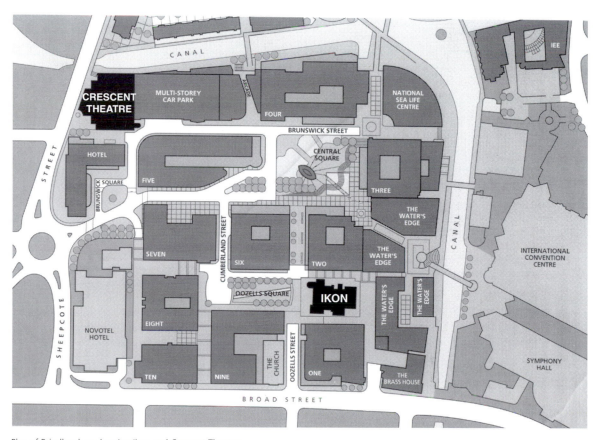

Plan of Brindleyplace showing Ikon and Crescent Theatres

Glass lift and stairway

theatres and art galleries, and was approached directly by Elizabeth Macgregor to undertake the initial feasibility study long before Lottery funding became available. She added, 'we chose the architects deliberately, as a practice that was genuinely interested in issues of access. You can't always guarantee that architects are particularly interested in these issues.'

As Paul Clark, the lead architect said:

[the client] didn't go through any of the big name arts-type architects and her reasoning was that she didn't want to be bullied into something she might not want. She likes the attitude of Levitt Bernstein.

As well as being contracted to design the interior of the Ikon, Levitt Bernstein were employed under a separate contract by Argent to work on the external refurbishment of the former school building. As Paul Clark commented, 'this gave us an intimate knowledge of the building'. By the time that Clark became involved with the actual conversion of the school to an art gallery, 'the brief was fixed [for the interior] but the design wasn't there. My role was to sit down and work up the design with my director and the Ikon.' The exterior of the building was preserved and refurbished, including having two towers built onto the outside containing a glass lift and stairway plus a service lift which allowed the maximum gallery space to be utilised.

The interior was in a very poor state of repair and was substantially rebuilt to create three floors, including 440 square metres of gallery space on the first and second floors, with the ground floor housing workshops, the gallery shop, café and kitchen. This internal layout, with the galleries on the upper floors, did cause some concern over the question of access and the route to the galleries. However, as Clark noted, 'because it's a public building, a lot of people will be there for the first time and the routes through and to various parts have to be very clear and simple. So immediately this has to make it

better access for disabled people was one of the key criteria for moving, together with being in a better location and in a building that provided more suitable visitor services. She added, 'one of the issues that was in our brief was whether it was possible to make this building accessible for people with disabilities, and by that we meant right across the board, not just physical disabilities'. As such, the attitude of the client informed the design and development team, ensuring that disabled people's access needs were taken on board as an integral part of the scheme. This attitude also underpinned the client's choice of Levitt Bernstein as architects. The practice has a history of arts projects, including easier for anyone with a disability because things are clear and straightforward.' He added, 'it was just a question of how clear is the route and how wide is the stair, so we had to re-jig the stair a bit to get it wider'. In addition, the glass passenger lift positioned beside the main staircase allows visitors level access to all floors.

One requirement of the lottery award was the obligation to set up, or consult with, an access committee or disability organisation. Ikon approached Artlink, a West Midlands-based arts agency working to involve local disabled people in the arts. Artlink was involved at an early stage in the design process (1:100 scale drawings) and had a number of meetings with the architect and Ikon. Given that there were certain limitations working within an existing shell, and that art galleries require features such as white walls,* both the client and architects felt that Artlink needed to be prepared to be flexible and not too dogmatic about designing 'by the book'. For example, Artlink gave the architects a paper about how to deal with light and colour on walls but, as Paul Clark said:

we heeded this where we could, but there were inevitable conflicts when it came to the galleries themselves, which had to be painted white. Also, rather than starting with a blank canvas, we were working with an existing listed building. The fact that it was listed meant that approval from the local authority planning department was required for every material alteration to the fabric of the building. We were able to create certain contrasts in materials and colours with the new additions and insertions: the main staircase is glass and matt grey steel within an exposed brick enclosure, the secondary stair is timber and steel, the first floor toilet is painted a vibrant blue and there is a vertical 'circulation and orientation' shaft over the entrance which is finished in a smooth exposed concrete.

Nevertheless, other features were able to be incorporated into the building.

The internal glass staircase

Artlink had asked for an accessible toilet which was larger than the Part M requirements and this was provided. The reception desk and shop counter were designed by the architects and these both had access committee input. They suggested a wheelchair turning circle behind both counters and for them to be set at a height suitable for a wheelchair user. One of the main issues of concern for Artlink was the glass staircase. As Paul Clark said:

It's sand blasted, it's not slippery and you can't see through it. We had a hell of a time with the glass treads, to make them apparent for anybody who is in any way visually impaired. At the

---

* The requirement for white walls was seen as being particularly important in the case of a gallery such as Ikon where there is no permanent collection and they are constantly changing their exhibitions.

The internal glass walkway

front of the treads there is a painted insert and we spent a long time with that and went through a number of samples showing Artlink how it might be dealt with.

Certain issues, such as the painted tread on the glass stairs, caused problems, both in getting samples made up and in reaching agreement with the access committee. This caused some delays in the development schedule for both the architects and, particularly, the contrac-

tors. In the end, as Clark intimated, Artlink 'went for a terracotta colour because they thought it would match the brickwork. If it had been black it would have been just as good.'

While the architects found consulta-tion with Artlink to be useful they were also frustrated by certain aspects of the process, particularly arranging meetings and getting feedback from the group. It proved difficult to get the group together at short notice and to have them come to a decision. Both the gallery director and the architects felt there should have been a stricter framework for consultation with Artlink. This was the case with the stair tread where the architects were under pressure from the contractors for a quick response. Levitt Bernstein also consulted with Artlink over samples for handrails in the building which, again, caused some delays in the construction schedule. As Clark said:

> we wanted stainless steel handrails because this huey-type coloured plastic looks hellish and it just shouts 'local authority' or 'sheltered housing'. Your normal polished stainless steel is too corporate but a dull one doesn't necessarily give enough grip. So we got samples for Artlink of what was called a short piened finish which is grit-blasted stainless steel and which we used in the end. It looks great and it works very well [but] we got them this sample and they kept it for a couple of weeks.

The consultation process was also a little problematic in that, as Clark said, 'the numbers in the access committee kept changing and it seemed difficult to get everybody together. I don't think we ever had the same people twice and then it started getting smaller and smaller.' Two-thirds of the way through the project, Artlink went out of business when their funding was stopped. This resulted in Ikon and the architects liaising with a Birmingham-based disability consultant who had been contacted by one of the Artlink members, although, by this stage, most of the major access issues had been addressed. As the gallery director said, 'although I think the results were very good I don't think that the [consultation] process was as good as it could have been'. Nevertheless, the input from Artlink was seen as beneficial to the design of the Ikon and this, combined with the hands-on approach of the gallery director and the awareness of the architects, meant that access issues were to the fore throughout the design and building process and have resulted in a building which offers good access throughout.

6 Shaping access through institutional and project team dynamics

Introduction

> The biggest difficulty in architecture is the fact that you develop the brief with the client, have an idea, produce all the information but you're entirely dependent on a host of other people to implement it.
>
> (architect interview)

As Haviland (1996: 55) notes, 'it has always been convenient to view building design as a coherent and bounded activity that starts at a specific moment'. For Haviland, this conception of the design process is at odds with the organisation of many development projects (see also Bentley, 1999; Hill, 1999; Imrie, 2000a; Morton, 1992). Design is not a linear process which begins with a client's brief to the architect and ends with the occupancy of a building. Rather, it is characterised by a myriad of, often conflicting, interactions between professionals with different views of what design is or ought to be (Bentley, 1999). For instance, the most significant design decisions are often made well before the project ever reaches the architect, or, as Rabinowitz (1996: 34) suggests, 'developers have grown more sophisticated . . . and much more concerned about management – including design management'. Haviland (1996: 52) notes that 'these owners may have substantial facilities management expertise; dictate the terms of engagement for design professionals; set high expectations for design services; and assure a partner role in design and construction'.

Such ideas indicate that the attitudes and practices of owners, property developers and related professionals are shaped within a complex nexus of institutional and agency-level interests and relations (Cadman and Topping, 1997; Guy and Henneberry, 2000; Haviland, 1996; Jackson, 1996; Ratcliffe and Stubbs, 1996). For Haviland (1996: 56), 'owners, occupiers, financiers, regulators, and the citizenry at large have substantial roles in establishing design parameters and negotiating design concepts', thus raising issues about the relative roles and relevance of a range of actors and agencies in influencing the details of design for disabled people's access needs (see also Ball; 1998, Guy, 1998). How disabled people's access requirements are defined and drawn into projects is dependent on the social interactions between the variety of agents and agencies involved in project design and development processes. There are no typical responses to the needs of disabled people; rather, as previous chapters have suggested, there is a range of possible responses contingent on the socio-institutional particularities of development projects.

These responses are, however, framed within broader 'structures of building provision' which serve to safeguard investments while maximising market opportunities (to build and let property) (see Chapter 1). As Guy (1998: 268) notes, buildings, as an investment medium for pension funds and insurance companies, are increasingly characterised by standardised designs 'which provide flexibility of use, thereby lowering valuation risks for developers'. Such designs are, as Harvey (1989) suggests, the product of a broader series of socio-institutional relations which serve to (re)produce the built environment as a mechanism of, and outlet for, profit. For Harvey (1989, 2000) and others, transformations in design culture can be explained, first and foremost, 'by reference to the roles they play in the capital accumulation process' (Bentley, 1999: 134). However, the design process is not wholly reducible to a socio-economic and institutional logic. Rather it is, as Bentley (1999: 75) suggests, 'ultimately a process of regula-tion and struggle in which all protagonists have at least some power, no matter how limited, to affect the outcomes on the ground'.

This chapter amplifies and illustrates some of these ideas by drawing on the interview and case materials previously outlined and discussed in Chapter 4 (see Appendix 1). These document a variety of development practices and attitudes in relation to three themes:

i the importance of the procurement route in influencing project speci-fications, particularly in relation to design and build;
ii the role of the client and other members of the project team in deter-mining attitudes and practices to access; and,
iii the growing importance of access consultants in influencing property professionals' responses to disabled people's building needs.

We discuss each of these themes in turn, and conclude by noting that the marginalisation of disabled people's design considerations in the develop-ment process is not attributable to any single factor.

Procurement programmes and contracts: the case of design and build

An important dimension in the development of the built environment relates to procurement systems, or the formulation of a project strategy, or building contract arrangements, by the development company and/or client (see Cadman and Topping, 1997; Franks, 1998). Construction schedules, financial and management responsibilities and team dynamics are determined, in large part, by the procurement route undertaken on building projects. These, in turn, have the potential to affect how and when access issues, amongst others, are addressed, and by whom. In the UK, traditional systems of building procurement, where the design is fully developed before going out to tender, have, over the last decade or so, been increasingly superseded by 'fast track' forms of contract such as construction management, management contracting and, in particular, design and build (Franks, 1998).[1]

Design and build (hereafter DB), in a variety of forms of contract, offers clear advantages to the client, 'through reducing the time taken from the client's briefing to his occupation by overlapping the design and construction periods rather tnan going to tender with completed drawings and specifications' (Franks, 1998: 2; see also Akintoye and Fitzgerald, 1995).[2] While time savings reduce costs, the client is also assured price certainty early on in the project and the financial risk, should the project go over time and budget, is shifted to the contractor. As one developer, in interview, said, 'DB fixes the cost for us at the time we enter into the contract. Development is a risky enough business as it is without carrying the risk of construction costs running over.' A contractor also commented that:

> with DB a lot of the responsibility is on the contractor and most criticism of design and build is that you'll always get the cheapest the contractor can get away with, which is true, because we are a business that is seeking to make money. We have a contract and we will do the works the cheapest way we can, within the scope of the contract itself . . . that is the minimum we are going to give them and also the maximum.

DB, then, is characterised by a contractual route underpinned by a guaranteed maximum price (GMP). This route, as interviewees have suggested, has the potential to sideline a range of design details, including providing for disabled people's access requirements. The GMP is premised on the specification of design details in advance of contractual commitments, with the contractor committed to providing the building for a known cost (and taking the risk in doing so). The DB route requires the contractor to submit drawings and specifications to the developer for approval, with the understanding that they (the contractor) are responsible for taking the financial risk if designs are altered during the course of construction. The incentive, then, is to provide tried and tested design packages which are simple and, as Cadman and Topping (1997: 213) note, 'to a standard design which has been used by the contractor elsewhere'.

However, DB is not a singular approach to development but is characterised by at least eight different types of contract, and clients can retain some control in a context where the architect is novated to the contractor.[3] In such cases, the client employs an architect 'to design and specify the building to the extent that the client's needs and intentions are clearly stated' (Franks, 1998: 20; see also Akintoye, 1994; Cadman and Topping, 1997). Tenders are then sought based on these drawings and the client novates the design consultants to the contractor who assumes responsibility for completion of the project. This, as Franks (1998: 20) notes, 'facilitate(s) the client's quest for ''best'' design and single-point responsibility'. As such, it would be wrong to suggest that DB is inherently flawed and will, necessarily, result in poor quality architecture.

Nevertheless, a number of respondents did acknowledge the need to ensure that good management of the schedule, and clear designation of responsibilities at the outset was vital. A developer, for instance, suggested that 'as long as people are clear where their responsibilities lie at each stage then it's a perfectly acceptable way of procuring buildings'. A contractor also added that 'I wouldn't say that design and build is flavour of the month but things do go in a cyclical nature . . . it's just a question of how the client can tease out the best possible product within the design and build form; that's where the expertise comes in.' For another, the GMP route was problematical because, as a project manager noted, 'they're not really set up for variations. The whole point is that there's a fixed sum of money and you have to do it for that. If you then have the client come in with a major variation the contract is just not set up for it.'

A number of the cases we investigated were DB (see example 6.1 over-leaf), with a range of respondents expressing reservations about it (see Akin-toye, 1994; Akintoye and Fitzgerald, 1995). For one architect, 'I have little or no time when I work with DB . . . not enough time to produce decent design'. Similar views were voiced by a developer who commented that:

> there's clearly a temptation [to cut corners] – no two ways about it. People are in business to make money. Let's face it, why is the client doing it? He wants to make his percentage of savings, and you're relying on the contractor's professional attitude in where do you draw the line between making legitimate savings which are going to benefit [both] the client and contractor and cutting corners? It's a fine line to tread.

Others expressed similar feelings, with another developer noting that:

> the design and build contract tends to eliminate design changes once a contract is let, at least from the builder's side, and any changes that are made on the client's side are usually punitive. Whereas in a traditional contract with a design contingency sum there, the architect and the client can make design changes as they go along, especially at the lack of detail, and it's the detail which is what really makes a building work or not.

Respondent architects also commented on the impact of DB on their role within the project team. As an architect suggested, 'it has had a huge shift in the change of power for the architect. He's working for the contractor now. Somebody who he was independent from is now our client.' Such views correspond with Akintoye and Fitzgerald's (1995) survey of architects' views of DB. As they suggest, architects were dissatisfied with 'imprecise briefings' and 'poor communications leading to misunderstanding of requirements' (Akintoye and Fitzgerald, 1995: 39). Indeed, an important part of the process relates to chains of command and responsibilities in projects. For one access consultant, the design and build procurement route is fraught with difficulties in attaining access because, as she commented:

> it gives your contractor scope to, not alter design as such – or they may not see it as altering the design – but just a slight tweak in the material . . . but from our perspective it might become a bit more of, for example, a slip hazard. It might not be as fit for its intended purpose as we would have liked it to if there had been the previous material that we'd agreed on.

Example 6.1 Design and build as a procurement route: the case of the Armadillo

The 3,000-seat Clyde Auditorium conference centre in Glasgow, colloquially known as the 'Armadillo', opened in September 1997. The development of the Centre, located adjacent to the existing Scottish Exhibition and Conference Centre (SECC), is a key part of Glasgow City Council's economic development strategy through fostering the growth of the business service sector. The Centre was planned to be a 'landmark' building for the city; a prestige development which would raise the profile of the city in both national and international terms. As the client's project manager said, 'the building had to make a statement. It had to be a feature for Glasgow by day and night and it had to make a significant contribution to the architecture of the city.' The client, Glasgow City Council and the SECC, wanted a clear, simple-to-use building that would enable a large number of people to get in and out of it as easily as possible. In reality, the City Council and the SECC received an acoustically-sealed auditorium enclosed in an armadillo-shaped structure.

The total cost of the development was £30 million with Glasgow City Council funding 90 per cent of the development costs. Other funding came from the European Regional Development Fund and Glasgow Development Agency. The conference centre was constructed using a design, manage and build contract with a guaranteed maximum price (GMP). The practice was novated to a management contractor, Bovis, and the appointed architect was Foster and Partners. The contractor, Bovis, was signed up to the project in July 1995 following a general competition. From July until December, Bovis worked with the client and their existing team to devise the budget. Peter Jacobs, project director for Bovis, said, 'the SECC always had a strict budget of £30 million but when we got on board the cost plan – the price of the design – was up to about £38 million, so we spent the first six months working with them to get the design budget down to £30 million'.

The Armadillo

Foster and Partners were appointed after the project had been tendered in the *European Journal*. This was Foster's first scheme under a design and build contract, and one that the company had certain reservations about. For the project architect, 'the problem with a GMP is getting the right quality of design information at the time of going to tender' (quoted in Cook, 1996: 39). As he suggested, design and build is 'not a traditional route that the architect takes because you lose a certain degree of responsibility. We were in the position where we were appointed by the client [but we were also working for the contractor]'. Others recognised some of the risks of the DB route, or as one of the contractors said, 'It's unusual to do a GMP job that is a landmark, one-off, highly technical building. I think everybody recognised the risks of that as we went into it. If it hadn't been for the team pulling together it could have been a nightmare job.' These words were, in part, prophetic given that, as Cook (1996: 38) observed, 'eight months into the project, the budget restraints of a GMP contract mean some of the internal finishes are being downgraded from the first specifications'.

An element of the project, which the architects felt was affected by the procurement route, was the quality of the finishings. As one of the architects said, 'there were items where we lost out on quality of finish which we probably could have improved on with a different form of procurement, but the building would have been more expensive and have taken longer to design. Given a fixed budget and programme I think we did the best we could.' Others concurred, with a project director noting that the quality of the building's finish was limited by the project's cost constraints. As he said: 'the one downside, or sour taste in the mouth, the one thing I think we all wish the architect had more money to be able to afford better finishes inside . . . it's a pretty industrial sort of building'. The architects tended to agree, with one of the project architects noting that 'the trickiest thing here was the fact that we had to guarantee the price so early. The earlier you guarantee the price the more risk there is to put against that price, so you're buying less building effectively and more risk.'

In relation to responding to disabled people's access needs, the building, as a project director noted, provides a range of features and, as he said, 'there are wheelchair spaces in the auditorium, so all of that was quite clear and that was allowed for in our GMP'. However, reservations were expressed by some of the appointed professionals about their ability to adapt design features once the process was underway. As an architect said, about consultations with an appointed access consultancy, 'our later meetings with Disability Scotland . . . the ability to change the building once it had been firmed up . . . the scope to change the slopes and the access was quite small, so we never actually got talking about huge issues on disability'. For another project director, part of the difficulty relates to the timing of discussions about access. From his recollection, access issues were being discussed very late in the process, or, as he said, 'the thing about disability issues is that they tend to come very late and as with any late change this causes problems . . . the client is normally eager to respond to the disability issues as long as it's not something ridiculous'.

In the event, the facilities provided for disabled people include a mixture of features: level access from the car park to the entrance, with colour contrasts between the pavements and road; the provision of four lifts with braille and 'talking' features; an induction loop system in the auditorium; short pile carpets to enable trolleys and wheelchairs to move freely; automatic doors internally; demountable stairs and ramps to the stage with disabled access, toilets and lifts backstage. In addition, stewards and first aid staff receive training on access issues.

Others concurred in noting how design was being reduced to a technical, engineering exercise where costs, and not user needs, were the defining criteria. In particular, the price fixity of DB schemes was commented on, time and again, by interviewees as the single biggest reason for disabled people's access needs being compromised in building projects. As an access consultant said, about the effects on access of design and build contracts, 'if buildings are being put up in that kind of way, one of the first things that goes is disabled access which is seen as one of those frills that's cutable'.

Reservations about the ability of DB to deliver access for disabled people are evident elsewhere too. For instance, like their British counterparts, Swedish professionals are concerned about the design implications of the GMP. In interview, a Swedish architect suggested that 'clients are more interested in the fixed price than in an extremely good building. They would rather take a fixed price and a rather good building than an uncertain price and an extremely good building.' For another Swedish architect, the use of quality assessment procedures, to ensure a minimum level of building design, is a misnomer in the context of projects driven by fixed-price criteria. As he commented:

quality systems focus on how the processes are made, what you write down on paper and how you manage your design work, not how the final product is. It's not focussed on that. In some ways it seems strange that the title is quality controller, it should be paper controller, it's got nothing to do with the quality of the building, it's just ensuring that the routine [the DB route] has been followed.

Another architect described the DB system as 'a disaster for the architecture [in Sweden]' while some were sceptical about control over detailed design issues. For a project manager, DB is questionable because 'the client has less control over the outcome – the final detailing of it – because they've given the ownership or the responsibility to the contractor . . . with the nitty-gritty and the nuts and bolts, a lot of the onus now goes to the contractor'. Others felt likewise, with a Swedish architect expressing misgivings about the inability to control some of the professional staff. As he said, 'the technical engineers have been engaged by the builder so we haven't had the control we usually have over a project for designing technical systems in a complete package with the builder'.

These testimonies, then, indicate that the type of procurement route is a critical factor in influencing aspects of the design process. In particular, DB is, potentially, a mechanism for cost control and, as a UK architect said, 'they [clients] need to appreciate that price is not everything in buildings and that really good design does not come with the cheapest price tag. You get what you pay for and sometimes you get less than you expect from DB' (quoted in Akintoye and Fitzgerald, 1995: 42). The implication for disabled people's design needs are that anything perceived to be 'additional' cost will be squeezed or, as an architect, in interview, commented, 'DB isn't the route for enlightened design and it isn't going to help give disabled people what they want and need'.

Project team dynamics and interactions

While the procurement route can influence developers' responses to the building and design needs of disabled people, such routes are determined largely, as Chapter 4 intimated, by needs specified by the client. There is no singular type of client, yet much of the literature on property development fails to differentiate between different types of clients and their diverse building requirements. This is particularly the case with what Ball (1998) refers to as mainstream neo-classical models of the development process. As Chapter 1 suggested, these tend to either ignore the determinate role(s) of clients in influencing building design and development or reduces their influences to a cost-calculating rationality. However, the case and other material is characterised by a diversity of clients seeking contrasting outcomes, and operating under a variety of different constraints and opportunities. Such contextual variation is, we would argue, critical to the ways in which the access needs of disabled people are approached and addressed within the development process.

The increasing importance of clients, in influencing design and development processes, was highlighted time and again by interviewees. As an architect commented, 'the big development projects tend to be client-led rather than architect-led. The client identifies what has to be done.' Another concurred in noting that 'at the end of the day, if the client's paying then the client's always right, I suppose'. A commonly held view, amongst property professionals, is that clients tend to do little in responding to disabled people's access needs. As an architect suggested:

> the client is everything. S/he tells you and you do what s/he says and putting in the minimum for the legislation would normally be the answer. I can rarely think of any clients that wanted better than the minimum.

A range of respondents felt constrained by the financial strictures that they operate within and commented on the client's perceptions of disabled access representing a cost as a factor in disabled people's needs often being overlooked. Indeed, some clients see disabled people as literally a waste of space. For instance, one project manager commented that client and developer behaviour can be influenced by 'perceptions of increased costs, related to the loss of usable space/seating capacity for a minority group which do not pay a commercial rate for benefits provided'. Others feel that the sheer ignorance of clients and/or developers is critical to the lack of provision for disabled people, or, as an architect suggested, the problem is that 'clients generally are either unaware or uneducated in details of disabled people's problems of access'. Others considered clients to be minimalistic with a willingness only to provide the legal minimum or, as one respondent said, 'as little as they can get away with'. For one respondent, access has to be sold to the client as a commercial concern or, as she commented, 'most clients are made aware of the marketing potential of providing facilities for all forms of disablement'.

However, while many clients tend to maximise space and minimise costs, a number of respondents felt that this was not only due to the nature of the industry but also because of a lack of understanding of the issues involved in accessible design. As one commented, 'I feel that there is a need to raise awareness of the needs of disabled people and of the techniques available to meet them, not only [for] architects but also engineers and clients'. Another agreed in suggesting that 'it is always useful to have information on specific problems and how to deal with them. However, architects are not the only ones who need this information – put clients and developers at the top of the list.' Project managers expressed their frustration in commenting on how clients have to be led towards specific design solutions. As a project manager said:

> you begin to build up a picture of what they need and they know they need it but they just haven't been able to tell you – you say 'What do you want in your building?' and their eyes glaze over, it all seems too complicated.

Others concurred, with another project manager noting that:

> at the moment we've got one client who shall remain nameless, but every time you talk to him it's this vague cloud that's moving around in the ether somewhere, it's like trying to pin a jelly to the wall, you can never get to the core of 'What exactly do you want?'.

Such responses are echoed by others, with Bentley (1999) referring to clients' inabilities to articulate themselves except in the most vague terms. Similarly, Magnano Lampugnani (1991: 117), in referring to clients, notes, perhaps unfairly, that they are 'not capable of expressing precise, concrete and unequivocal demands'. These frustrations with clients are not confined to the UK but are evident elsewhere. For instance, developers in Sweden referred to the resistance of clients to access issues. One developer commented that 'growing awareness in society has raised not only expectations but also legal requirements and often these are not fully appreciated by clients who seek cost effective minimum solutions'. Others agreed, or as a Swedish respondent argued, 'it is useful to be aware but at the end of the day the client makes the decisions on economic grounds . . . you look after your client. The customer is everything and if he says he wants this and not that you supply it because if you don't he'll go to another guy.'

Clients are only one part of the process and it would be problematical to reduce poor access solely to their (lack of) knowledge and motivations. As significant, we would argue, is the nature and composition of the development team in influencing how far, and in what ways, access issues feature as an integral part of a project. Its quality and motivations can have a significant influence upon the form and content of building provisions for disabled people. Indeed, for Haviland (1996: 56), 'design management spans the entire facilities cycle and involves coordinating and reconciling many diverse and competing issues, organisations, and ways of operating'. As a UK developer argued, the major constraint in responding to access relates to the attitudes and disposition of the project team. As he suggested, in relation to a major mixed-use development:

it would be very simple just to say cost but that's not the factor. I don't think the cost is the problem at all. I think it's getting the rest of the consultants to take on board the importance of it, or to recognise that it's one of the criteria to be satisfied when designing a building properly. It shouldn't always be aesthetic factors ... I think it's just a bringing together of everyone and getting them to recognise that it's the right thing to do.

Other professionals, particularly access consultants, commented on their difficulties in trying to persuade the myriad of actors in development teams to incorporate access facilities. As an access consultant said, 'every time a query was raised they moved by an inch, building control had to struggle to get things through and I felt the same, that you had to work quite hard to establish why you wanted particular things'. Similar experiences were evident in Sweden, with a range of respondents commenting on the resistance of members of project teams to incorporate access beyond their (self-) understanding of disability as a form of mobility impairment. As a project manager noted:

when you meet the architect at the building permission meetings we have here in Sweden you will not see anything about those with impaired sight or hearing and so on. They have no knowledge of this. I think it's worse today and disabled people complain a lot about this, especially about the colour of signs, electrical lights, and so on. It's not good I don't think. For example, the little details; there's no attention to these.

For this respondent, a critical part of the development process is raising professional awareness within the development team: 'I spend a lot of time talking with the various partners about what we have to achieve and why it's important'. Respondents in the UK expressed similar reservations about lack of knowledge and empathy within key segments of project teams. Thus, one client commented on the appointed developer:

well, there was an awareness. Yes, they knew they had to provide good car parking and accessible car parking, but what they didn't realise was that it's not good enough for it to be over the other side of the site. I just don't think they thought it through.

This client also expressed frustration with the lack of knowledgeability of access issues by some of her main contractors. As she remarked:

the contractor was very open to it but hadn't really thought it through. But then they hadn't thought through the fact that I would want to see all the kind of fittings and all the stuff to make sure. I mean, for example, they would say here's your white fitting and it had a red thing on it and I'd say well that's not acceptable and they'd say well it's white, so for them working with us was a trying experience, never mind access.

For other property professionals a constraint in engaging with access issues is their estrangement from elements of the development process and not knowing how best to intervene at the key stages. As an architect commented, 'I think we need to know more about the building process in terms of the fact that there are obvious stages, and at what points during the process are the best points for consultation [about access]?' This, then, relates to the operationalisation and implementation of access directives for specific building projects. A range of access consultants, and other professionals, commented on how disabled people's needs are often not met at the point of implementation, whatever the knowledge base and/or good intentions of clients, developers and other participants in development teams. According to one access consultant:

> certainly experience from other buildings has been down to a question of following the guy around with the screwdriver putting the handrails on . . . is there a need for someone to be there on the day that they are fitting out the toilets, for example? Because every single disabled accessible toilet I look at seems to have something wrong with it. I make jokes about it, about doing a big scale plan of where to put hand rails and the soap dispenser and things because nobody ever seems to be able to get it right.

Even when consultation and discussions about access occur at formative stages of the process, this is no guarantee of a satisfactory outcome. As a member of the City of London access group commented, in relation to their experiences of seeking to influence access:

> even if you get in thoroughly at the planning application stage, and even if you convince the architects and developers, it's the chap with the hammer and the trowel who needs to know. It's the fine detail. But how do you make sure that he knows that it can matter?

Similar observations were made by Swedish access consultants who were often highly critical about the absence of debate and explicit consideration of disabled people's needs by members of project teams. In the development of a public swimming pool, for example, an access consultant was important in redressing the architect's ignorance of wheelchair users' needs. As he recounted, 'they [the architects] were not looking at the swimming pool for disabled people's use, when you have lots of people swimming who are disabled. It was impossible to get to the pools . . . it was interesting that they hadn't thought about this.'

These observations highlight the importance of developing clear communicative and interactive structures between members of development teams as a prerequisite in responding to items such as disabled people's access needs. For one project manager, for instance, the extent to which access directives were complied with depended, in part, on his chain of command and professionals' understanding of his directives. As he said, 'different professionals will interpret the design parameters [concerning access] in different ways and they never see eye-to-eye, so I have to resolve this'. Others concurred in noting that different professional stances on, and understanding of, access was sometimes difficult to reconcile. As an architect said, 'I see access as a design challenge, but others will dismiss it as an extra cost . . . most don't think about it'. This, then, poses a dilemma for disabled people in seeking to intervene in, and influence, the development process. In particular, which professionals should disabled people seek to influence, and what means should they deploy to gain professionals' understanding of their needs? This is a theme we turn to now.

Consultative processes and the role of access consultants

As the previous section has indicated, the development process is characterised by a myriad of actors, often with contrasting levels of understanding of access issues. For Bentley (1999), contrasting actors carry out their work according to different views and values, with the potential for conflicts of interest to arise. Thus, as Morton (1992: 10) notes, while most architects prioritise aesthetics as the primary design value to be pursued, surveyors have 'a primary concern with market efficiency and value for money where value itself is defined in monetary terms'. Moreover, the task specialisms, underpinning the development process, are a potential source of mutual ignorance between members of development teams. Such circumstances are increasingly leading to the appointment of specialist consultants, seeking to create generic understanding and responses by professionals in relation to specific aspects of the development process. This is particularly so in relation to the needs of disabled people, in which anecdotal evidence suggests that the use of access consultants is becoming more common (Noble, 1999, 2000).[4]

The use of specialist advisers concerning access issues is, as Chapter 3 noted, being stimulated by changing external circumstances. For instance, the funding of development projects by the National Lottery and other groups such as, for example, the Arts Council for England, the Scottish Arts Council and English Heritage, are beginning, in part, to change client attitudes and responses to the building needs of disabled people. As a Scottish Arts Council project officer, responsible for the capital programme, said:

> if access is not seen to be properly provided in proposals, then they won't get funded. These are public buildings and if a building is not accessible in as full a sense as it can be then it doesn't deserve to be funded. On several occasions, projects where access maybe hadn't been thought about as fully as it could have been, have been deferred or even refused.

Changes to funding regimes, coupled with the directives of the DDA, are, in part, stimulating professionals' increasing use of access advisers or consultants (see Noble, 1999). As a respondent said, 'I think that access auditing is the one thing that is actually going to help most architects to raise their game to actually begin to appreciate the minutiae of these things – colour contrast, visibility and acoustics – all these things which actually help people get about'. However, in interview, clients expressed some reservations about the use of access consultants. Indeed, most clients who use access consultants tend to do so only after initial design parameters have been agreed between them and the appointed developer and architect. As one client commented, about using an access consultant:

> [we brought him in] I would say midway through the process, just prior to putting a planning application in but when the design is pretty well there from the landscape architect's perspective and we've got a keen idea of what materials we want to use. If the consultant then comes in – and I see that as an appropriate time to do so – they must understand our wants and requirements.

For some clients, the use of an access consultant, while informative and important in addressing legal issues, provides a source of legitimation or accreditation. As a client/developer said, about employing an access consultant:

> having someone like that not only helps you do the right thing it also helps add credence to what you've done when it comes to the planning stages because each authority has its own access committee who tend to go overboard in terms of what should be done. And by having someone there who actually has problems of his own in terms of access and has the knowledge of all the regulations there's an educated response to some of the more quirky things they're asking us to do.

In the case of Bluewater, for instance, an important feature was the development of consultative and participative procedures which were continuous throughout the development process (see also pages 84–91). Such inclusivity was apparent in relation to disabled people with the appointment of, at the very earliest stages, an access consultancy to advise the development team of the specificities of designing for the needs of disabled people. The consultancy acted as a fulcrum point for members of the project group, disseminating advice and seeking to ensure that all project members were aware of the access requirements and of how to implement them. As the project manger said:

> in terms of how we manage that process, what we've got the access consultants to do is a series of appraisals for the different elements of the job, stairs, floors, cinemas, each of the villages, and we've taken these and they've gone to the design teams to talk with them about how to implement the features and we try and follow it up with an audit of that appraisal . . . they have a wide ranging remit to talk to the design teams and analyse what they're doing and come back and give us feedback.

The access consultant concurred, and noted that:

> we lead them through the design process [about access] and there is a four-meetings process where we have them in first and they tell us what they want to do and we take it away and we tell them this is what we think you could do and we try and take them through it . . . we want them to talk about what they're creating here and actually push back the bounds.

The access consultant was important in establishing procedures and mechanisms with the contractors to diminish the possibilities of non-implementation of access directives concerning fittings and fixtures. Indeed, for the project manager, the consultant's advice and appraisal role was pivotal in that, as he said, 'now that we're down the track [the appraisals help us know] how far we've strayed from that and if there is something we've fundamentally got wrong, can we put it right?' In concurring, one of the access consultants described her involvement at the conceptual stages of the process:

> at that stage quite often in terms of it being a water coloured drawing, they may involve myself as well and say . . . 'this is the concept for this particular part, cast your eye on this and give us some feedback', and so quite often the feedback would be given on prospective-type drawings.

An important consideration in designing for the needs of disabled people is to ensure that project plans are followed through and implemented. However, some research indicates that disabled people's needs are often not met at the point of implementation, whatever the knowledge base and/or good intentions of clients, developers and other participants in development teams (Imrie, 1996). This may be for a range of reasons but is often because of poor project management and/or a lack of effective monitoring of fitting procedures. This was recognised by the developer and client of Bluewater, Lend Lease who, in responding to the access consultants, devised systems to monitor access compliance. As a respondent from Lend Lease said: 'we don't just talk the talk, we make sure it's implemented as well. The developer and access consultant actually audit the development every month.'

However, Lend Lease tends to be an exception and a number of access consultants expressed disquiet about their involvement only in a limited range of projects. As one consultant said, 'many of the projects I'm involved in are funded by the National Lottery . . . speculative developers will rarely come to us which is a pity. We don't deal with them and they don't come near us.' Most consultants feel side-lined and have to push to get any notice. As a consultant commented:

> the architect is great, but again like everybody else he's got loads of pressures . . . it's constantly me having to you know prod him, is this design done yet, is this . . . ? It's down to chance that something is actually developed and I've then commented on it rather than actually been included in the design process, which is not really to our liking I must admit.

Another consultant concurred, or as he said, in relation to consultative processes concerning the development of a leisure centre:

> I think there was just a feeling of being fobbed off. There's a feeling of jumping through the hoops, 'Oh, yes, we're obliged to have this meeting with the disability groups so we'll have it and then we'll just go back to doing what we were going to do anyway.'

For others, consultative processes between developers and/or their agents and disabled people are, at worst, irrelevant, and, at best, often little more than public relations exercises. As one access consultant said, 'it does seem to be that for these big boys in the architectural world that the needs of people, let alone disabled people, are not really part of the point, people's needs don't really come into it'. However, a contractor argued that protracted meetings with consultants were problematical or, as he said, 'unfortunately in the modern construction process you can't make decisions by committee. You have to be very positive because things are moving so quickly [and] at the end of the day it's the programme and the costs which drive everything.'

In particular, a critical issue is the timing of entry of access consultants to a development project. There were few examples of access consultants being appointed at the inception of projects; rather, they were usually appended at later stages to save development costs. Interviews with access consultants conveyed an impression of them being 'the poor relations' of the development process or, as one consultant said:

> I wasn't brought in at the beginning of this project and some of the materials they are using are not all that good from an access point of view. They originally overestimated how much it was going to cost them to get me involved, that's why the late entry. They also keep forgetting about me and I have to keep on at them and remind them that I'm around. I need to build up a relationship with the curator and hopefully he'll bring me in.

Moreover, access consultants are not necessarily seen by disabled people as being best able to provide relevant advice and guidance to developers on access issues. There is an issue about who and what the consultant is seeking to represent. Thus, for a member of a focus group, employed by a developer to feed into a retail project, the 'consultant was there to listen to us but just seemed to take our ideas away and re-present them to the developer ... they were getting paid to do this and we weren't and we had no idea how our opinions were being used'. For others, in the same group, the access consultant was no more than a 'talking shop ... representing the developer and not that interested in taking on our ideas'. Disabled people tend to see consultants as conforming to the minimum rules, or, as a disabled person suggested, 'it was really a question with them that they were particularly hot on the regulations and sticking to them and any deviation from that was difficult to argue for. The trouble is, you'll know this, that from our side of the fence you're appealing to people's goodwill.'

Conclusions

The complexities of property development are such that no single professional attitude or practice is able to determine the content of building projects; rather, the form and content of projects is broadly conditioned by the development context which is defined by an array of variables, including, amongst others, site-specific or locational details, individual and agency interactions, the fiscal and contractual conditions of the project, and the procurement route. In particular, the evidence suggests that DB, as a procurement route, is increasingly a preferred choice for development projects, in which the details of design are itemised and costed in advance of the contractural commitment. Fixing costs, in advance of construction, implies that significant changes to design will often be resisted by contractors after the commencement of a project. For many architects, this is a retrograde change which is, as Akintoye and Fitzgerald (1995: 42) suggest, contributing to 'reduced standards and lower professional fees'.

It also renders irrelevant the consultative processes which characterise most projects and, consequentially, contributes to the potential estrangement of disabled people from the development and design process. Some projects might involve architects presenting plans to access groups, but how useful is this if the contractural route has already determined, in advance, the design specifications of the building? The nature of DB, as a procurement-type, implies that disabled people and access consultants ought to be involved in consultative processes at the formative or conception stages of a project if they are to have any influence. Moreover, seeking to influence architects to incorporate access may be irrelevant if their contribution to the design process is limited by a broader 'design management' approach to projects. As an architect, in interview, said, 'I've had to go to the meetings [of the access group] but I'm only a mouthpiece and I have little control over the final design . . . but try telling that to them [disabled people]'.

The determinants of design are related, in part, to the myriad of professional values and interactions in the development process. Such values are diverse and often contradictory, and it is not always obvious to any person, disabled or not, as to who or what ought to be influenced (see Bentley, 1999). One implication, for disabled people, is that professionals, other than just architects, ought to be drawn into consultative processes, particularly investors, clients and development companies. Other observers, such as Guy and Henneberry (2000), note that one of the key actors, the institutional investor, is perhaps the hardest for people to influence, given that they are often non-local or remote to where a project is being built. However, this is relevant to the development industry as a whole, whereby non-local firms dominate development and construction activities. In this context, then, what value are local negotiations or forms of dialogue which, ultimately, are subject to ratification by often remote extra-local parties?

Further reading

The best introduction to the development process is Cadman, D. and Topping, R. (1997) *Property Development*, published by E & FN Spon. It provides details of the main contractural routes underpinning property development with examples of how they operate in practice. For a critical appraisal of design and build, readers should look at the research by Akintoye, A. (1994) and Akintoye, A. and Fitzgerald, E. (1995). In addition, readers should refer to Franks, J. (1998) *Building Procurement Systems: A Client's Guide*, Longman, Harlow.

Case study
Crescent Theatre, Birmingham, UK

The Crescent Theatre

The Crescent Theatre is one of Birmingham's oldest theatre companies and was founded in 1924 by a group of City Council employees. An amateur organisation, the company currently has a membership of over 250 actors, technicians and designers and stages upwards of 15 productions a year. The company was originally based in a converted building on Cambridge Crescent but, due to redevelopment, relocated to a purpose-built theatre in Cumberland Street in 1964. History repeated itself in the late 1980s when the ground lease in Cumberland Street was disposed of by the City Council to developers. With Cumberland Street, and the surrounding area, coming within the Brindleyplace development area, the 1960s architecture of the Crescent was seen as outdated in the context of the proposed prestigious development scheme for Brindleyplace (see also the Ikon case study, Chapter 5). In particular, the theatre occupied a prime location within the site, which the developers wanted for a 90,000 square foot office development. As one of the developers, in interview, said:

> the theatre sat on one of the most important elements of the Brindleyplace site as far as we were concerned. It was an ugly building and deserved to be knocked down; it was crap in terms of the accommodation provided. We wanted the site and agreed to build them a new theatre.

After long negotiations, the developers, Argent plc, agreed to finance and build a new theatre on an adjacent canal-side site fronting onto Sheepcote Street (see the map of Brindleyplace, Ikon case study, page 115). The new theatre was to be built on a 'like-for-like' basis in terms of size and seating capacity, and to include upgraded features where required by current legislation, such as Part M. Any extra facilities beyond those agreed with the developer were to be paid for by the Crescent through a proposed Lottery bid. In itself, this was an unusual project for a commercial developer to undertake, in

that it is extremely rare, if not unheard of, for the private sector to fund and build a theatre. Nevertheless, both parties stood to benefit from the deal; Argent by gaining a prime site for development, and the Crescent by getting a new £4 million theatre with additional fixtures and equipment.

The scheme was developed under a negotiated design and construction contract by Norwest Holst (the contractors) on a partnership basis with the Argent Group (the client). This procurement route was used throughout Brindleyplace and, for Argent, this 'fast track' contract allowed them to get the Crescent project underway and to resolve detailed design issues whilst on site, as well as giving them price certainty. Argent employed a concept architect, John Chatwin, to develop an outline scheme for the theatre. This appointment was partly because of his work on the master plan for the Brindleyplace project, and due to his specialisation and interest in theatre design. As with other schemes in Brindleyplace, John, as concept architect, was retained by Argent throughout the development process. Argent also appointed a theatre consultant, Martin Carr of Carr & Angier, to oversee the more technical requirements, such as stage lighting and electricals. Norwest Holst also appointed their own architects, Temple Cox Nicholls, under the Design and Build procurement route, to produce the construction drawings.

The Crescent had originally planned to apply for Lottery funding to allow for a number of enhancements to the theatre above and beyond those offered by the developers in their contract. However, following consultation with a number of arts bodies, the Lottery bid, submitted in July 1996, was increased in scope and cost to £3,500,000. This was to facilitate a number of capital investments, including an extended foyer on two levels, and enhanced technical installation and a provision to endow a youth education programme. The initial bid was almost rejected outright, before the Crescent was asked to resubmit their plans at a lower cost. The design was revised a number of times before the Crescent received approval in October 1997 for funding at a much-reduced level of £500,000. Crescent trustees felt that the climate of Lottery funding had changed after the initial burst of large capital grants and that their bid had suffered accordingly. The Lottery application process was time consuming for all concerned and, by the time the final decision was announced, building work, which had commenced in February 1997, was well underway.

Given the reduced Lottery funds, the main features to be cut out of the scheme were the extension of the front foyer, and proposals for a separate bar and café. Instead, a smaller foyer, and combined bar and café have been built. For John Chatwin:

this compromise was a direct result of a very delayed Arts Council decision. Although the reduced foyer spaces work well in most respects, there is

one point where a column had to be included to allow for either foyer layout to be built. This causes a bottle-neck which can make it difficult for disabled people to get around when the theatre is crowded.

The episode concerning the Lottery bid and proposed foyer extension, together with contractual obligations, impacted upon access to the main control room in the theatre. The extended foyer was intended to have provided facilities to allow a large platform lift into the control room, and disabled people's access into it. However, under the pro-curement contract, it had been agreed that the Crescent would put the plat-form lift in as part of their Lottery appli-cation, as opposed to it being in the contractor's contract. With the foyer extension cut from the Lottery funding, the contractor's argued that it was not their responsibility to provide the lift. Simultaneously, Building Control in Birmingham City Council requested

Crescent Theatre bar featuring split-level counter

Reception area featuring split-level counter

that wheelchair access be provided to the lighting and sound desks in the control room. With Building Control withholding approval under Part M of the Building Regulations, Argent agreed to a compromise by providing a hoist up the four stairs into the control room which, while not perfect, provides some measure of access for wheelchair users.

Both the contractors and Argent felt that the Lottery application took people's eye off the ball until a very late stage in the development. The Lottery board took longer than anticipated to come to a final decision as to the level of funding, while the design base build got lost in aspirations of (Lottery) money coming in. As John Chatwin said, 'a number of key decisions were taken in the belief that because the Lottery application had been so favourably received, most aspects of it would be approved. When the funding was substantially reduced, considerable re-design had to be undertaken within the reduced resources then available.' Nevertheless, for the Crescent trustees, the Lottery funding, albeit at a much reduced level, was welcomed in that it provided for a number of extra features, including the conversion of the rehearsal room into a studio theatre and sound equipment for the Main House.

From an access point of view, the Lottery paid for an additional wheel-chair lift backstage to assist disabled performers and technicians with access to all operational parts of the theatre, except for the flytower and upper technical galleries.

For some of the development team, the project was complicated as the Crescent committee members were unsure as to what they wanted from the new theatre. The appointment of Jacqueline Green as full-time general manager in January 1998 saw her bring extensive knowledge of access to theatres, in both physical and general terms. As John Chatwin noted, 'her previous job had been organising the move into a new theatre and she avoided many potential mistakes by having first hand experience of what designing for the disabled means, rather than simply following published guidelines without understanding the real problem'. This understanding of access ranged from broader issues such as signed performances and multi-format information, down to detailed design issues such as colour contrasts, handrails and signage. As Jacqueline commented, 'you can make a huge difference on the small details', such as fixtures and furnishings. Nevertheless, she added that Argent, not the Crescent, were the client on the base project and controlled key decisions concerning issues such as access. As she said: 'we actually had no legal right to say "Can you change this?"'

For many of the design and development team, the project was a steep learning curve and, according to the client's representative, people were caught out by the complexity of the building, particularly some of the sub-contractors. Given the complex nature of a theatre, the use of design and build was questioned by some of those involved. As a member of the contractor's team said, 'we tried to develop this single [contractual] document which everybody was happy with. I know the architect had some concerns ... the way that it was pushed along for commercial reasons.' Others were concerned that the DB route had placed cost constraints on the design. As a respondent said, 'there's a lot of commercial constraints on us because the building has been done very cheaply ... we tried to keep these [disabled people's access features] to a sensible level'. Others referred to development team dynamics as a factor in inhibiting aspects of the design process. Thus, for another respondent, 'there's still situations where we failed because we didn't fully understand exactly what the theatre needed, silly things'.

Moreover, the DB route was such that all of the critical design decisions, as intimated above, had been made prior to the confirmation of the level of Lottery monies. As the concept architect said: 'because of the slightly unusual situation of the Crescent where the building had been designed and was going to be built in any event, irrespective of Lottery money, all the critical decisions about access had already been made'. However, for the developers, Argent, the Crescent was completed on schedule, in October 1998, and within budget which, as a number of people commented, is unusual. As the contractor noted, 'I think that Martin [Carr – theatre consultant] is of the opinion

that it's one of the few theatres that have been done almost in line with the budget and to the programme that was initially set. It's the nature of the beast; they always overrun in terms of time and cost', while Michael Whittall, one of the Crescent trustees, noted that Argent were 'very good on cost control'. However, as John Chatwin said:

> In some respects, the technical aspirations for the theatre were more appropriate to a £5 or £6 million building than the £4 million contracted; consequently, limited funds meant that preference was given to creating volume and installing the basic technical infrastructure. As was admirably demonstrated in the separate Lottery-funded fitting out, this means that the internal finishes and higher specification theatre equipment can always be added at a later date. Above all, the Crescent would never have had another opportunity to gain such flexible performance and ancillary space.

From an access point of view, the Main House can accommodate up to six wheelchair users and the Studio up to two. There is an infrared sound transmission system and access in the front of the house and backstage, including lifts in both areas, neither of which were available in the old theatre. The appointment of a general manager, and the expansion of the operation of the Crescent, has also led to a sponsorship deal with British Telecom to provide signed performances and the setting up of an audio description service. Programme information is available in large print and on disc and tape and, amongst the staff there is an awareness of improving access for all. Although there were some technical and contractual problems which did impact upon access issues, Jacqueline Green feels that, at the time of writing, the Crescent is the most successful theatre in Birmingham from an access point of view.

PART III
Reflections

7 Alternative directions in property development, disability and design

Introduction

> The use of services such as shops, cinemas, restaurants and libraries is something most people enjoy without a second thought. Many disabled people cannot take access to such services for granted. If we are to achieve an inclusive society where the contribution of disabled people is allowed to flourish and is valued, and where everyone can enjoy the facilities and services on offer – independently and more conveniently – we must strive for comprehensive rights of access.
>
> (Disability Rights Task Force, 1999: 53)

The DRTF's observation is apt in a context in which the property industry is generally insensitive to the building needs of disabled people. While there are some examples of knowledgeable and good practice, these are few and far between. They are more likely than not to be over-shadowed by poor design and a lack of engagement between property professionals and disabled people (see Imrie, 1996, 2000a). As the research in this book suggests, professionals rarely exceed the legislative minima in providing access, and most regard the provision of access as a cost (whatever the contrary evidence might suggest). Access features and facilities are rarely seen as enhancing the value of development projects, while access tends to be an after-thought, rather than integral to the design and development of a building (Gleeson, 1999a; Imrie, 1996). This is compounded by legislation which, arguably, defends the profit-seeking motives of professionals, while providing a range of exclusions from its provisions.

Inclusive development and design will not be attained as long as reductive conceptions of disability remain at the core of professionals' knowledge of disabled people. Property professionals tend to (re)produce an understanding of disability as impairment-specific, or a medical condition that can, potentially, be corrected through cure and rehabilitation. As earlier chapters suggest, this conception is problematical because it fails to situate the limitations of impairment, or the ways in which bodies operate, in the broader context of socio-cultural values and attitudinal relations or structures. Given this, professionals are unlikely to conceive of their attitudes and practices as the primary determinant of disabled people's experiences of the built environment. Rather, they are more likely to see such experiences as directly connected to the specific incapacities, or functional limitations, of disabled people's bodies. This leads to a prognosis that what ought to be corrected are the 'personal difficulties' of disabled people.

Similarly, professionals' understanding of disabled people is usually stereotypical and, as a consequence, inaccurate. Thus, disability is often counterpoised to ability, or where the abnormal body is contrasted to the normal, the invalid to the valid, the mental or mad with the sane, etc. These binary divisions perpetuate an understanding of disabled people as deficient and disordered, or as victims in need of help. Such conceptions see disabled people as requiring 'special assistance', and reinforce socio-cultural conceptions of disabled people as 'dependent, childlike, passive, and sensitive' (Linton, 1998: 25). This essentialism deflects attention from the complexity of disabled people's minds and bodies, and as Linton (ibid.) suggests, from the 'lack of opportunity, discrimination, institutionalisation, and ostracism' which underpins and gives shape to their lives. This, then, suggests that the attainment of inclusive design will require significant changes in social, cultural and political attitudes and practices.

In this final chapter, we develop the proposition that the value and knowledge systems underpinning property development inhibit professionals in responding to the diverse design needs of disabled people. From architects' reductive conceptions of the human body, to project managers' concerns with cost control, the property industry is implicated in perpetuating what Gleeson (1999a) terms environmental injustice. We develop and discuss this proposition in the next part of the chapter, and consider alternative directions for the design and development of the built environment. In particular, we focus on the possibilities for the development of an inclusive design philosophy underpinned by current ideas about civil rights. We conclude by itemising some of the practical possibilities for transforming the social relations of property development, in directions which are knowledgeable of, and sensitised to, the needs of disabled people.

Environmental injustice and the civil rights of disabled people

As a range of authors note, the form of the built environment is primarily driven by professionals' financial criteria; users' functional demands are generally of less importance (see, for instance, Guy, 1998; Henneberry, 1988). Thus, as Edwards (1990: 175) suggests, 'private property development is driven more by investment demand and suppliers' decisions than by final user demand – even less by any sort of final user needs'. Likewise, investment decisions by property professionals are connected to a particular way of conceiving of property development processes. For Fischler (1995: 21), such perspectives are 'a direct function of people's background, in particular of their professional culture. One's professional culture gives one a pre-disposition to frame situations and problems in particular ways.' Similarly, Guy and Henneberry (2000: 2415) note the difficulties in changing the value-bases of the development process, in that 'investment theory and practice are not sensitive to challenge from without their own terms of reference'.

These professional values and practices, underpinned by investment pressures, tend to (re)produce development processes which are insensitive to the environmental needs of a myriad of different users. In the context of property development, disabled people are subjected to injustices which can, after Young (1990), be defined as oppression and domination. As Chapter 2 intimated, oppression refers to institutional processes which prevent (disabled) people exercising their capacities and expressing their experiences. This reflects, in part, broader social structures which, by the absence of consultation with disabled people, result in inappropriate forms of service provision. Likewise, domination is a facet of disabled people's lives, or where institutional conditions inhibit (disabled) people from participating in determining their actions, or the conditions of their actions.

The oppression and domination of disabled people underpins the (development) processes which give shape to the built environment. For some commentators, the resultant environments are unjust (i.e. oppressive and dominant), in perpetuating socio-institutional contexts which deny disabled people the means to influence the conditions of their movement, mobility and access (Gleeson, 1999a; Hine, 1999; Hine and Mitchell, 2001; Imrie, 2000c; Laws, 1994; Sibley, 1996; Young, 1990). Thus, from the poorly designed nature of public transportation to the dependence of many disabled people on under-funded 'dial-a-ride' bus services, environmental injustices serve to perpetuate inequalities by failing to accommodate, or respond to, the range of human needs in the built environment.[1] The social spaces of disability are compounded by the institutional 'rules' of the development process which tend to reduce users to asocial categories. As a consequence, disabled people rarely feature as an explicit category in project proposals or plans.

For Gleeson (1999a), the creation of enabling environments ought to be a priority; that is, the development of social spaces which, in Hahn's (1987: 188; quoted in Gleeson, 1999a: 149) terms, 'accommodate a broader range of human capabilities than the present environment' (see also the arguments by Gleeson, 2001; Kitchen and Law, 2001). In amplifying, Gleeson (1999a: 149) suggests that an enabling environment will aim 'to establish social independence for all inhabitants' by empowering people to determine the conditions of their own existence through non-hierarchical social relationships and mutually supportive networks (see also Fraser, 1995; Swain *et al.*, 1993). Others concur with Oliver (1990, 1993), for instance, noting that what disabled people want is social inclusion and cultural respect, and as Gleeson (1999a: 149) notes, the upholding 'of the right of all to have their material needs guaranteed, while insisting on the necessity of freedom from cultural–political forms of disability oppression'.

These ideas are core to a broader politics of disability which is premised on the eradication of ascribed needs, or processes whereby policy experts and professionals assess disabled people's needs and ascribe the relevant policy prescriptions (e.g. the provision of special transport or equipment to facilitate access). For Oliver (1990, 1996), ascribed need reinforces the power of experts to determine the quality of disabled people's lives. This, according to Oliver, maintains disabled people's dependence on others and does little to create the conditions for self-determination.[2] In contrast, Oliver (1996) notes that a politics of disability ought to work from a position of self-defined needs as a basis for rights claims (see also Abberley, 1987; Gleeson, 1999a; Handley, 2000; Imrie, 2000b; Oliver, 1990, 1996; Young, 1990). As Oliver (1996: 74) suggests, 'it is rights to appropriate their own self defined needs that disabled people are demanding, not to have their needs defined and met by others'.

In relation to development and access, disabled people are increasingly seeking to assert their self-defined needs in relation to their claim that they have the right to equality of opportunity in gaining entry and access to places. This, though, is far from an unproblematic position and process (Handley, 2000; Oliver, 1990, 1996). As Handley (2000: 318) notes, 'if everyone is demanding the satisfaction of their self-defined needs by right, then how are we to sort out the inevitable conflicts that this will generate? How are we to prioritise all of these competing claims, and who will arbitrate between them?' This is the crux of seeking to politicise access with reference to 'individuated' claims to rights or through a framework which is, potentially, oblivious to the points of conflict and the possible need for compromise or even an acceptance on particular limits to, and limitations of, a person's access to the built environment.

Indeed, while one might accept that disabled, and other, people have the moral right to access, the issue becomes more difficult in thinking about how this might be translated into practical or legal terms, or into a set of policies underpinned by legal rights. As Handley (2000: 319) asks, should such rights be ones which last in perpetuity, that is, civil or political rights, or should they be 'special' or compensatory in form? How should limits to rights claims be assessed or gauged, and how far should one respond to Ramsey's (1998: 229; quoted in Handley, 2000: 321) observation that 'needs cannot be inferred from what people say they need or from what people actually do'? Moreover, how does one deal with Beiner's (1992, 147; quoted in Handley, 2000: 321–2) claim that 'part and parcel of rights discourse is a tendency towards forms of social life that are exclusively adversarial, litigious, and geared towards modes of self assertion'?

Such debates are, as Swyngedouw (2000: 67) notes, part of a current obsession with a politics of identity or seeking to activate 'voices from the margins'. For Swyngedouw (ibid.), the politics of difference is 'an apparently progressive liberal and non committal politics' that provides the illusion of resistance while failing to shift or transgress power. It is increasingly linked to a politics espousing a 'something for something' philosophy, or where governments seek to activate the liberal ideal by holding people responsible for the exercise of the rights conferred upon them (see Raco and Imrie, 2000). For disabled people, this may hold little or nothing for them, given that their material capacities, with which to exercise their rights, are often absent or weakly developed. For instance, the material means for disabled people to exercise their rights are limited, in part, by their precarious position in the labour market. Indeed, given employers' prejudices towards disability, how far can disabled people exercise a right of access to work when the right is denied to them by those who predominantly control the workplace?

There are no easy answers nor programmatic or prescriptive resolutions to these, and related, issues and it is only through the development of a 'politics of access' that such questions can come to the fore as the basis for developing new perspectives and political programmes. This, though, is a long way from realisation. Disabled people lack rudimentary levels of participation and involvement in civil society and a pre-condition for transforming their access to the built environment is, we would argue, opportunities for participation in 'the discourse and associations of the public sphere' (Gould 1996: 181). This ought to be more than just the installation of deliberative democratic fora or procedural enactments that, potentially, do little to transform the social and institutional fixities of disablist attitudes and practices. In particular, discourses (of access) ought to move beyond just public sector participative networks, towards the development and propagation of private or corporate sector responsibilities.

Changing the social relations of the development process

As we indicated at the start of the chapter, development practices need to be sensitised to definitions of disability which transcend the limitations of reductive models of disability. Thus, while disability is related to an individual physical and/or mental impairment, it is not necessarily reducible to it; disability is also a socio-cultural construct. This distinction is critical because the contrasting conceptions of disability have different implications for the form and content of the development process. Reductive models of disability imply that disabled people should 'fit' themselves to the pre-existing built environment; that developers, and related professionals, have little responsibility in producing or overturning inaccessible environments. In contrast, conceptions of disability which seek to contextualise it as part of broader socio-cultural values and practices are more likely to consider property professionals' attitudes and actions as constituting, in part, the problem to be redressed.

Related to this is the fact that development practices tend to reflect societal stereotypes of disabled people as being mobility impaired. This is usually translated into policy practices which revolve around creating accessible spaces primarily for wheelchair users. This is problematical because it fails to recognise the diversity of physical and mental impairments in society along with the often conflicting and different access and other requirements of different categories of disabled people. Thus, the development process ought to develop some sensitivity to the heterogeneous nature of disabled people (and design accordingly). In part, this can be facilitated by education and training. Architecture, estate management and land economy courses, including surveying, should develop and teach modules which seek to sensitise professionals to the diverse building needs of users. Such courses should be more than technical in content but raise moral and ethical issues and, in doing so, seek to relate debates about access to broader questions concerning quality of life issues (see also MacDonald, 1991).

However, few property professionals receive education or training about access, and what does occur is ad hoc and aimed at particular members of development teams (i.e. usually the architect). In interview, a typical response was given by a course director of an architectural degree pro-gramme: 'in terms of disability, as far as I'm aware, I can't think of a particular project that's run since I've been here that actually focusses pri-marily, in the degree, on disability'. Similar responses were given by other course directors of architectural degree programmes. As a director said, 'I think that they [the students] probably don't learn a huge amount actually. There isn't a course that specifically deals with that [disability].' Others con-curred in noting that it was more than permissible for students to ignore access issues. Thus, as a course tutor commented, 'We would consider it acceptable for them [the students] to say, "Well, look, I've not considered accessibility in this project at all and I'm aware of that but I've done that because I wanted to explore other issues."'

Moreover, most design theory and practice is problematical in conceiv-ing of the human body as 'a normal type', or a form that fails to capture the complexity of bodily shapes, interactions and movements. Thus, as a lecturer in an architectural school said about his students' conception of the human body, 'you could say this is narcissistic on a certain level because it is centred on the person's own body, and it is also related to work in the art world which has quite a strong tradition'. Others con-curred, with another lecturer commenting that, 'I've been thinking about what do we do about the body here and I guess we don't do a great deal practically, perhaps not enough'. For others, little knowledge was being conveyed about the complexity of impairment. As a course tutor said, 'we don't teach anything much about disability and rarely say anything about the design needs of disabled people. It's not something we think about.' Architects' education and training is often dismissive of engagement with topics or substantive matter, such as access, that might clutter the curricu-lum or compromise creative thinking. As the director of an architectural school said:

> The difficulty with architecture is that there's a hell of a lot of issues, from the very aesthetic artistic issues to complex technical issues, accessi-bility, all those kinds of things have to be taken on board, and in each project, if the student tries to satisfy realistically all of those issues, that can be a hindrance to them thinking creatively.

For others, the lack of response to the building needs of disabled people was seen as a function of a busy routine. As an architect said:

> If it's not law it's not really going to filter back down into architectural education because it's not something we have to absolutely consider, and there are a lot of things . . . I mean, I'm not saying that we blindly turn our backs on it but there are lots of things that are legal that we have to consider and as such we've only got a limited amount of time.

Such responses are indicative, in part, of practical constraints on profes-sionals' abilities to incorporate access into aspects of the development process. These situations require, we would argue, the development of a practical politics of access; that is, a politics which is broadly defined as seeking to work within the existing, structural constraints of the development process, while seeking to push it towards attitudes and practices which have, at their core, a commitment to disabled people's access needs. A broad range of interrelated issues need to be addressed; and we will consider them now.

- A consistent response from disabled people, and some property professionals, is that regulatory control is the key in seeking to secure an accessible environment. While the building regulations, and aspects of the DDA, leave a lot to be desired, they provide a basis for securing access. However, much more needs to be done. The underlying medicalised definitions of the legislation remain intact and, with them, a 'blame the victim' understanding of disability. This requires redress by seeking to (re)define disability, as intimated earlier, as a product of the interface between impairment and socio-institutional relations and processes. Professionals are also confused by the legislation in that it is unclear how the building regulations interface with the DDA. As some respondents noted, this has the potential to inhibit or confuse development and design responses to access.

- Most development teams will often do no more than is legally required. Accordingly, Part M of the building regulations should be revised to raise standards of access beyond the presently prescribed minimum standards, and to develop a stronger (legal) formulation than that which presently only requires 'reasonable provision' to cater for disabled people's access needs in new buildings and/or substantial renovations. As Goldsmith (1997: 115) suggests, the regulations are 'a pragmatic and shaky response to political concerns' and retain a vagueness which permits more or less any combination of responses (to access) by developers. As the regulations are pivotal in shaping disablism in design processes, their restructuring ought to be the focal point for challenges to, and transformations of, contemporary attitudes and practices towards the design needs of disabled people.

- However, the facilitation of access depends on much more than the development and use of regulatory controls. As Steinfeld *et al.* (1977) argue, the success of a building depends on its acceptance by those who use it. For Steinfeld *et al.* (ibid.: 10), the experiential knowledge of building users is critical in directing formative building design, but also in helping 'to conceptualise and direct later changes and to keep a place adapted to current needs'. Urban design is, however, generally characterised by task specialisms dominated by professionals in which user views are residual or rarely permitted to filtrate into design and development processes (Imrie, 1996, 1999b, 2000a). For Bentley (1999: 250), 'there are serious problems inherent in design culture's systematic devaluation of lay knowledge' which ought to be redressed.

- These ideas are suggestive of a series of pragmatic transformations to the development process with the potential to sensitise professionals to the needs of disabled people. For instance, the use of access consultants or specialists is critical although, as Chapter 6 notes, they need to be integral parts of a development team rather than 'add-ons' to the process (as most were in our case examples). The more progressive development companies also seek to consult, up-front, with disabled people and their organisations. Participative structures, with disabled people being involved continuously in the development cycle, can have benefits to all parties. Thus, evidence from the research shows that the experiential knowledge of disabled people is an educative tool, as well as providing professionals with useful guidance on which to take access matters into consideration.

- The development of user-knowledge through consultative and/or participative networks is not a straightforward task and requires the local mobilisation of disabled people. As our research indicates, development companies will only respond to disabled people if they have a coherent and well informed set of opinions based on a knowledge of the development process. This is, for understandable reasons, singularly lacking amongst disabled people and the onus should be on local authorities to provide the context, and resources, for disabled people to become key informants and participants in the development process. Here, access officers have a role to play, particularly in informing disabled people about the potential design and cost implications of different types of procurement routes. Similarly, the onus should be on professionals to communicate project plans in non-technical terms, or in ways which facilitate disabled people's ease of understanding of the development process.

- Information, in and of itself, is insufficient if the mechanisms for disabled people to provide professionals with their views are absent or weakly developed. Previous research shows that there are significant physical and socio-institutional barriers to disabled people's participation in the development process (Gleeson, 1999a; Imrie, 1996; Imrie and Kumar, 1998). Thus, too many consultative meetings, between professionals and disabled people, are held in rooms without induction loops for hard-of-hearing people, or other facilities to enable the independent movement of mobility-impaired people (Imrie, 1996; Imrie and Kumar, 1998). Similarly, meetings held in the evening are often 'off-limits' to vision-impaired people because of their difficulty in seeing after dark, while transport to get disabled people to venues is not always available. It is important, then, that the timing of meetings, and their venues, are appropriate in facilitating the participation of disabled people.

- A practical politics of access should also defend the importance of aesthetic values in development and design. A commonly held position in the development industry is to decry access facilities and features, on the grounds that they lack aesthetic appeal or detract from particular design or aesthetic principles. Indeed, the categories of 'aesthetic' and 'access' are often seen as mutually exclusive (see Foster, 1997; Imrie, 2000a). However, disabled people demand a quality of environment that is commensurate with the highest aesthetic standards, and this ought to be an underlying principle of designing for access. In this, we agree with Bentley (1999: 152) who suggests that 'the aesthetic experience is not merely a kind of icing on the cake of urban experience as a whole. Rather, it unavoidably permeates users' agendas throughout.'

- While substantial research is required to itemise the potential and actual costs to the development industry, in providing accessible buildings, most of our respondents agreed that designing access into new buildings at the outset of the process minimises developer costs. In a context whereby the DDA, potentially, requires the costly re-adaptation of existing buildings, designing for access ought to be encouraged as a standard practice at the inception of a project. This, then, places an onus on the development team to become knowledge-able of where to obtain appropriate features and fittings to facilitate access. However, professionals have incomplete knowledge of where to obtain alternative design features to those that are regularly supplied as part of the building process. Professional institutions, such as the British Property Federation, or the RIBA, could play a part in producing lists of appropriate suppliers of accessible design features, and disseminating such information to their respective memberships.

- While the remit of the research was confined to property professionals' attitudes and practices, such attitudes were revealing of the role of local planning authorities in seeking to secure accessible environments. As some respondents suggested, planning officers operate in variable and inconsistent ways in relation to access matters (see also Gleeson, 1999a; Imrie, 1996; Imrie and Kumar, 1998). By law, officers are responsible for ensuring that access is brought to the attention of a development team; that is, that access is a forethought and discussed at the initial, pre-planning, application stages of the process. However, this is not always done. Similarly, local planning authorities are inconsistent in their interpretation of statutory duties with regard to access (see Imrie, 1996). As Imrie's research shows, this has the potential effect of leading to an uneven provision of access facilities and features.

- While we have not been able to quantify the costs to developers of refurbishing buildings to accessible standards (which was not an objective of the research), anecdotal evidence suggests that designing access into older buildings may well be prohibitive and a disincentive to developers. More information and research about costings is required, yet there is sufficient evidence to suggest that some form of public subsidy should be made available to encourage developers to incorporate access into the refurbishment of older buildings. As Chapter 3 indicates, fiscal subsidies are provided to developers in a range of countries, including Singapore. In particular, subsidies ought to be provided where the provision of access leads to a substantial and demonstrable loss of commercial floorspace. The amount of subsidy should also reflect, amongst other things, the degree of technical difficulties in achieving access standards, and the public benefits to be gained from attaining an accessible scheme.

- The development process ought to respond to the DRTF's (1999: 3) caution against a simplistic understanding of meeting the needs of disabled people purely in monetary terms. As they suggest, 'the bene-fits of a tolerant, inclusive and diverse society cannot easily be expressed in pounds and pence'. For the DRTF, disabled people have every right to independence of mobility, movement and access, a right that ought not to be infringed by a cost/profit balance sheet approach to the provision of goods and services. However, it is unrealistic to expect professionals to operate outside of a profit/cost maxim and, given this, the development profession ought to recognise disabled people's valuation as an untapped market resource. This is the crux of retailers' positive responses to the 'disabled pound' which, while potentially reducing disabled people to the category of a commodity, may well be a basis for one element of a practical politics of change.

Conclusions

The emergence of non-disabling environments, or places which facilitate the movement, mobility and access of disabled people, is far from being realised. While a practical politics of disability, as itemised in the last section, can address immediate, tangible concerns about access in the built environment, it needs to be aligned to a broader agenda of change (see, for example, UPIAS, 1976). This agenda, at its root, ought to consist of a programme of fundamental transformations in attitudinal and value systems towards disability (see Barnes *et al.*, 1999; Oliver, 1990, 1996). For Gleeson (2001), the 'architecture of apartheid', as he terms it, can be overthrown by seeking to democratise the values and practices which shape the 'good city'. This, for Gleeson (2001: 256), involves, in part, the political scrutiny and (democratic) control of 'masterplans, markets, professional codes, and other constructed certitudes'. It also involves a rejection of a set of accessibility regulations which, so Gleeson (2001: 257) argues, 'simultaneously *controls* and *protects* the forces that produce exclusionary places and spaces'.

For others, non-disabling environments ought to respond to the diversity of bodily needs by (re)producing 'a fluid urban form that will affirm ambivalence and irony' (Gleeson, 2001: 263; see also Robins, 1995). Thus, for White (1990), architects ought to proceed by rejecting motives of domination and acquisition, and, instead, respect cultural fluidity and the differences of others. Gleeson, in referring to Beck (1998: 119), conjures up the idea of a reflexive architecture or, in Beck's terms, an architecture which is 'open-minded' and without boundaries or borders. Similarly, Bentley (1999) refers to the notion of 'robustness' to describe his normative ideal of a 'good city'. As Bentley (ibid.: 15) suggests:

> if we are to create new places which appeal as widely as possible across this spectrum of unpredictable and ever-changing differences, we have to find ways of making settings which have the potential to accept a wide and unpredictable range of alternative activities which different people with different values might want to pursue.

Mumford (1938: 48) notes that the 'good city' ought to be underpinned by the reorganisation of 'neighbourhoods and corporate organisations' in order to activate the 'political functions of the community'. This appeal, to the (re)activation of a local polity is, in part, expressed through contemporary debates about citizenship and empowerment. As Bookman and Morgen (1988: 4) note, empowerment begins when (disabled) people 'change their ideas about the causes of their powerlessness, when they recognise the systemic forces which oppress them, and when they act to change the conditions of their lives'. However, for disabled people, the disabling values and practices of society have tended to undermine their capacity to govern themselves, by blocking or defusing consciousness or actions which might precipitate self-help or empowerment (see Cruikshank, 1999; Imrie, 1996). This, then, represents the challenge, in which property and spatial development are exposed to the values and lives of disabled people in ways which will enable the diminution of disablist development and design processes.

Further reading

Ian Bentley's book, *Urban Transformations* (1999), is a beautifully written, subtle and engaging text which will provide the reader with insights into the interrelationships between property professionals and users. For debates on civil rights, difference and justice, readers should refer to the excellent book by Young, I. (1990) *Justice and the Politics of Difference*. In relation to disabled people, such debates are well developed by Handley, P.'s (2000) article 'Trouble in paradise – a disabled person's right to the satisfaction of a self-defined need: some conceptual and practical problems', and especially in Mairian Corker's (1998) book, *Deaf and Disabled or Deafness Disabled*. Indeed, Corker's book is passionate and well argued and ought to be a compulsory read. Likewise, Brendan Gleeson is foremost in geography in providing insights into the social spaces of disability, and his excellent writings will repay a careful reading. Readers should especially refer to his book, *Geographies of Disability*. Finally, Cruikshank, B.'s (1999) book, *The Will to Empower*, is a penetrative analysis of the interrelationships between citizenship, rights and well being.

Endnotes

Chapter 1

1 A good example of this has been set out by the DIY store, B & Q. In their Norwich store, a range of access features have been pioneered, including wider aisles, lower checkouts, improved use of colour, use of icons as well as words, sign language and subtext as videos in the store, and induction loops for hearing-impaired customers. Every member of staff was given Disability Awareness Training. Since 1999, B & Q have opened 16 new stores, all of which have been built to the Norwich store standard.

2 Part of the research underpinning this book was a postal survey of chartered surveyors. Full details of the research objectives and methods are contained in Appendix 1.

3 The institutions primarily responsible for the development of principles of universal design are the Center for Universal Design based in the School of Design at North Carolina State University of Raleigh, and the Adaptive Environments Center, a non-profit organisation based in Boston and founded in 1978 (see Appendix 2).

4 As Turner (1987) suggested, despite the poverty of people living in squatter settlements, their flexibility, adaptability and self-determination were all important ingredients in enabling them to express themselves about their living environments. For Turner, such environments were far superior to American standardised housing.

Chapter 2

1 Between 1936 and 1976, the Swedish state carried out a policy of the forcible sterilisation of 63,000 women considered to be socially unfit. Such women included those released from prison, people with learning difficulties, the poor, epileptics, alcoholics and women of 'mixed social quality'. The Swedish sterilisation programme of the 1930s was similar to that occurring in Nazi Germany and appeared to gain its impetus from some of the ideas underpinning Nazi ideas about race (see Drake, 1999). Many other countries also performed sterilisation programmes based on eugenics ideas linked to the Nazis, including

Austria, France, Finland, Norway and Switzerland (see, for example, the accounts by Drake, 1999).

2 The medicalisation of disability is evident even in those countries thought to be bastions of best practice towards disabled people. For instance, in Sweden, welfare policies are premised on medical cure and rehabilitative programmes or what Curtin and Higgins (1998: 23) refer to as 'growth and an effective use of human and natural resources'. If medical rehabilitation is ineffective or inappropriate, additional measures include various types of disability pensions, annuities from employment injury insurance and special employment programmes. As a Swedish Liberal MP, interviewed by the authors, noted: 'the municipality or government gave them what they thought was good for them. I think there was no will. It was a paternalistic way . . . in the past it was more "This is good for you and you should be grateful".' Social attitudes and practices are compounded by policy responses and measures which often assume that disabled people are 'to blame' for their situation or that, at the very least, they are implicated in their dependent status (see Curtin and Higgins, 1998).

3 The Disability Rights Task Force was set up by the Labour Government in 1997. Their remit was to consider 'the full range of issues that affect disabled people's lives and to advise the government on what further action it should take to promote comprehensive and enforceable civil rights for disabled people' (DRTF: 2). Their biggest impact to date has been the recommendation, and subsequent appointment, of the Disability Rights Commission (DRC), a body set up to ensure compliance with disability rights legislation.

4 For instance, a survey conducted by Ohara (1991), of 460 Japanese architects (with a response rate of 43 per cent, or 198 architects), shows that half felt that barrier-free design would increase costs while reducing the developable area.

5 The Disability Discrimination Act (DDA, 1996) is a piece of UK civil rights legislation which seeks to provide disabled people with powers to challenge discriminatory practices by employers and providers of goods and services. Chapter 3 provides a fuller account and appraisal of the DDA.

6 DETR's (1998) impact assessment of the extension of the building regulations to dwellings notes that there is a potential saving of £14,000 per year for every elderly person who is able to live in their own home as a result of the implementation of the regulations. DETR also suggest that other benefits will accrue. Thus, the proposals for wider doors and circulation spaces will make it more convenient to move furniture, while accessible switches and sockets will benefit those who find bending difficult.

Chapter 3

1 ASEAN is an organisation of 10 South East Asian countries seeking to pursue regional cooperation. It was formed in 1967 and comprises Brunei, Cambodia, Indonesia, Laos, Malaysia, Myanmar, Philippines, Singapore, Thailand and Vietnam (see: www.asean.or.id/ for further details).

2 The United Nations (1996: 2) Standard Rules state that:

> governments, in collaboration with organisations of people with disabilities and the private sector, should work towards the equalisation of opportunities so that people with disabilities can contribute to and benefit from full participation in society. Policies concerning people with disabilities should focus on their abilities rather than their disabilities and should ensure their dignity as citizens.

3 The Council on Tall Buildings and Urban Habitat (1992: 10) have described the legal situation rather differently in suggesting that 'many countries have adopted standards which are quite idiosyncratic and without much regard for international equivalence'.

4 Such reformism has, however, done little to transform the material lives of disabled people who remain disadvantaged in comparison to non-disabled individuals. Thus, in 1978, 6 per cent of the severely disabled working population in Sweden was unemployed compared to 3 per cent of non-disabled people. By the late 1990s, little had changed and, if anything, the socio-economic and political status of disabled people had deteriorated (Petersson *et al.*, 1998). As Petersson *et al.* (ibid.: 43) have argued, public sector cuts 'brought vital constitutional problems to the fore in relation to the social rights of citizens'. In particular, they point to the ever lengthening queues for residential care for the elderly and disabled, noting that, 'less than half of the municipalities had adopted the recommendations of the Swedish Association of Local Authorities [*Kommunforbudet*] concerning the rights of the elderly and the handicapped to move to special housing in other municipalities' (p. 42).

5 Developers appoint 'quality controllers' (who are usually architects) to provide guidance on how to conform with the legal directives concerning access. The new system, for one respondent, is generating new layers of responsibilities between property professionals. As he commented, 'self control [*egenkontroll*] creates a different responsibility in the property developer and it requires good advice and support during the planning of the scheme'. A range of interviewees were, however, sceptical about the control system, with an architect noting that, 'disabled access in the buildings is not reviewed when building permits are given. Many actors in the process do not have knowledge.' Others concurred, with one developer noting that 'a lot depends on how the architect reviewing the building permit is acting'.

6 As Doyle (1995: 221) notes, the philosophy of reasonable accommodation is enshrined in most anti-discrimination legislation. The definition of 'reasonable' usually revolves around considerations of cost and/or the practicalities of making physical adjustments to a premise.

7 However, there is recognition, in some statutes, of the social construction of disability. In New South Wales, Australia, 'statute requires regard to be had to community attitudes relating to a physical impairment and to the physical environment' (Doyle, 1995: 175).

8 This provision in the building code is, as McAuley (1996) observes, limited because the continuous path of travel does not have to be to

the main entrance of a building. Disabled people, then, can still be confronted with a 'back-door' approach to design.

9 The government provides the loans at special interest rates for the improvement of facilities, including corridors, stairs and elevators. For joint ventures between the government and the private sector, no interest is charged.

10 The development plan is a document produced by local authorities and comprises a series of statements about the future spatial development of given areas of land (see Rydin, 1993, for further details). If the document is approved by central government, through the Department of the Environment, Transport and the Regions, it becomes a legal document and its provisions may be binding on developers. The development plan is a material consideration when local planning authorities make decisions about planning applications submitted by developers.

11 Local authority planners have the power to set specific conditions of development on approvals of planning permission. These tend to comprise worded statements such as, for example, 'the permission is conditional on satisfying Part M of the Building Regulations'.

12 Since the Lottery-funded capital programme was launched in 1995, 2,108 projects have received more than £1,000 million from the Arts Council for England.

13 In commenting on broader social attitudes towards disabled people, a Swedish government official, charged with implementing the UN's Standard Rules in Sweden, noted that 'people with disabilities are not employed to the extent they could be, the shops are not accessible, and they [the public authorities] don't do anything about it. So in that way you could say the attitudes are not that good.' In particular, some commentators in Sweden regard the absence of anti-discrimination legislation, or the means for disabled people to claim legal redress, as a fundamental flaw. As a spokesperson for the Swedish Liberal Party stated, in interview, 'the problem is that in many ways disability policy is social policy and welfare policy and not a question of democracy and participation. Accessibility is much more about democracy and participation in society and we haven't focussed on that like in the USA . . . people here don't see inaccessibility as discrimination.'

14 Some estate agents have already responded. For instance, the DRTF (1999: 66) provide the example of Cardiff Accessible Housing Register, 'a joint initiative between the Voluntary Action Cardiff Housing Access Project and a number of estate agents in Cardiff'. As the Task Force note, estate agents, using an access guide, inspect each other's property to identify the barrier-free elements. Properties are categorised into one of four types to indicate levels of accessibility: negotiable, visitable, liveable and universal. This information is included as an integral part of the property details made available to the general public.

Chapter 4

1 The National Lottery was set up by the British government in 1994 as a means to raise funding for projects of benefit to the public. These

range from the support of new sports stadia developments to the funding of the refurbishment of art galleries and theatres.

2   Attitudes towards costs are more pragmatic in countries like Sweden. As a Swedish developer said, 'access is a standard requirement and we design it in from the very start, always and every time we do a scheme . . . so, it's not an additional cost'. Indeed, Swedish developers, of whatever complexion, rarely see the provision of access as an additional cost item, but rather as a standard requirement that has to be fulfilled in order to satisfy the building regulations. As a respondent said, 'I've heard tenants say, "is it really necessary for us to take an expensive area of our office to make a disabled person's toilet?". But you have to do it, it's a regulation.'

3   The Arts Council for England and English Heritage have vested interests in influencing the development of specific buildings, and are able to provide development funds to appropriate applicants.

4   Access groups have proliferated since the early 1980s with the Access Committee for England (ACE, 1994) estimating that 401 were operating in England in 1993. Most are small scale in terms of staffing, resources and political leverage, yet apart from the ACE (1994) report, there is little written documentation about them (although, see Imrie, 1999b). Access groups tend to be dominated by wheelchair users and elderly people. This reflects the voluntary nature of the groups whereby elderly people have more disposable time to devote to voluntary work. Many members of access groups feel that the groups do not appeal to younger disabled people because of a staid and outdated image (ACE, 1994). Very few hard-of-hearing or deaf people are involved in access groups, likewise ethnic minorities. Access groups, then, seem to be partial in terms of membership and representation (ACE, 1994)

5   The Silver Jubilee Committee (1979) recommended that local authorities appoint an officer with responsibilities for addressing the access needs of disabled people. By the mid-1990s, 259 local authorities had appointed a person with responsibilities for access issues (Imrie, 1996). However, most appointees are employed as full-time planning or building control officers, with the responsibility to devote a small proportion of their time to access duties (see Imrie, 1996, Chapter 5, for a full account of the roles and responsibilities of access officers).

Chapter 5

1   For instance, Milner (1995: 31) quotes an opinion poll of 1,382 people, conducted by the Henley Centre, which concludes that 'in two out of three building categories the public thought architects were unaware of their tastes and needs'.

2   The final response rate was adjudged to be 28 per cent after adjusting the sample from 770 to 739 respondents. The questionnaire was returned from thirty-one practices for a mixture of reasons, including the retirement of the architects, architects not known at the address the questionnaire was sent to, and, in one case, the recent death of an architect.

3　It is, however, impossible to infer from the data that no definition is used by those practices that did not define disability. It may be that a formal definition is used but not known about by the particular respondent. Moreover, the absence of a formal definition does not necessarily indicate a lack of knowledge, or sensitivity, on the part of the architectural practice towards disabled people and their needs. The data, therefore, have to be treated as indicative and interpreted with caution.

4　Note that some respondents gave more than one answer and identified a range of training mediums that they had used. This accounts for a response figure greater than the sixty-two respondents who said that they had received training on access matters. Moreover, of the sixty-two respondents, fifty-nine (or 95 per cent) said that the training had covered technical requirements for ensuring access. Fifty-two (84 per cent) said that they looked at access legislation and forty-two (68 per cent) said that training covered raising awareness. Costing and access auditing were only covered in eighteen (29 per cent) and seventeen (27 per cent) of cases respectively.

5　Similarly, a minority of Swedish (thirty-eight, or 36 per cent) respondents feel that there is no need for training relating to access. Many regard the regulations and general information as being sufficient. As a Swedish respondent commented, there are 'laws, directions of applications and handbooks for further education'. Another echoed these sentiments, suggesting that, 'the documents of law are pretty clear. In most cases the industry is working well in Sweden.'

6　From the survey of Swedish architectural practices, half regarded their building regulations as sufficient in providing for the needs of disabled people. One respondent commented that 'I have never come across any complications between the building regulations and the wishes of disabled organisations'. Some respondents offered more cautious approval, suggesting that 'regulations cannot cover everything' and that 'legislation is never better than its application'. Twenty-two (21 per cent) respondents felt that the regulations are insufficient. For one architectural practice, the regulations are 'too general – one needs supplementary literature' and that 'it invites far too many arbitrary interpretations'.

7　One's optimism about architects' positive attitudes towards legal controls has to be tempered by the fact that the majority of our respondents (138, or 65 per cent), while aware of the DDA, had few opinions on how it is affecting their work. Of those that did (seventy, or 34 per cent), the majority (fifty-three, or 76 per cent) said that the DDA is not affecting their work at all and was unlikely to do so.

Chapter 6

1　As Cadman and Topping (1997) suggest, there are three main categories of procurement (with many variations in each type). Foremost is the standard form of contract or the Joint Contracts Tribunal (JCT). Here, the main contractor carries out the construction following the design guidance of the developer's professional team. Design and build, as the chapter indicates, places most of the responsibilities for design with the contractor, while a third route, management contracting, is similar to JCT although the building work is divided into specialised trade contract packages. The management contractor 'co-ordinates and supervises the various subcontractors on behalf of the developer' (Cadman and Topping, 1997: 201).

2   Akintoye's (1994: 159) survey of seventy-seven construction firms shows that 54 per cent of his respondents 'claimed that the use of design and build for project procurement can account for up to 20 per cent reduction in overall project time compared to traditional JCT80 contracts'. Similarly, Akintoye and Fitzgerald's (1995: 157) survey of construction contractors indicates that 21 per cent of the workload of private contractors in 1994 was procured by a design and build route.

3   The term 'novated' is used by building professionals to describe the transfer of appointment contracts. In design and build schemes, for example, the developer may appoint an architect to undertake design work upon which tenders will be sought from building contractors. On agreement of contracts, the architect may be transferred (novated) to the building contractor who then assumes (legal) responsibility for the architect's employment on the scheme.

4   The assent of the DDA has stimulated a growing demand for access consultants to provide advice to providers of goods and services about the impacts and implications of the legislation on business behaviour and responsibilities. However, as Noble (1999) notes, the quality of consultants is variable and the sector is unregulated. For Noble (ibid.: 43), consultants tend to fall into one of three types: 'the enthusiastic amateur, the cowboy, and the trained professional'. In seeking to control for quality, the Centre for Accessible Environments has produced a National Register of Access Consultants (Centre for Accessible Environments, 1999) which is formally approved by DETR and DfEE. The objective of the register is to help clients identify appropriate consultants to use, to inform and educate clients about access consultancy and to provide a learning forum for those interested in access matters. To this end, access consultants are able to apply to be considered for inclusion on the register. The first part of the process involves a simple screening to filter out those who do not have the basic requirements. The second stage is the preparation of reports by applicants and a professional interview. By April 2000, over ninety applications for the Register had been received (Noble, 2000).

Chapter 7

1   Dial-a-ride is a 'special needs' public bus system that operates in many UK towns and cities. It is usually funded by the local authority and provides a door-to-door service for disabled people at pre-booked times. However, the service is seen, by many disabled people, as continuing segregated services which are inferior to mainstream provisions. As Barnes (1991) notes, dial-a-ride services are irregular, underfunded, inconvenient and provide little independence for its users.

2   However, this is not to decry expert knowledge, or the expertise vested

in property professionals. Rather, it is to acknowledge the limitations of particular ways of knowing and, as White (1990: 257) notes, to throw 'into question our sense of ourselves, our language, of others'. Thus, in seeking to respond to the needs of disabled people, it is important for professionals to recognise the fluidity of disabled people's views and values rather than, as Bentley (1999: 145) notes, to assimilate 'the positions of all users, in regard to all given settings, into some homogenised, sanitised commonality of experience'.

APPENDICES

1   Research design and methods

Most of the research in the book was generated from a project funded by the Economic and Social Research Council and carried out in the period from November 1997 to July 1999. The original remit of the research was:

a   to compare and contrast the role of the property development industry in two different countries, Sweden and the UK, in facilitating and/or constraining disabled people's access in the built environment;

b   to assess the various roles of key professionals in the development process, such as architects, project managers, surveyors, clients and end user groups, in influencing the provision of access for disabled people;

c   to describe and evaluate the significance of disabled people's participation in the development process and their impact in influencing the attitudes and practices of property developers (and related professionals); and

d   to utilise and develop practitioner networks to help guide and formulate the research and to use them as mechanisms of dissemination.

The research was divided into three parts: postal surveys of key property professionals; depth interviews with property developers; case studies to provide illustrations of professionals' responses to the building and access needs of disabled people. In total, the research team conducted 202 interviews, 90 in Sweden and 112 in the UK, and administered 1,463 postal questionnaires.

The first part of the research comprised three postal surveys seeking to gain broad-based information about the attitudes and practices of key property professionals in responding to the building needs of disabled people. Architects and chartered surveyors were identified as key professionals in the development process, so too property development companies. The first survey, of a 10 per cent (or 770) sample of UK architectural practices, took place between December 1997 and March 1998. As Chapter 5 intimates, the sample was derived from a Royal Institute of British Architects (RIBA) database of RIBA registered architectural practices with questionnaires sent to named individuals. The sample was random although proportionally weighted to reflect the geographical distribution of architectural practices. The second survey, of 50 per cent (or 263) of Swedish architectural practices registered with the Svenska Arkitekters Riksforbund (SAR), was undertaken in the period from February to May 1998.

The sample was derived from the SAR directory on the same basis as the UK survey. A response rate of 105 (or 40 per cent) practices was attained.

In addition, a survey of a 5 per cent (or 430) sample of chartered surveying practices in the UK was administered from February to April 1998 (Hall and Imrie, 1998). Names of surveying practices in the building surveying, general practice, planning and development, and quantity surveying divisions were obtained from the 1997 Royal Institution of Chartered Surveyors (RICS) directories and a proportional sample was taken for each county to ensure UK-wide coverage. A response rate of 120 (or 28 per cent) practices was attained. After taking advice from Swedish property experts, a postal survey of Swedish surveyors was not undertaken owing to the lack of a directly comparable role and organisational body within the Swedish development system. To encourage a high response rate, all postal surveys followed the same procedure: the initial letter and questionnaire were sent out; a follow-up reminder letter and questionnaire were sent out four weeks later to non-respondents; a telephone reminder to non-respondents occurred two weeks after the initial follow-up.

On the advice of members of a user network, set up to provide advice and guide the research, it was decided not to administer a postal questionnaire to property development companies (as originally envisaged) but to conduct depth interviews to generate detailed opinions and information. This decision was also based on:

a   the probability of a low response rate to a postal survey;
b   the lack of research time to devote to what would have been the fourth large-scale postal survey of the research programme; and
c   the need for the research team to prioritise time, effort and resources towards the case research.

In total, thirty-nine depth interviews with development companies were conducted over the period from May 1998 to March 1999, twenty-four in the UK and fifteen in Sweden. The focal part of the research comprised case studies of commercial development projects. Ten UK and six Swedish case studies were undertaken and, as Chapter 4 notes, a diversity of key actors and agents were interviewed.

To help guide and steer the research, a user network was established at the outset with a mixture of architects, chartered surveyors, access officers, developers and private (disabled) citizens. The network variously fed into the research by commenting on surveys, the original research proposal, initial research findings, etc. In addition, a wider network of contacts (organised around the Access Officers Association) was used to collect comments on various parts of the research as well as providing a means for disseminating research findings. For instance, the postal surveys were drafted by the research team and sent out for comment to both networks. The draft postal survey of chartered surveyors was sent to members of the RICS Working Party on Disability. The draft postal survey of architects was sent to a variety of individuals within the user network, including members of the Architectural Association. Final surveys were drawn up after this period of consultation and user feedback. The choice of case study areas was also influenced by discussions held with participants in the user networks.

The project generated more material about the UK context than the Swedish for a number of reasons. Foremost, most of the interviews in Sweden were conducted in the English language and there were linguistic limitations placed on the pursuit of intricate and depth debates. Many respondents also tended to provide terse and short responses and felt that access provision for disabled people was not an issue because, as one Swedish developer said, 'they [disabled people] are fully provided for'. Our research indicates that this is far from the case, yet it proved to be difficult to get participants 'to open up' or reveal some of the depth and complexity underpinning professionals' responses to the needs of disabled people. In seeking to convey an accurate understanding of professionals' attitudes and responses to the needs of disabled people, we feel more confident in using the UK material as the basis for the book, supplemented, where appropriate, with reference to specific examples from Sweden.

A follow-up project, funded by The Leverhulme Trust, generated additional data. The objective of this research was to document the contrasting ways in which western (or modern) architectural theories, traditions and practices conceive of the human body and of its multiple differences and with what implications for the design and use of buildings and the wider built environment. Two specific aims were itemised:

a to relate investigations about the body in architecture to the relative estrangement, marginalisation and exclusion of disabled people in architectural theories and practices; and,
b to consider the practical possibilities for changing architectural ideas and practices concerning building design, disability and disabled bodies.

In developing the research, a project advisory group, comprising architects, was formed at the beginning of the project and an initial, one-day workshop was held in London on 1 July 1999. The workshop was a mechanism to enable the development of the research objectives and to gain advice and direction about research design and methods. It also provided the project with a point of entry into the architectural profession and with key contacts for future interview-based research.

A two-fold research design was developed and implemented in the period from August 1999 to April 2000. First, a sample of architectural schools were chosen as a basis for investigating how and where issues relating to the body are addressed in architects' educational training. On the advice of the advisory group, an initial sample of twelve architectural schools were contacted for course and curricula details. This documentation was used as a basis for choosing five schools (Bartlett, Canterbury School of Art, Strathclyde, Oxford Brookes and Sheffield) for detailed scrutiny, through a mixture of methods including interviews with course directors, tutors and the inspection of a range of course materials. Second, using a Royal Institute of British Architects (RIBA) database, a sample of architectural practices, largely based in London, were chosen as a basis for detailed investigation. In total, forty-one interviews were conducted with architectural firms using a semi-structured interview schedule. Interviews varied in length between one and three hours. Supporting documentation, such as drawings and architectural plans, were acquired and are an important item of evidence in understanding architects' conceptions of the human body.

2   Useful contacts

i Useful information about UK policies and programmes in relation to disabled people can be found at: www.disability.gov.uk

ii To obtain up-to-date information about access issues in the UK, readers should contact the following organisation:

The Centre for Accessible Environments
Nutmeg House
60 Gainsford Street
London SE1 2NY

They are responsible for producing the UK National Register of Access Consultants.

Tel: +44 (0) 20 7357 8182
e-mail: cae@globalnet.co.uk
Web site: www.cae.org.uk

iii One of the most innovative access groups in the UK is in the City of London. Their contact details are:

City of London Access Group
Milton Court
Moor Lane
London EC2Y 9BL

Tel: + 44 (0)20 7332 1995/1933
Text tel: 020 7332 3929
e–mail: julie.fleck@corpoflondon.gov.uk

iv Access consultancy is an important part of seeking to create accessible environments. One of the foremost organisations is the Joint Mobility Unit:

Joint Mobility Unit
Royal National Institute for the Blind
225 Great Portland Street
London W1N 6AA

Tel: +44 (0) 20 7387 2233
Web site: www.rnib.org.uk/jmu/welcome.htm

v   The DDA in the UK is being enforced by the Disability Rights Commission. Their contact details are:

Disability Rights Commission
222 Grays Inn Road
London
WC1X 8HL

Web site: www.drc-gb.org

To develop some understanding of international differences in access attitudes, policies and practices, the following contacts are useful:

vi An important campaigning group for disabled people is:

Disabled Peoples' International
11 Belgrave Road
London
SW1V 1RB

Tel: +44 (0) 20 7834 0477
Fax: +44 (0) 20 7821 9539
Webs site: www.dpi.org

vii Adaptive Environments Center, Inc. is a non-profit organisation founded in 1978. It seeks to promote universal design through education, technical assistance, training and consulting.

Adaptive Environments Center, Inc.
374 Congress Street
Suite 301
Boston
MA 02210,
United States

Tel: + 617 482 8099
e-mail: adaptive@adaptenv.org
Web site: www.adaptenv.org

viii The Center for Universal Design

NC State University
School of Design
Box 8613
Raleigh
NC 27695–8613
USA

Tel: + 919 515 3082
e-mail: cud@ncsu.edu
Web site: www.ncsu.edu

ix Building Code of Australia 1990

Australian Building Codes Board
GPO Box 9839
Canberra ACT 2601
Australia

Tel: 6 276 1000

x   Disability Discrimination Act 1992

Australian Government Publishing Service
GPO Box 84
Canberra City ACT 2601
Australia

Tel: + 6 295 4411

xi World Health Organisation

Assessment, Classification and Epidemiology
CH-1211
Geneva 27
Switzerland

Web site: www.who.int/icidh/

References

Aalto, A., 1940, 'The humanizing of architecture', *The Technology Review*, November, 14–16.

Abberley, P., 1987, 'The concept of oppression and the development of a social theory of disability', *Disability, Handicap, and Society*, 2, 1, 5–19.

Abberley, P., 1993, 'Disabled people and "normality" ', in Swain, J., Finkelstein, V., French, S. and Oliver, M. (eds) *Disabling Barriers – Enabling Environments*, Open University, Milton Keynes, 107–15.

Access Committee for England, 1994, *National Research Project on Local Access Groups, Summary*, ACE, London.

Access Committee for England, 1995, *Response from ACE concerning the DOE's proposals for Part M, New Dwellings* (January 1995), ACE, London.

Adair, A., Berry, J., Deddis, B. and Hirst, S., 1999, 'Evaluation of investor behaviour in urban regeneration', *Urban Studies*, 36, 12, 2031–45.

Adler, D. (ed.) 1999, *Metric Handbook: Planning and Design Data*, Second edition, Architectural Press, Oxford.

Akintoye, A., 1994, 'Design and build: a survey of construction contractors' views', *Construction Management and Economics*, 12, 2, 155–63.

Akintoye, A. and Fitzgerald, E., 1995, 'Design and build: a survey of architects' views', *Engineering Construction and Architectural Management*, 2, 1, 27–44.

Albrecht, G., 1992, *The Disability Business: Rehabilitation in America*, Sage, London.

Americans with Disabilities Act (ADA), 1991, 'Rules and Regulations', *Federal Register*, 56, 144, 26 July.

Appleton, I., 1996, *Access to Arts Buildings: Provision for People with Disabilities; Management Policy and Design Standards*, The Scottish Arts Council, Edinburgh.

Arts Council for England, 1998, *National Lottery Funding Capital Programme: Access Guidelines and Checklist*, Arts Council for England, London.

Arts Council for England, 2000, *Annual Report*, Access Committee for England, London.

Atkinson, D. (ed.) 1993, *Past Times: Older People with Learning Difficulties Look Back on Their Lives*, Open University Press, Buckingham.

Ball, M., 1981, 'The development of capitalism in housing provision', *International Journal of Urban and Regional Research*, 5, 145–77.

Ball, M., 1985, 'The urban rent question', *Environment and Planning A*, 17, 503–25.

Ball, M., 1998, 'Institutions in British property research: a review', *Urban Studies*, 35, 9, 1501–17.

Ball, M. and Harloe, M., 1992, 'Rhetorical barriers to understanding housing provision: what the "provision thesis" is and is not', *Housing Studies*, 7, 1, 3–15.

Ball, M., Harloe, M. and Martens, M., 1988, *Housing and Social Change in Britain and the USA*, Routledge, London.

Barnes, C., 1991, *Disabled People in Britain and Discrimination*, Hurst and Company, London.

Barnes, C., Mercer, G. and Shakespeare, T. 1999, *Exploring Disability: a Sociological Introduction*, Polity, Oxford.

Beck, U., 1998, *Democracy Without Enemies*, Polity, Cambridge.

Beiner, R., 1992, 'The moral vocabulary of liberalism', in Chapman, J. and Galston, W. (eds) *Nomos XXXIV: Virtue*, New York Press, New York, 145–84.

Bentley, I., 1999, *Urban Transformations: Power, People and Urban Design*, Routledge, London.

Birkenbach, J., 1993, *Physical Disability and Social Policy*, University of Toronto Press, Toronto.

Blomley, N., 1994, 'Mobility, empowerment and the rights revolution', *Political Geography*, 13, 5, 407–22.

Bloomer, K. and Moore, C., 1977, *Body, Memory, and Architecture*, Yale University Press, Yale.

Bookman, A. and Morgen, S. (eds) 1988, *Women and the Politics of Empowerment*, Temple University Press, Philadelphia.

Boverket, 1987, *Swedish Planning and Building Act*, Boverket, Karlskrona.

Boylan, E., 1991, *Women and Disability*, Zed Books, London.

Bruner, J., 1986, *Actual Minds, Possible Worlds*, Harvard University Press, Cambridge, MA.

Bury, M., 1996, 'Defining and researching disability: challenges and responses', in Barnes, C. and Mercer, G. (eds) *Exploring the Divide: Illness and Disability*, Disability Press, Leeds, 17–38.

Bury, M., 1997, *Health and Illness in a Changing Society*, Routledge, London.

Butler, R. and Bowlby, S., 1997, 'Bodies and space: an exploration of disabled people's experiences of public space', *Environment and Planning D: Society and Space*, 15, 411–33.

Butler, R. and Parr, H. (eds) 1999, *Mind and Body Spaces: Geographies of Disability, Illness and Impairment*, Routledge, London.

Cadman, D. and Topping, R., 1997, *Property Development*, Third edition, E & FN Spon, London.

Canadian Human Rights Commission, 1983, *Human Rights Act*, CHRC, Ottawa.

Center for Universal Design, 1995, *Principles of Universal Design*, Center for Universal Design, North Carolina State University.

Center for Universal Design, 2000, Web site: www.design.ncsu.edu/cud /index.html

Colomina, B., 1994, *Privacy and Publicity: Modern Architecture as Mass Media*, MIT Press, Cambridge, Massachussetts.

Connell, B. and Sandford, J., 1999, 'Research implications of universal design', in Steinfeld, E. and Danford, G. (eds) *Enabling Environments*, Kluwer Academic, London, 35–57.

Cook, A., 1996, 'Shell shock', *Building*, 2 August, 37–40.

CORAD (Committee on Restrictions Against Disabled People), 1982, *Report*, HMSO, London.

Corker, M., 1998, *Deaf and Disabled or Deafness Disabled*, Open University Press, Buckingham.

Council on Tall Buildings and Urban Habitat, 1992, *Building Design for Handicapped and Aged Persons*, McGraw-Hill, New York.

Cousins, C., 1998, 'Social exclusion in Europe: paradigms of social disadvantage in Germany, Spain, Sweden and the United Kingdom', *Policy and Politics*, 26, 2, 127–46.

Crow, L., 1995, 'Including all of our lives: renewing the social model of disability', in Barnes, C. and Mercer, G. (eds) *Exploring the Divide: Illness and Disability*, Disability Press, Leeds, 55–74.

Cruikshank, B., 1999, *The Will To Empower: Democratic Citizens and Other Subjects*, Cornell University Press, Ithaca.

Curry, D., 1993, *Letter to David Rose*, Director, Public Affairs, RTPI, 9 June.

Curtin, J. and Higgins, W., 1998, 'Feminism and Unionism in Sweden', *Politics and Society*, 26, 1, 69–83.

Curtis, W., 1994, *Modern Architecture Since 1900*, Phaidon Press, London.

D'Arcy E. and Keogh, G., 1997, 'Towards a property market paradigm of urban change', *Environment and Planning A*, 29, 4, 685–706.

Darke, J., 1984a, 'Architects and user requirements in public sector housing: 1. Architects' assumptions about the users', *Environment and Planning B: Planning and Design*, 11, 389–404.

Darke, J., 1984b, 'Architects and user requirements in public sector housing: 2. The sources for architects' assumptions', *Environment and Planning B: Planning and Design*, 11, 405–16.

Davies, C. and Lifchez, R., 1987, 'An open letter to architects', in Lifchez, R. (ed.) *Rethinking Architecture*, University of California Press, Berkerley, California, 35–50.

Dempsey, I. and Foreman, P., 1997, 'Towards a clarification of empowerment as an outcome of disability service provision', *International Journal of Disability, Development and Education*, 44, 4, 287–303.

Department for Education and Employment, 1999, *Labour Force Survey, Autumn, 1999 – Great Britain*, DfEE, London.

Department for Education and Employment, 2000, *Survey of Employers' Responses to the DDA*, DfEE, London.

Department of the Environment, 1985, 'Access for the Disabled', *Development Control Policy Note 16*, DoE, London.

Department of the Environment, 1992, *Planning Policy Guidance (PPG1): General Policy and Principles*, HMSO, London.

Department of the Environment, 1995a, 'Draft proposals to extend Part M of the Building Regulations to dwellings', *unpublished consultative paper*, DoE, London, copy available from Rob Imrie (r.imrie@rhul.ac.uk).

Department of the Environment, 1995b, *Circular 11/95*, Department of the Environment, London.

Department of the Environment, Transport and the Regions, 1998, *Regulatory Impact Assessment (Final) of the Proposed Extension of Part M (Building Regulations) to Dwellings*, HMSO, London.

Department of the Environment, Transport and the Regions, 1999a, *Planning Policy Guidance 12,* HMSO, London.

Department of Environment, Transport and the Regions, 1999b, *Building Regulations 1991 Approved Document M: Access and Facilities for Disabled People*, HMSO, London.

Dickens, P., 1980, 'Social science and design theory', *Environment and Planning B: Planning and Design*, 6, 105–17.

Disability Discrimination Act, 1996, *Code of Practice: Rights of Access to Goods, Facilities, Services and Premises*, Department of Social Security, London.

Disability Rights Task Force, 1999, *From Exclusion to Inclusion, Final Report of the Disability Rights Task Force*, Department for Education and Employment, London.

Doyle, B., 1995, *Disability, Discrimination and Equal Opportunities: a Comparative Study of the Employment Rights of Disabled Persons*, Mansell, London.

Drake, R., 1999, *Understanding Disability Policies*, Macmillan, London.

Dun and Bradstreet, 1997, *Key British Enterprises*, Web-based dataset, www.kbe.uk.dnb.com

Edwards, M., 1990, 'What is needed from public policy?', in Healey, P. and Nabarro, R. (eds) *Land and Property in a Changing Context*, Gower, Aldershot, 175–83.

Ellis, K., 2000, 'Welfare and bodily order: theorising transitions in corporeal discourse', in Ellis, K. and Dean, H. (eds) *Social Policy and the Body*, Macmillan, London, 1–22.

English Sports Council, 1998, *Access for Disabled People: Guidance Notes*, English Sports Council, London.

European Commission, 1996, *How is the European Union Meeting Social and Regional Needs?*, EU, Brussels.

Finkelstein, V. and Stuart, O., 1996, 'Developing new services', in Hales, G. (ed.) *Beyond Disability: Towards an Enabling Society*, Sage, London, 170–87.

Fischler, R., 1995, 'Strategy and history in professional practice: planning as world making', in Liggett, H. and Perry, D. (eds) *Spatial Practices*, Sage, London, 13–58.

Fleck, J., 1996, 'City shows way forward on access for disabled people', *Access*, 1183, 23 August, 8.

Foster, L., 1997, *Access to the Historic Environment: Meeting the Needs of Disabled People*, Donhead, Shaftesbury.

Franks, J., 1998, *Building Procurement Systems: a Client's Guide*, Third edition, Longman, Harlow.

Fraser, N., 1995, 'From redistribution to recognition? Dilemmas of justice in a post-socialist age', *New Left Review*, 212, 68–73.

French, S., 1993, 'Disability, impairment, or something in-between?', in Swain, J., Finkelstein, V., French, S. and Oliver, M. (eds) *Disabling Barriers – Enabling Environments*, Sage, London, 17–25.

Fry, E., 1986, *An Equal Chance for Disabled People: a Study of Discrimination in Employment*, The Spastics Society, London.

Gathorne-Hardy, F., 1999a, 'Expert bodies', *Scroope: Cambridge Achitecture Journal*, 11, 1–7.

Gathorne-Hardy, F., 1999b, 'The miniature and the monstrous', *Landscape Design*, 280, 21–3.

Ghirardo, D. (ed.) 1991, *Out of Site: A Social Criticism of Architecture*, Bay Press, Seattle.

Gleeson, B., 1997, 'The regulation of environmental accessibility in New Zealand', *International Planning Studies*, 2, 3, 367–90.

Gleeson, B., 1999a, *Geographies of Disability*, Routledge, London.

Gleeson, B., 1999b, 'Can technology overcome the disabling city?', in Butler, R. and Parr, H. (eds) *Mind and Body Spaces: Geographies of Illness, Impairment and Disability*, Routledge, London, 98–118.

Gleeson, B., 2001, 'Disability and the open city', *Urban Studies*, 38, 2, 251–66.

Goldsmith, S., 1997, *Designing for the Disabled: the New Paradigm*, Architectural Press, Oxford.

Gooding, C., 1994, *Disabling Laws, Enabling Acts: Disability Rights in Britain and America*, Pluto Press, London.

Gooding, C., 1996, *Blackstone's Guide to the Disability Discrimination Act 1995*, Blackstone Press, London.

Gordon, E., 1983, 'Epithets and attitudes', *Archives of Physical Medicine Rehabilitation*, 64, 234–5.

Gould, A., 1996, 'Sweden: the last bastion of social democracy', in George, V. and Taylor-Gooby, P. (eds) *European Welfare Policy: Squaring the Welfare State*, Macmillan, Basingstoke, 72–94.

Graham, P., Jordan, A. and Lamb, B., 1990, *An Equal Chance or No Chance*, Spastics Society, London.

Greed, C. (ed.) 1999, *Social Town Planning*, Routledge, London.

Greer, N., 1987, 'The state of art design for accessibility', *Architecture*, January, 58–60.

Grosz, E., 1994, *Volatile Bodies: Towards a Corporeal Feminism*, Indiana University Press, Bloomington.

Guy, S., 1998, 'Developing alternatives: energy, offices, and the environment', *International Journal of Urban and Regional Research*, 22, 2, 264–82.

Guy, S. and Henneberry, J., 2000, 'Understanding urban development processes: integrating the economic and the social in property research', *Urban Studies*, 37, 12, 2399–416.

Guy, S. and Shove, E., 1993, *Leaping the Barriers*, BSA Risk and Environment Study Group Meeting, University of York, December, paper available from S. Guy, Centre for Urban Technology, Department of Town and Country Planning, University of Newcastle, Newcastle upon Tyne, NE1 7RU.

Habinteg Housing Association Ltd, 1999, *Annual Report 1999*, HHA, London.

Hahn, H., 1987, 'Civil rights for disabled Americans: the foundation of a political agenda', in Gartner, A. and Joe, T. (eds) *Images of the Disabled/Disabling Images*, Praeger, New York, 181–204.

Hall, E., 1999, 'Workspaces: re-figuring the disability–employment debate', in Butler, R. and Parr, H. (eds) *Mind and Body Spaces: Geographies of Illness, Impairment and Disability*, Routledge, London, 138–54.

Hall, J., 1999, 'Touch – "the very life of things in the mind"'?, *The Independent*, 8 July, 7.

Hall, P. and Imrie, R., 1998, 'Disability rights and wrongs', *Chartered Surveyor Monthly*, 8, 2, 42–3.

Handikapp Ombudsmannen, 1997, *The Situation of the Functionally Limited Persons on the Labour Market – a Pilot Study*, Office of the Disability Ombudsman, Stockholm, Sweden.

Handley, P., 2000, 'Trouble in paradise – a disabled person's right to the satisfaction of a self-defined need: some conceptual and practical problems', *Disability and Society*, 16, 2, 313–25.

Harris, S. and Berke, D. (eds) 1997, *Architecture of the Everyday*, Princeton Architectural Press, New York.

Harvey, D., 1989, *The Condition of Postmodernity*, Blackwell, Oxford.

Harvey, D., 2000, *Spaces of Hope*, Edinburgh University Press, Edinburgh.

Hatch, R. (ed.) 1984, *The Scope of Social Architecture*, Van Nostrand Reinhold, New York.

Haviland, D., 1996, 'Some shifts in building design and their implications for design practices and management', *Journal of Architecture and Planning Research*, 13, 1, 50–62.

Hawkesworth, M., 2001, 'Disabling cities and the regulation of visible differences', *Urban Studies*, 38, 2, 299–318.

Hayden, D., 1985, 'What would a non sexist city be like: speculations on housing, urban design, and human work', *Ekistics*, 52, 310, 99–107.

Healey, P., 1992, 'The reorganisation of state and market in planning', *Urban Studies*, 29, 3/4, 411–34.

Healey, P. and Barrett, S.M., 1990, 'Structure and agency in land and property development processes: some ideas for research', *Urban Studies*, 27, 1, 89–104.

Healey, P. and Nabarro, R. (eds) 1990, *Land and Property in a Changing Context*, Gower, Aldershot.

Heiser, B., 1995, 'The nature and causes of transport disability in Britain and how to remove it', in Zarb, G. (ed.) *Removing Disability Barriers*, Policy Studies Institute, London, 49–63.

Henneberry, J., 1988, 'Conflict in the industrial property market', *Town Planning Review*, 59, 241–62.

Hester Jr, R., 1987, 'Participatory design and environmental justice', *Journal of Architectural and Planning Research*, 4, 4, 289–300.

Higgens, P., 1992, *Making Disability*, Charles Thomas, Springfield, Illinois.

Hill, R., 1999, *Designs and their Consequences: Architecture and Aesthetics*, Yale University Press, New Haven.

Hilpern, K., 2000, 'New moves to combat inequalities in the jobs market', *The Independent*, 8 October, 9.

Hind, F., 1996, *Interview conducted by R. Imrie with Fiona Hind*, Rehabilitation Officer with the Society for the Blind, 12 August.

Hine, J., 1999, 'Transport policy', in Allmendinger, P. and Chapman, M. (eds) *Planning Beyond 2000*, Wiley, London, 151–74.

Hine, J. and Mitchell, F., 2001, 'Privatised concerns: individual worlds and travel experiences', *Urban Studies*, 38, 2, 319–32.

Hobbes, T., 1996, *Leviathan*, Oxford University Press, Oxford.

Holmes-Siedle, J., 1996, *Barrier-Free Design*, Butterworth-Heineman, London.

House Builders Federation, 1995, 'The application of building regulations to help disabled people in new dwellings in England and Wales', *unpublished paper*, available from R. Imrie, Department of Geography, Royal Holloway, University of London, Egham, Surrey, TW20 0EX.

Hubbard, R., 1997, 'Abortion and disability: who should and should not inhabit the world', in Davis, L. (ed.) *The Disability Studies Reader*, Routledge, London, 187–200.

Hunt, J., 1998, 'Builders hit disabled plan', *Sunday Business*, 15 March, 8.

Huxley, M., 1997, 'Ecologically sustainable cities, environmentally friendly transport or just "more work for mother"', Conference Proceedings, *Women on the Move*, TransAdelaide, 1–4.

Imrie, R., 1996, *Disability and the City: International Perspectives*, Paul Chapman Publishing, London, and St Martin's Press, New York.

Imrie, R., 1997, 'Challenging disabled access in the built environment: an evaluation of evidence from the United Kingdom', *Town Planning Review*, 68, 4, 423–48.

Imrie, R., 1999a, 'The body, disability, and Le Corbusier's conception of the radiant environment', in Butler, R. and Parr, H. (eds) *Mind and Body Spaces: Geographies of Disability, Illness and Impairment*, Routledge, London, 25–45.

Imrie, R., 1999b, 'The role of access groups in facilitating accessible environments for disabled people', *Disability and Society*, 14, 4, 463–82.

Imrie, R., 2000a, 'Responding to the design needs of disabled people', *Journal of Urban Design*, 5, 2, 199–219.

Imrie, R., 2000b, 'Disability and discourses of mobility and movement', *Environment and Planning A*, 32, 1641–56.

Imrie, R., 2000c, 'Disabling environments and the geography of access policies and practices in the United Kingdom', *Disability and Society*, 15, 1, 5–24.

Imrie, R. and Hall, P. 1999, 'Property developers' attitudes to access in Sweden and the UK', *Access by Design*, 79, 9–12.

Imrie, R. and Kumar, M., 1998, 'Focusing on access in the built environment', *Disability and Society*, 13, 3, 357–74.

Imrie, R. and Wells, P., 1993, 'Disablism, planning and the built environment', *Environment and Planning C: Government and Policy*, 11, 2, 213–31.

Jackson, A., 1996, *Reconstructing Architecture for the 21st Century*, University of Toronto Press, Toronto.

de Jong, G., 1983, 'Defining and implementing the independent living concept', in Crewe, N. and Zola, I. (eds) *Independent Living for Physically Disabled People*, Jossey Bass, London, 4–28.

Joseph Rowntree Foundation, 1997, *Foundations: Building Lifetime Homes*, JRF, York.

Kavka, G., 1986, *Hobbesian Moral and Political Theory*, Princeton University Press, New Jersey.

Kitchen, R. and Law, R., 2001, 'The socio-spatial construction of (in)accessible public toilets', *Urban Studies*, 38, 2, 287–98.

Knesl, J., 1984, 'The power of architecture', *Environment and Planning D: Society and Space*, 1, 3–22.

Knox, P., 1987, 'The social production of the built environment – architects, architecture, and the post modern city, *Progress in Human Geography*, 11, 3, 354–78.

Lamb, B. and Layzell, S., 1994, *Disabled in Britain: A World Apart*, SCOPE, London.

Laws, G., 1994, 'Oppression, knowledge, and the built environment', *Political Geography*, 13, 1, 7–32.

Lefebvre, H., 1991, *The Production of Space*, Blackwell, Oxford.

Lévi-Strauss, C., 1955, *Tristes Tropiques*, Penguin, New York.

Lifchez, R. and Winslow, B., 1979, *Design for Independent Living*, University of California Press, Berkeley.

Linton, S., 1998, *Claiming Disability: Knowledge and Identity*, New York University Press, New York.

Luccarelli, M., 1995, *Lewis Mumford and the Ecological Region: the Politics of Planning*, Guilford Publications, London.

Luithlen, L., 1994, *Office Development and Capital Accumulation In the United Kingdom*, Avebury, Aldershot.

McAuley, H., 1996, 'One step ahead down under', *Access by Design*, 65, 8–11.

MacDonald, N., 1991, *Democratic Architecture*, Whitley Library of Design, New York.

MacDonald, R., 1995, *Disability and Planning Policy Guidance*, paper presented to the Access Sub-Committee, Oxford City Council, 7 March.

McGlynn, S. and Murrain, P., 1994, 'The politics of urban design', *Planning Practice and Research*, 9, 3, 311–20.

Madanipour, A., 1996, *Design of Urban Space*, Wiley, London.

Madanipour, A., 1998, 'Social exclusion and space', in Madanipour, A., Allen, J. and Cars, G. (eds) *Social Exclusion in European Cities*, Jessica Kingsley, London, 75–89.

Magnano Lampugnani, V., 1991, 'The architect as client', *Lotus International*, 70, 43–51.

Major, J., 1993, House of Commons debate, *Hansard*, volume 217, column 485, 22 January.

Marks, D., 1999, *Disability: Controversial Debates and Psychosocial Perspectives*, Routledge, London.

Matrix, 1984, *Making Space: Women and the Man-Made Environment*, Pluto Press, London.

Michailakis, D., 1997, *Government Action on Disability Policy: a Global Survey*, Office of the United Nations Special Rapporteur on Disability, Geneva.

Milner, J., 1995, 'Disabling design and the dinosaurs', *Housing*, June, 31–3.

Monahan, J., McMullan, E. and Jentle, J., 1998, *Free For All: Access for Disabled People to Sadler's Wells*, report commissioned by the London Boroughs Grants Committee, London.

Morris, J., 1991, *Pride against Prejudice: Transforming Attitudes to Disability*, Women's Press, London.

Morris, J., 1993, *Independent Lives*, Macmillan, Basingstoke.

Morton, R., 1992, 'Professional ideologies and the quality of the British environment', *Proceedings of the Bartlett International Summer School*, University College London, London.

Mumford, L., 1928, 'Towards a rational modernism', *New Republic*, April, 297–8.

Mumford, L, 1938, *The Culture of Cities*, Harcourt, New York.

National Council on Disability, 1993, *ADA Watch – Year One: A Report to the President and Congress on Progress in Implementing the Americans with Disabilities Act*, NCD, Washington DC.

Neufert, E. and Neufert, P., 2000, *Architects' Data: Third edition*, Baiche, B. and Walliman, N., (eds) Blackwell Science, Oxford.

Niesewand, N., 1999, 'Have I been here before?', *The Independent*, *Monday Review*, 22 February, 9.

Noble, M., 1999, 'Surveyors must understand disabled access rules', *Chartered Surveyor Monthly*, July/August, 8, 42–3.

Noble, M., 2000, 'National register of access consultants', *Access by Design*, 83, 21–2.

Office of Population Censuses and Surveys, 1987, *The Prevalence of Disability in Great Britain*, *Report 1*, HMSO, London.

Office of Population Censuses and Surveys, 1993, *National Population Projections*, *1991–based*, HMSO, London.

Ohara, K., 1991, *Architects and Barrier-free Design*, research report, Department of Architecture, Yokohama National University, Japan.

Oliver, M., 1990, *The Politics of Disablement*, Macmillan, Basingstoke.

Oliver, M., 1993, 'Disability and dependency: a creation of industrial societies', in Swain, J., Finkelstein, V., French, S. and Oliver, M. (eds) *Disabling Barriers – Enabling Environments*, Sage, London, 49–60.

Oliver, M., 1996, *Understanding Disability: from Theory to Practice*, Macmillan, Basingstoke.

Ostroff, E., 2000, 'Mining our natural resources: the user as expert', *Adaptive Environments web site*: www.adaptenv.org

Pawley, M., 1983, 'The defence of modern architecture', *RIBA Transactions* 2, 50–5.

Petersson, O., Hermansson, J., Micheletti, M., Westholm, A. and Widfeldt, A., 1998, 'Democracy and leadership: report from the democratic audit of Sweden', *Democratisation*, 5, 3, 35–51.

Pieda, 1996, *A Cost–Benefit Analysis of Lifetime Homes*, Pieda plc, 52 Queens Road, Reading, RG1 4AU.

Potts, P., 1989, 'Working report: the People's Republic of China', in Barton, L. (ed.) *Integration: Myth or Reality*, Falmer Press, London, 168–81.

Prak, N., 1984, *Architects: the Noted and the Ignored*, Wiley, Chichester.

Prescott Clarke, P., 1990, *Employment and Handicap*, Social and Community Planning Research, London.

Rabinowitz, H., 1996, 'The developer's vernacular: the owner's influence on building design', *Journal of Architectural and Planning Research*, 13, 1, 34–42.

Raco, M. and Imrie, R., 2000, 'Governmentality and rights and responsibilities in urban policy', *Environment and Planning A*, 32, 12, 2187–204.

Ramsey, M., 1998, *What's Wrong with Liberalism? A Radical Critique of Liberal Political Theory*, Leicester University Press, Leicester.

Ratcliffe, J. and Stubbs, M., 1996, *Urban Planning and Real Estate Development*, UCL Press, London.

Robins, K., 1995, 'Collective emotion and urban culture', in Healey, P., Cameron, S., Davoudi, S. and Madanipour, A. (eds) *Managing Cities: The New Urban Context*, Wiley, London, 45–62.

Roulstone, A., 1998, *Enabling Technology: Disabled People, Work and New Technology*, Open University Press, Buckingham.

Rowe, A., 1990, *Lifetime Homes: Flexible Housing for Successive Generations*, Helen Hamlyn Foundation, London.

Royal Institute of British Architects, 1998, *Examinations in Architecture, Description and Regulations*, RIBA, London.

Royal Institute of British Architects Client Forums, 1999, 'Therapeutic environments for mental health', *report of a symposium held at the RIBA*, 28 January 1999, RIBA, London.

Royal National Institute for the Blind (RNIB), 1995, *Building Sight*, HMSO, London.

Rufford, N., 1995, 'China moves to ban babies with defects', *Sunday Times*, 5 February, 17.

Rydin, Y., 1993, *The British Planning System: An Introduction*, Macmillan, London.

Rydin, Y., 1997, 'Planning, property and the environment', *Planning Practice and Research*, 12, 1, 5–7.

Salmen, J. and Ostroff, E., 1997, 'Universal design and accessible design', in Watson, D. (ed.) *Time-saver Standards for Architectural Design Data: the Reference of Architectural Fundamentals*, McGraw Hill, New York, 1–8.

Sandercock, L., 1998, *Towards Cosmopolis*, Wiley, London.

Sangster, K., 1997, *Costing Lifetime Homes*, Joseph Rowntree Foundation, The Homestead, 40 Water End, York, YO3 6LP.

Scherer, M., 1993, *Living in the State of Stuck: How Technology Impacts the Lives of Disabled People with Disabilities*, Brookline, Cambridge, MA.

Schull, A., 1979, *Museums of Madness: The Social Organisation of Insanity in Nineteenth-Century England*, Allen Lane, London.

Scotch, R., 1989, 'Politics and policy in the history of the disability rights movement', *Millbank Quarterly*, 67, 52, 380–400.

Scott, V., 1994, *Lessons from America: a Study of the Americans with Disabilities Act*, Royal Association for Disability and Rehabilitation, London.

Sennett, R., 1990, *The Conscience of the Eye: The Design and Social Life of Cities*, Faber and Faber, London.

Shakespeare, T., 1993, 'Disabled people's self-organisation: a new social movement?', *Disability, Handicap and Society*, 8, 3, 249–64.

Shakespeare, T. (ed.) 1998, *The Disability Reader: Social Science Perspectives*, Cassell, London.

Shantakumar, G., 1994, 'The aged population of Singapore: Census of Population 1990', *Monograph No. 1*, Department of Statistics, Singapore.

Sibley, D., 1996, *Geographies of Exclusion*, Longman, Harlow.

Silver Jubilee Committee, 1979, 'Can disabled people go where you go?' *Silver Jubilee Access Committee Report*, Department of Health and Social Security, London.

Slavin, T., 1999, '"Till death do us part" hits home', *The Observer*, *Cash Section*, 31 October, 8.

Smith, M., 1999, 'Designing for living', *Mental Health Care and Learning Disabilities*, 2, 11, 367–9.

Sokolowska, M., Ostrowska, A. and Titkow, A., 1981, 'Creation and removal of disability as a social category: the case of Poland', in Albrecht, G. (ed.) *Cross-national Rehabilitation Policies: A Sociological Perspective*, Sage, London, 223–34.

Sommer, R., 1972, *Design Awareness*, Rinehart Press, San Francisco.

Sommer, R., 1983, *Social Design: Creating Buildings with People in Mind*, Prentice Hall Inc., New Jersey.

Steinfeld, E., 1994, 'The Concept of Universal Design', *unpublished paper* presented at the Sixth Ibero-American conference on accessibility, Center for Independent Living, Rio de Janeiro, 19 June.

Steinfeld, E. and Danford, G. (eds) 1999, *Enabling Environments*, Kluwer Academic, London.

Steinfeld, E., Duncan, J. and Cardell, P., 1977, 'Towards a responsive environment: the psychosocial effects of inaccessibility', in Bednar, M. (ed.) *Barrier-free Environments*, Dowden, Hutchinson and Ross Inc., Pennsylvania, 7–16.

Stone, D., 1984, *The Disabled State*, Macmillan, Basingstoke.

Swain, J., Finkelstein, V., French, S. and Oliver, M., 1993, 'Introduction', in Swain, J., Finkelstein, V., French, S. and Oliver, M. (eds) *Disabling Barriers – Enabling Environments*, Sage, London, 1–7.

Swyngedouw, E., 2000, 'Authoritarian governance, power, and the politics of rescaling', *Environment and Planning D: Society and Space*, 18, 63–76.

Tesco, 2000, *web site*: www.tesco.com

Thamesdown Borough Council, 1994, *Access: Design for Life*, Thamesdown Borough Council, Swindon.

Thomas, C., 1998, 'The body and society: some reflections on the concepts of "disability" and "impairment"', paper presented at the British Sociological Association conference, *The Body and Society*, Heriot Watt University, Edinburgh, 6–8 April, copy available from the author, e-mail, C.Thomas@lancaster.ac.uk.

Thomas, H., 2000, *Race and Planning: the UK Experience*, UCL Press, London.

Thompson, P., Itzin, C. and Abendstern, M., 1990, *I Don't Feel Out: the Experience of Later Life*, Oxford University Press, Oxford.

Touche Ross, 1993, *Profiting from Opportunities – a New Market for Tourism*, Touche Ross, London.

Towers, G., 1995, *Building Democracy: Community and Architecture in the Inner Cities*, UCL Press, London.

Tschumi, B., 1996, *Architecture and Disjunction*, MIT Press, Cambridge, MA.

Turner, J., 1987, 'The enabling practitioner and the recovery of creative work', *Journal of Architectural and Planning Research*, 4, 4, 273–80.

Union of the Physically Impaired Against Segregation, 1976, *Fundamental Principles of Disability*, UPIAS, London.

United Nations, 1975, *Declaration of the Rights of Disabled People*, UN, Geneva.

United Nations, 1987, *An Evaluation of the Rights of Disabled People*, UN, Geneva.

United Nations, 1995, *Promotion of Non-handicapping Physical Environments for Disabled Persons*, UN, New York.

United Nations, 1996, *The Standard Rules on the Equalisation of Opportunities for Persons with Disabilities*, UN, New York.

US General Accounting Office, 1998, *Building Audit*, GAO, Washington DC.

US General Accounting Office, 1999, *Building Audit*, GAO, Washington DC.

van der Krabben, E. and Lambooy, J.G., 1993, 'A theoretical framework for the functioning of the Dutch property market', *Urban Studies*, 30, 8, 1381–97.

Ventre, F.T., 1997, 'Architecture and regulation: a realization of social ethics', in Watson, D. (ed.) *Time-saver Standards for Architectural Design Data: the Reference of Architectural Fundamentals*, McGraw Hill, New York, 9–20.

Ventriss, C., 1987, 'Critical issues of participatory decision making in the planning process: a re-examination', *Journal of Architectural and Planning Research*, 4, 4, 281–8.

Venturi, R., 1966, *Complexity and Contradiction in Architecture*, The Museum of Modern Art, New York.

Wajcman, J., 1991, *Feminism Confronts Technology*, Polity, Oxford.

Walker, A., 1995, 'Universal access and the built environment', in Zarb, G. (ed.) *Removing Disabling Barriers*, Policy Studies Institute, London, 38–48.

Ward, A., 1996, 'The suppression of the social in design: architecture at war', in Dutton, T. and Hurst Mann, L. (eds) *Reconstructing Architecture: Critical Discourses and Social Practices*, University of Minnesota Press, Minneapolis, 27–70.

Wates, N., 1976, *The Battle for Tolmers Square*, Routledge and Kegan Paul, London.

Wates, N. and Knevitt, C., 1987, *Community Architecture – How People are Creating their Own Environment*, Penguin, London.

Weisman, L. (ed.) 1992, *Discrimination by Design*, University of Illinois Press, Illinois.

Weisman, L., 1996, 'Diversity by design: feminist reflections on the future of architectural education and practice', in Agrest, D., Conway, P. and Weisman, L. (eds) *The Sex of Architecture*, Harry N. Abrams Inc., New York, 273–86.

Weisman, L., 1999, 'Creating justice, sustaining life: the role of universal design in the 21st century', *Keynote address*, Adaptive Environments Center, 20th anniversary celebration, The Computer Museum, Boston, 10 April

White, J., 1990, *Justice as Translation: An Essay in Cultural and Legal Criticism*, Chicago University Press, Chicago.

Wilkoff, W. and Abed, L., 1994, *Practicing Universal Design*, Van Nostrand Reinhold, London and New York.

Willis, D., 1990, 'Towards an architecture of responsibility', *Journal of Architectural and Planning Research*, 8, 15–22.

Wolfe, T., 1981, *From Bauhaus to Our House*, Penguin, London.

World Health Organisation, 1980, *International Classification of Impairments, Disabilities, and Handicaps*, WHO, Geneva.

World Health Organisation, 1999, *ICIDH-2: International Classification of Functioning and Disability*, Beta-2 draft, Full Version, WHO, Geneva.

Wright, F.L., 1992, 'Architecture as a profession is all wrong', in Pfeiffer, B. (ed.) *Frank Lloyd Wright: Collected Writings*, volume 1, 1994–1930, Rizzoli International Publications, New York, 333–6.

Wylde, M., Baron-Robbins, A. and Clark, S., 1994, *Building for a Lifetime: the Design and Construction of Fully Accessible Homes*, Taunton Press, Newtown, Conn.

Young, I., 1990, *Justice and the Politics of Difference*, Princeton University Press, Princeton, New Jersey.

Young, J., 1999, *The Exclusive Society: Social Exclusion, Crime, and Difference in Late Modernity*, Sage, London.

Index

Aalto, Alvar, 12, 13
abnormality, 29–30, 43
Access Committee for England, 41, 58, 158
access consultants, 70, 74, 78, 80, 121, 123, 129, 130, 131–4, 135, 149, 160
access groups, 20, 25, 81–83, 89, 90, 103–5, 106–8, 130, 135, 158, 165
access officers, 71, 82, 104–5, 106–8, 130, 135, 158, 165
Access Officers Association, 163
access standards, 52, 58, 59, 61, 89, 151
accessible toilets, 69, 97, 100, 117
Americans with Disabilities Act (ADA), 39, 42, 48, 50–1, 52, 53, 54, 55, 57
adaptable environments, 16
Adaptive Environments Center, 154, 166
aesthetics, 36, 103, 129, 131, 150
affordability, 40
ageing, 37, 100
architects and:
    access groups, 103–5, 107, 135
    achitecture of apartheid, 152
    attitudes to building codes, 51
    attitudes towards access, x, 7, 20, 26, 95–101
    awareness of disability, 101–3
    body conceptions, 10, 143–4, 148
    consulting with users, 103–5, 109
    design and build, 123, 126
    disabled practitioners, 6
    education of, 36, 101–3, 164
    holistic approach to design, 39
    Japanese practices, 155
    novation, 122, 124, 160
    one dimensional practices, 4

    perceptions of users, 3
    procurement, 125
    quality control (in Sweden), 156
    relations with building control, 76–7
    resisting minority design, 71
    statutory regulations, 109–11
    surveys of, 162–3
    users, 93–5, 103–5, 109
Architectural Association, 163
architectural schools, 101, 102, 148, 164
architecture of the everyday, 13
Argent plc, 114, 116, 137, 139–40
Armadillo, 70, 76, 124–5
art galleries, 70, 107, 113–19, 158
artificial light, 12
Arts Council for England, 42, 61, 62–3, 77, 131, 157
ascribed need (also, see *need; self defined need*), 145
assistive technologies, 17, 45, 55
asylums, 28, 29
Auckland, New Zealand, 55
audio, 23, 42, 78, 97, 140
Australia, 21, 31, 50, 54, 55, 66, 156
Austria, 155
autism, 98

B & Q, 154
barriers, ix, 6, 18, 25, 27, 30, 32, 34, 36, 39, 44, 46, 150
biosocial model of disability, 34–5
Birkenbach, Jerome, 34, 37
Birmingham, 69, 70, 113–19, 136–40
blame the victim, 30, 149
Blindness; also, see vision impairment, 4, 35, 72, 105
Bluewater, 70, 86–91, 132, 133

bodies and:
    architects conceptions of, 92, 96
    biological conceptions of, 35
    complexity of, 44
    impairment, 35, 45
    liberty of, 5
    multiple physiologies of, 3
    normality of, 43–4
    reductive conceptions of, 10, 19, 27, 72, 143–4,
      148
    universal design, 15
    western conceptions of, 164
Bovis, 124
Braille, 57, 72, 125
Brindleyplace, 114, 115, 137
Building Act (1991), New Zealand, 54
building control, 25, 53, 56, 70, 76, 80, 87, 89, 90,
    110, 139, 158
building regulations and (also, see entries for *access
    standards, ADA, law, legal frameworks, Part M,
    regulations, statutory regulation*):
    access standards, 52
    developers responses to, 74, 77, 79–81
    enforcement of, 107, 133, 139
    evaluation of, 54–7
    housing (UK), 38–9
    international comparisons of, 49–58
    limitations of, 43, 90, 97, 110, 157
    medicalisation of, 30–1
    minimum standards, 66, 82
    securing access with, 111, 149, 157
    UK system of, 57–65
    variations in, 7
built environment and:
    access directives, 9
    access legislation, 49–66, 146
    architects attitudes to access, 92–112
    barriers, ix, 6, 27
    bodily interactions with, 35
    changing design configurations of, 31
    costs in providing access, 40–3
    design of, 4
    developers attitudes to access, 69–91
    Disability Discrimination Act, 111
    disabled people's exclusion from, 3, 27, 38, 47, 145
    disabled people's use of, x
    enabling justice, 33
    enabling technology, 45–6
    estrangement from, 24
    human needs in, 12

    human well being, 112
    illegibility of, 15–16
    inaccessible design, 30, 110
    inclusive design, 18–20, 24, 144
    legibility of, 16
    medical model of disability, 44
    mobility impairments, 43
    modernism, 94
    multiple uses of, 19
    non disabling spaces, 152
    politics of access, 147
    procurement, 121–6
    provision of access, 37
    urban fabric, 7

Canada, 5, 50
car parking, 91, 129
Cardiff Housing Access Project, 157
Center for Universal Design, 15, 166
Centre for Accessible Environments, 160, 165
charity, 18, 28, 47
China, 50
Chronically Sick and Disabled Persons Act (1970), 58
cinema, 76, 105, 132, 143
Circular 11/95, 59
citizenship, 33, 71, 152
City of London Access Group, 105, 106–8, 130,
    165
civil rights, 42, 49, 50, 50–1, 53, 57, 59, 65, 144,
    153, 155–6
clients and:
    attitudes towards access, 7, 16, 77, 81, 84, 86–91,
      116, 131
    collaborating with users, 20
    consulting with disabled people, 81–3, 135
    design and build, 121–6
    design intentions of, 133
    ignorance of, 111
    impact of DDA on, 111
    interactions with architects, 93, 95, 103, 120
    project design and implementation, 124–5, 127–31,
      139–40
    providing access, 109
codes of practice, 51, 58, 61, 79
colour contrasts, ix, 73, 97, 105, 125, 131, 139
construction, 3, 8, 20, 53, 87, 107, 110, 119
construction schedules, 121–2
consultation, 23, 81–3, 99, 104–5, 106, 117–19, 125,
    130, 145, 163
Continuing Professional Development, 152

contractors, 70, 115, 119, 122, 123, 124–5, 129, 133, 134, 137, 138, 140
costs and:
  access audits, 158
  clients' attitudes towards, 111, 128
  control of, 144
  design and build, 121–6, 135
  designing for disabled people, 91
  economics of real estate, 74–7
  lottery funding, 137–40
  Part M, 110
  participative processes, 20
  procurement routes, 150
  profit margins, 9
  providing access, 6–7, 36, 40–3, 73–4, 84–5, 100, 130–1, 134, 143, 158
  provision of universal design, 14
  reasonable accommodation, 156
  refurbishments, 151
  regulation, 55–8, 79–81
  time pressures, 26
  unreasonable burdens, 47, 55
Council on Tall Buildings and Urban Habitat, 41
Crescent Theatre, 136–40
Curry, David, 58

Dartford, 69, 70, 86, 87
Disability Discrimination Act (DDA), 55, 58, 61, 64–5, 66, 79, 82, 88, 111, 131, 151, 155, 159
deafness, 57, 158
democracy, 18, 24, 156
design and build, 70, 121–6, 137, 159–60
design culture, 10–14
design management, 94, 120, 128, 135
design theory, 4, 93–4, 148
Department of the Environment, Transport and the Regions (DETR), 31, 52, 155, 160
development control, 25, 58, 70
Development Control Policy Note 16, 58
development cycle, 150
development plan, 59, 107, 157
development process and:
  access consultants, 131–4
  aesthetic principles, 150
  architects role in, 92–119
  attitudes of developers to access, 69–91
  changing social relations of, 84–5, 147–52
  commercial imperatives of, 82
  conceptions of disability, 147

consultations with disabled people, 81–3, 131–4
domination of disabled people, 145
enabling environments, 145
environmental injustice, 144–7
equality of opportunity, 146
lack of responsiveness to disabled people, 8–10, 112, 121
medical model of disability, 31
planning processes, 151
procurement contracts, 121–6
project team interactions, 127–31
regulatory control, 77, 79–81, 149
responding to disabled people, 74–7
social and attitudinal barriers of, 36–47
use of access consultants in, 149
dial-a-ride, 145, 160
difference, ix, 3, 9, 10, 15, 17, 24, 26, 33–4, 44, 71, 146, 152, 164
disability and:
  access legislation (see, *law, legal frameworks*)
  accessible housing, 38–9
  architects attitudes towards (see, *architects*)
  biosocial model of, 34–5
  clients' attitudes towards (see, *clients*)
  definitions of, 17, 19, 43–4, 71–4, 143, 147
  design culture, 10–14
  developers attitudes towards (see, *development process*)
  development costs (see, *costs*)
  effects of design on, 4, 6
  immobility, 5
  medical model of, 30–1, 32, 33, 34, 44
  models of, 34
  pejorative conceptions of, 9–10, 28–31, 36, 38–9
  politics of, 146, 150
  professional awareness of, 129
  reasonable adjustments, 41
  social attitudes towards, 27, 28–35, 46–7
  social inclusion, 145
  social model of, 31–4
  universal design, 14–17
  wheelchair reductive model of, 43–4
Disability Awareness Training, 154
Disability Rights Commission (DRC), 65, 155, 166
Disability Rights Task Force (DRTF), 59, 64, 65, 143, 151, 155
Disability Scotland, 125
Disabled Persons Act, 58, 109
Department of the Environment (DoE), 38, 59
domination, 145, 152

Donald and Warn, 21
door handles, 72, 99
doors, 22, 23, 44, 52, 62, 99, 125, 155
Dunedin, New Zealand, 56
Dyslexia, 96

education, 6, 9, 28, 32, 36, 101–3, 112, 148, 159,
    164
elderly, 3, 21, 51, 72, 98, 155, 158
empowerment, 145, 152
enabling environment, 145
enabling justice, 33
end user, 3, 162
English Heritage, 77, 131, 158
English Sports Council, 62–3, 77
environmental injustice, 18, 144
epileptics, 154
equality of opportunity, 66, 146
escalators, 44, 56
ethics, 13, 74, 79, 85, 93
eugenics, 154
European Commission, 4
European Regional Development Fund, 114, 124
European Union, 78
exchange value, 8
experiential knowledge, 20
expert knowledge, 81, 160–1

facial disfigurement, ix, 54
Finland, 13, 155
fittings, 9, 16, 45, 129, 133, 151
fixtures, 9, 16, 45, 133, 137, 139
Fleck, Julie, 106
floor surfaces, 23
Foster & Partners, 124, 125
France, 155

gender (also, see *women*), 3, 12, 102
genes, 29
Germany, 27, 154
Glasgow City Council, 76, 78, 124
Glasgow Development Agency, 78, 124
Guaranteed Maximum Price (GMP), 122, 123, 124–5,
    126
Goldsmith, Selwyn, 17, 25, 54, 55, 57, 58, 59, 61,
    112, 149
Gooding, Caroline, 25, 46, 48, 51, 53, 55, 57, 58,
    61, 64, 66, 79
Gropius, Walter, 103

Guildhall Art Gallery, 107

Habinteg Housing Association, , 41
handrails, 8, 52, 99, 107–8, 119, 130, 139
hard of hearing (see *deafness*), 96
Harvey, David, 121
House Builders' Federation (HBF), 6, 8, 10, 38–9, 40
hidden lives, 105
historic buildings, 64, 70
Hobbes, Thomas, 5
Hong Kong, 51, 56
hotels, 37, 55
housing, 3, 20, 33, 36, 38, 41, 103, 154, 155, 157
Howarth, Alan, MP, 41
Human Rights Act, Canada, 54
Human Rights Act, New Zealand, 40, 53, 55

International Classification of Impairments, Disabilities,
    and Handicaps (ICIDH, 1980), 29–30, 31, 35
Ikon Gallery, 70, 113–19
impairment, x, 3, 5, 10, 14, 17, 18, 20, 22, 30, 31,
    34, 38, 40, 43, 47, 54, 58, 59, 60, 71, 72, 88,
    95, 96, 101, 104, 107, 129, 143, 156
inclusive design, ix, 3, 5, 18–20, 22–3, 24, 26, 71, 91,
    100, 107, 144
inclusive society, 143
independence, 5, 10, 16, 151, 160
India, 31
Indonesia, 31, 51
induction loops, ix, 23, 42, 73, 97, 150, 154
interior design, 10

Jackson, Alan, 94, 103
Japan, 52, 57, 155
Joint Contracts Tribunal (JCT), 115, 159
Joseph Rowntree Foundation, 41

Kennedy, Edward, 42
Kuhne, Eric, 87

Land market, 6
law, 14, 29, 48, 53–4, 55, 57, 61, 66, 73, 93, 111,
    148, 151, 159
Le Corbusier, 94
learning difficulties, 45, 96, 98, 103, 104, 112, 154
Lefebvre, Henri, 44
legal frameworks, 8, 9, 25, 48, 49, 51
leisure, x, 70, 75, 76, 107, 133
Lend Lease, 87–91, 133
level entry, 97

Levitt Bernstein, 116, 119
Lifchez, Raymond, 12, 93–4, 95, 96, 112
lifetime homes, 40, 41, 42
lifts, 31, 39, 63, 74, 82, 97, 116, 117, 125, 138, 139, 140
Lighthouse, 70, 77, 78
listed buildings, 64, 77, 114, 117
local authorities, 25, 43, 54, 56, 58, 61, 70, 80, 84, 87, 101, 104, 106–8, 110, 117, 150, 151, 156, 157, 160
London, UK, 3, 38, 69, 74, 98, 106–8, 130, 164

machine aesthetic, 12
Mackintosh, Charles Rennie, 78
mainstreaming, 17
Major, John, 58
Malaysia, 21, 50, 51, 155
Matrix, 3, 96
medical model of disability, 30–1, 32, 33, 34, 44
mental impairment, x, 5, 20, 22, 29, 31, 37, 44, 64, 71, 95, 104, 147
Metric Handbook, 10
Mies van der Rohe, Ludwig, 94
mobility and:
    access legislation (see, ADA; law; legal frameworks; Part M)
    access to housing, 10, 38
    bodily norms, 10
    Disability Discrimination Act, 64–5
    definitions of disability, 72, 88, 100
    movement around buildings, 8, 150
    restrictions on movement, 5, 112, 145
    special design features, 20
    stereotypes of, 147
    wheelchair use (see *wheelchair users*)
mobility rights, 5
modernism, 10, 12
morality, 14, 25, 28, 36, 57, 71, 73, 79, 84, 85, 146, 147
Morris, Jenny, 28, 33–4
Mumford, Lewis, 4, 13, 152

National Building Code (1992) of Australia, 56
National Council on Disability, 57
National Disability Council, 64
National Lottery, 22, 77, 84, 112, 131, 133, 157
navigational aids, 3
need (also, see *ascribed need; self defined need*), x
Neufert and Neufert, 10
New South Wales, 156

New Zealand, x, 40, 48, 50, 53–4, 55, 56, 66, 85, 109
Newhaven Downs House, 98–9
Noble, Mary, 131, 160
normal, 19, 28, 30, 44, 96, 144, 148
normalise, 71
Northern Ireland, 57
Norway, 27, 155
Norwest Holst, 137
Norwich, 154
Nottingham, 105
novated, 122, 124, 160

offices, x, 8, 55, 57, 70, 75, 76, 82, 108, 137, 158
Oliver, Michael, 4, 25, 29, 30, 31, 32, 34, 100, 111, 145–6, 152
Office of Population Censuses and Surveys (OPCS), 32, 43
oppression, 32, 34, 46, 145
Ostroff, Elaine, 14, 15, 17, 37
Ove Arup and Partners, 21

Part M, 8, 22, 48, 56, 57–8, 59, 60, 61, 62–3, 64, 66, 77, 79–80, 85, 90, 91, 100, 102, 109–10, 111, 117, 137, 139, 149, 157
participation, 4, 20, 31, 32, 33, 81, 147, 150, 156, 157, 162
passive stimulation, 99
pathology, 44
Penoyre & Prasad, 98–9
personal tragedy, 28, 34
Peters Hill, 107–8
Philippines, 51, 54, 155
Pieda plc, 38, 42
planning conditions, 56, 59
Planning and Building Act (1987), Sweden, 53
Planning (Listed Buildings and Conservation Areas) Act (1990), 64
Planning Policy Guidance 1, 58–9
Planning Policy Guidance 12, 59
political rights, 146
politics of access, 147, 148–9, 150
politics of disability, 145–6, 152
politics of identity, 146
Portugal, 50
procurement, 70, 115, 121–6, 135, 137, 138, 150, 159
project managers, x, 7, 80, 84, 87, 88, 123, 124, 126, 128, 130, 132, 144, 162
project team, 84, 120, 121, 123, 127–31

property development, x, 3, 6, 8, 9, 48, 81, 84, 85, 127, 134, 143, 144, 162
property markets, 7, 9, 73
property professionals and (also, see entries for *separate professionals*):
    attitudes towards disabled people, 8
    attitudes towards the client, 127–8
    conceptions of building users, 4
    costing access, 40–3, 47 (also, see *costs*)
    education and training of, 6
    expert knowledge of, 160
    investment decisions by, 145
    legal regulations, 61, 149, 155
    participation with users, 20, 24
    resisting access provision, 42–3
    responding to access issues, 30–1, 35, 44, 46, 51, 53, 73, 74–7, 129–30
    social inclusion, 24
public housing, 3
pure design, 94
pushchairs, 19

Queensland, 21

race, 154
Ralph Beattie and Partners, 21
ramps, 8, 10, 31, 39, 56, 62, 73, 87, 90, 97, 102, 125
reactionary architecture, 12
real estate, 8, 9, 74
reasonable accommodation, 157
reasonable adjustment, 41, 61, 64
reflexive architecture, 152
regulations, 9, 22, 38, 48, 51, 57, 58
rehabilitation, 25, 30, 50, 100, 155
retail, 9, 39, 61, 69, 75–6, 83, 84, 87, 91, 134
Royal Institute of British Architects (RIBA), 95, 101, 151, 160, 164
Royal Institution of Chartered Surveyors (RICS), 163
rights discourse, 146
Royal National Institute for the Blind (RNIB), 4, 18, 20, 41, 105
robustness, 152

Sadler's Wells, 22–3
Salmen, John, 14, 15, 17, 37
Scotland, 57, 70, 78
Scottish Arts Council, 62–3, 78, 131
segregation, 28, 31, 49
self defined need (also, see *need*), 146
shopmobility, 73, 88, 89, 90, 91

shops, 55, 143
sight loss, (also, see *blindness and vision impairment*, 17
signage, 23, 59, 105, 139
signs, 78, 99, 105, 129
Silver Jubilee Committee, 58, 158
Singapore, 49, 57, 151, 155
social architecture, 4, 12, 14, 26
social design, 14, 18
social exclusion, ix, 5, 14, 27, 93
social inclusion, 24, 145
social integration, 14, 17
social model of disability, 31–4
social space, 33, 145, 153
Sommer, Robert, 13, 18, 19, 24, 26, 92
South Down Health NHS Trust, 98–9
special assistance, 144
special education, 36
special employment programmes, 50, 156
speculative development, 70, 74–5, 133
stair lifts, 74
stairs, 52, 74, 82, 115, 117, 118, 125, 132, 139, 157
standardisation, 8, 10
statutory regulation, 57, 95, 109
Steinfeld, Edward, 14, 14, 16, 149
steps, 9, 98, 107–8
sterilisation, 29, 154–5
structures of building provision, 7–8, 70, 121
surveyors, chartered, ix, x, 9, 21, 25, 37, 70, 74, 79, 131, 154, 162, 163
Sweden, x, 32, 43, 48, 50, 52, 53, 61, 72, 83, 101, 102, 109, 126, 128, 129, 154, 155, 156, 158, 162–3, 164
Switzerland, 154

tactile paving, ix, 97
tactile signs, 105
Tarmac plc, 115
technology, 10, 19
Temple Cox Nicholls, 137
tender, 122, 125
Tesco plc, 39–40
texture, 16, 23
Thamesdown Borough Council, 38
theatres, 22, 70, 105, 116, 136–40, 158
toilets, 39, 63, 76, 82, 87, 100, 105, 125, 130
Touche Ross, 40
Town and Country Planning Act (1971), 58
training, 6, 9, 36, 95, 101, 112, 125, 147, 154
transport, ix, 3, 28, 33, 38, 40, 51, 55, 145, 150

Turner, John, 13, 17, 20, 24, 154

United Kingdom, 6, 8, 18, 23, 25, 27, 31, 33, 35, 37, 39, 40, 42, 43, 48, 49, 50, 52, 53, 54, 55, 56, 57, 62, 65, 66, 71, 72, 73, 74, 76, 77, 83, 95, 101, 102, 109, 121, 126, 128, 129, 155, 162, 163
Unitary Development Plan, 107
United Nations, 39, 49–50, 55, 66, 156
Universal design, 14–17, 45, 154
unmonumental, 14
Union of Physically Impaired Against Segregation (UPIAS), 31, 152
urban design, 10, 44, 83, 149
US General Accounting Office, 41
USA, x, 5, 14, 29, 37, 40, 42, 48, 50, 52, 53, 57, 157,
use value, 8
users, x, 3, 12, 14, 15, 17, 18, 19, 20, 24, 36, 73, 75, 85, 91, 92, 103, 105, 144, 145, 149, 150, 153

Venturi, Robert, 12, 20
Viipuri library, Finland, 13
vision impairment (also, see *blindness, sight loss*), 4, 17, 35, 96
visitable, 157
visual art, 12, 92
voluntarism, 25, 51, 53, 109

Wales, 28
Walpole-Nornalup National Park, Western Australia, 21
West Lambeth Community Care Trust, 98
wheelchair users, 3, 4, 9, 36, 43, 52, 63, 72, 88, 97, 104, 111, 130, 140, 147, 158
World Health Organisation (WHO), 30, 31, 35, 167
Wolfe, Tom, 94
women (also, see *gender*) 50, 154
Wright, Frank Lloyd, 4